NOBODY CARES
ABOUT YOUR
STUPID
PICTURES

NOBODY CARES ABOUT YOUR STUPID PICTURES

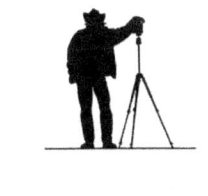

DALE O'DELL

For Bernadette, the Muse
&
Emmette, the Mentor

TABLE OF CONTENTS

INTRODUCTION

If you do a thing long enough eventually you get good at it. I've been hammering away on a nail called 'photography' for forty-seven years, thirty-six of them professionally, and I'm beginning to feel like I might be getting good at it. Might be. Early on I thought I was 'special,' that I had an innate artistic skill with a camera and in the darkroom that automatically made me better than most. That feeling carried me through college graduation and right up until I joined the profession of photography. Jumping into a business (both commercial photography and fine-art) already filled with many extremely talented practitioners and learning that the business is brutally competitive and cutthroat quickly exploded any feelings of specialness I had. In my mind, I went from *you're special to you suck* in a nanosecond. I suppose that's the difference between doing something for fun and doing something for a living — things get very serious, very fast. I've never achieved the recognition I thought I would when I thought I was special, but I kept at it because I really, really love what I do. I love every aspect of it — except the business/money part, which I find to be as ugly as the art-part is beautiful. As a still relatively unknown artist I've always felt I had more to give than was ever accepted by the art-world. Of all the photography books I've read none really told what it was like to be an actual working photographer, with all the pleasures and perils. As a photography student I never read a 'real world' photography book because there weren't any, so I wrote Photographic Memories in 2009 and now this book. This book expands upon, continues, and is a companion-volume to that book. These are some of the real things I've experienced, done and contemplated from the perspective of a non-famous, unknown, but serious full-time photographic artist. If you're an art or photography student reading this I hope it opens your eyes to what's just over your career horizon. If you're a photographer I bet you can relate. If you're not in the arts I hope this enlightens you about what life is like for the creative person.

Aside from doing this thing called photography for most of my life I've thought about it a lot too. Contemplation is important, it adds to the depth of knowledge. I've carefully considered the creative process and have tried to understand the mystery of it. I try to look at art from the perspective of both creator and consumer. I've got a pretty good idea of how the artist relates to art but I also want to understand the perspective of the gallerist, the art director, the collector and the critic. I think it's important to have these thoughts, to write them down and share them with others. Was it the same for you as it was for me? Is my experience unique? Perception is different for everyone — that's why there's such variety in art, but I wonder, does the viewer even see the same thing I do? The viewer responds to the image on the paper (or now, screen) but they seldom consider the thought process behind it. I'll tell you a bit about it in this book.

The business and art of photography has changed in extraordinary ways since I joined it in the 1970s. Technology has not only manifested profound changes to how a photograph is made but also to how it is published, or now, shared. The photograph's value has decreased due to the sheer volume produced. With over a trillion photographs made annually, it's hard to stand out in a sea of ever-changing pixels. As a professional image-maker it's easy to feel that nobody cares about your stupid pictures when really you're just lost in the crowd. What does make a photograph stand out? What's the value of a thousand 'likes' on Instagram compared to one person buying a print?

I'm always up for an engaging and lively discussion about art and life and cherish the rare opportunity when it happens. But all too often competition gets in the way and the conversation turns to money, or client and collector name-dropping, or banal consumerist discussions about equipment. It's difficult to have a deep conversation about art/photography/creativity outside of the academic environment. (And art-academia wants nothing to do with people like me.) In order to express those thoughts I'm compelled to write them down. I've put a lot of that material on my blog — which is lost among millions of other blogs and largely unread. This book is the 'blog greatest hits' collection.

Since I'm one of the photographic artists who lived and worked through the film-to-digital transition and was an early-adopter of digital-imaging, I've put a considerable amount of mental effort into understanding the profound nature of technology-driven change from the perspective of *being in the middle of it*. Almost a quarter century ago at the beginning of the digital revolution I attempted to define, early on, the difference between photography and digital art. *The Digital Art Manifesto* is presented as the very first chapter of this book. And it's pretty darned plain and simple. Aspects of the Manifesto were published in some of the leading photography publications as far back as the 1990s but no one, and I mean *nobody*, ever challenged it or responded to it in any way. Again, I've found it exceedingly difficult to engage anyone in a meaningful discussion about the artistic issues that I feel are important. Once I even paid a curator at a Major Museum (Portfolio Reviews chapter) for the opportunity to have the discussion but even she wouldn't engage.

Since too many photographers take themselves so *seriously* I've included humor when I've found it at *Photoshop World* and *Area 51* and *Bigfoot*. *True Photographer Tales* are included when I've been chased by tornados, or when I tried to sell out and failed. I've re-experienced the hideous clusterfuck of photography at Antelope Canyon and had a profound experience photographing the solar eclipse of 2017. I wonder if art-making might be related to having an obsessive-compulsive disorder? There is a longer chapter on the cell-phone video camera being an instrument for social change that (I know via my blog) has pissed-off at least one person in law enforcement (indicating that I'm *probably right*). This book includes some helpful math on limited-editions and pay-to-display scams. I've put the success and failures of Vincent Van Gogh and Thomas Kinkade (two names not often seen together) in perspective in a unique way. This book contains the very last thing I'll ever say about the shitty business of Stock Photography. And I've included some of the absolute weirdness I've encountered like being told *how to behave at my own gallery opening* and working with people so stinkin' rich they have no clue they don't have a clue. A lot of what I've written here is personal, but it's personal-universal, in that I'll bet you can relate to it.

All over the world there are artists just like me, unknown, unrecognized, hardworking, creative and thoughtful. They're just doing what they do, every day. Not everyone gets plucked from obscurity and many talented artists never gain the recognition they deserve. Thankfully modern technology in the form of self-publishing gives the voiceless a voice. Just because no one *asks* you to speak does not mean you have nothing to say.

CHAPTER

THE DIGTAL ART MANIFESTO

Digital Art is a new art form brought about by the digital imaging revolution. The approximate birth date of digital art is 1990, the year *Adobe Photoshop*™ brought digital image processing to the consumer via the personal computer. Because photographers were the early-adopters of digital technology and the (now) ubiquitous software application is called photo-shop, digital art is often confused with photography but they are not the same.

The definition of digital art is:
Any artwork that cannot be created without the use of digital technology (computer + program) can be considered 'digital art.' If digital technology is required for the production of a specific artwork, and that artwork cannot be created by any other means except by use of digital technology, then the artwork is 'digital art.'

It's that simple. We seem to have no trouble understanding how painting, drawing and sculpture are unique art forms distinct from each other but when 'digital' is mixed with photography there is confusion. We can clear that confusion by setting distinct boundaries that define when an image stops being a photograph and crosses the line into 'digital art.' One way to define an image as a photograph is whether or not you can go and see the scene depicted in the photograph in real life. If it exists in the real world

1

and reflects light that can be recorded on film or a digital camera's sensor, then it's a photograph. Even some composite images can be photographs. If the composite image came from a darkroom or uses digital processes that could be replicated in a darkroom, then that composite image is a photograph. If that composite image uses digital techniques without analog equivalents, then it is no longer a photograph and should be recognized as digital art. High Dynamic Range images, although a result of digital image processing, should be considered photographs because there are analog techniques that, however difficult to produce, emulate the HDR technique. Digital infrared photographs are photographs the same as their film forebears, only a different spectrum is used to create the image. Hybrid images combining computer-generated elements with photographic elements are digital art because a computer is required to make computer-generated imagery.

The photographic aspects of digital art are indeed confusing. When one describes their artworks as 'photographs' the viewer has a certain expectation about how that image should look. When the image is so manipulated that it violates the viewers' expectations I use the term 'photo/digital' to describe the artwork. 'Photo/digital' is an honest and descriptive term and cues the viewer.

It took over one-hundred years for photography to be recognized as a legitimate art form because, in the beginning, photography had no history. The same exact thing is occurring right now with the perception of 'digital art' because its history is less than thirty years. I predict that within one generation, 'digital' will be recognized as its own, legitimate, separate and distinct art form.

Until 'digital art' has its own unique history it will be perceived as 'photography' or an offshoot of photography.

As a photographic artist who worked during the film-to-digital transition I want to go on record and state unequivocally that 'digital art' or 'photo/digital' art are unique art forms separate from others. I know of no one in the exalted position of *curator*, *critic*, *director* or *gallerist* who has had the courage to go on record and define this new, digital, art form so I've done it for them. *If the art could not be created without the use of digital imaging technology, it's digital art.* If anyone would like to discuss or challenge this I'm more than willing to meet and debate the issue but I doubt there'll be any takers.

CHAPTER

WHAT IS PHOTOGRAPHY NOW?
COMPETITION WITHIN CONFORMITY

Whenever I speak to art and photography groups the audience is supposed to learn something from me. They usually do, but I always learn something from them. After a lecture I gave to a photography club I was asked to critique and judge their monthly assignment and I selected prints for first, second and third places. The first-place photograph was a lovely desert landscape image that I found very intriguing. As it goes with 'winners' (and I really don't like the concept of 'winning' and 'losing' in the arts, but that's the competitive system our society has provided for us) the creator of the first-place image wanted to talk to me after the 'judging.' As it turned out his image was of an obscure place in a State Park I've visited many times; *Valley of Fire State Park* in Nevada.

I told the photographer I've been there many times, I love the place, it's beautiful, and it can be seen in the backgrounds of over half the car commercials on TV today — but where'd he find that particular spot? I've never seen it and I am pretty darned familiar with *Valley of Fire.*

"Oh, just download the eBook about *Valley of Fire*, it's got all the obscure photo-spots identified complete with GPS coordinates," he told me.

I found the eBook online, paid the four bucks for it via PayPal, downloaded and printed it out. And sure enough, there were all those obscure locations, clearly marked with GPS coordinates —

easy to find! Perusing the eBook I decided I needed to go back and photograph some of those things.

I had the same thoughts a year ago when I was researching *The Palouse,* a beautiful area of farmland in eastern Washington. Yes, The Palouse was someplace I wanted to go to photograph and as I did online research I found a lot of information. There were numerous 'photo workshops' held at The Palouse, I also found 'photography maps' complete with marked locations of 'red barns,' 'lone trees,' 'abandoned buildings,' etc. etc. I downloaded and printed that map and used it when I was photographing the area.

I'm sure the *Valley of Fire* eBook will be just as helpful as The *Palouse* 'photography maps' I used when I was photographing that area. But what is going on? There are maps of photographic hotspots now?

For many photography is no longer an act of discovery.

I do online research before almost every location shoot and I'm more and more amazed by the sheer amount of photography-specific information available. There are workshops where 'experts' will take you to 'photogenic' locations where you can shoot all the same photographs for yourself that have been shot before. You can find maps where you're practically told where to place your tripod, which way to point your camera, which lens to use and what time of day to shoot.

I was once in Monument Valley — a place where photo-workshops are held nearly constantly, where city-dwellers can come and shoot the exact same 'western' photos everyone else does — and a fellow pointed to a photo on a brochure and told me, "I shot that!"

"Good for you," I replied, "Does the Park Service pay a decent license fee for using the photo?" He gave me a confused look and then said, "Oh I didn't shoot that photo; I shot one just like it."

"Good for you," I said again and then walked away, shaking my head and thinking, *yeah good for you, you shot a photo exactly like one in a brochure, how unoriginal.*

But to the amateur (and many pro) photographers, originality doesn't mean much, what they're trying to do isn't about being unique, creative or original, it's about *competition* and *conformity*. They see these pretty places, see other photographers' photos and think, *I can do that.* I'm sure some think they can do it better, but most just want to do it too, to shoot their own version of a time-worn, cliché image. They take zero risks whatsoever, they're shooting the same, pre-approved images and adding nothing of *their own vision* (assuming they have a personal vision) to the scene. These aren't the people who go to the Grand Canyon, point their cameras, look around in frustration and think, *what could I possibly photograph* that hasn't been done a zillion times? No, these are the folks who point their cameras at the same thing millions of other people have seen and think, *Yeah, now I can get my photo of it!*

It's competition-within-conformity. It's conformity because they're all shooting the same thing. It's competitive because photographers are thinking, *my picture is better than the other guys.'*

Competition-within-conformity isn't confined to the amateurs and camera-clubbers, we can find it among commercial and fine-art photographers too. Look at almost any energy company's annual report or capabilities brochure and you'll find the same stock-andstandard executive portrait and you'll also see there are only a few ways to photograph an oil well at sunset. Very few corporate or industrial photographers have a point of view (or need one) because they're all essentially interchangeable; there's only so many types of photographs that are acceptable to corporate clientele, and too much originality is too scary for them. We can't really blame the commercial photographers for this, they're in it to make money, earn a living and provide a service. Their 'success' isn't based on art or creativity but rather on figuring out just how far from the edges of the creative box they can get and still make an acceptable image for their client.

But we *can* blame the 'fine art photographers' because they're the very ones who call themselves 'fine artists' while safely staying within the comfortable bounds of what's accepted as 'fine art.' Like corporate photographers the fine artists also know their clientele, and for their 'success' they've also got to stay within their own box of acceptability. Right now, in terms of contemporary 'fine art' photography, the box is full of documentary photographers.

I once asked a curator at a Major Museum what it would take to get my photography noticed by someone in her position and she actually answered with: "Study what successful contemporary photographers are doing, and do that." *That advice* is institutionalized conformity at its worst, and very *bad advice too*!

I've examined all four corners and all six sides of that box and I've memorized it. There's nothing new in it for me (although it's a comfortable box, it's too crowded) and I don't want in. But where exactly is 'outside the box?' It's far from the crowd, on a trail blazed by yourself; it's alone and scary and original and outside the box is someplace where some people might not like your pictures because they're *different.*

If you're really trying to discover something original with your photography you won't find a map of all the cool 'photo spots' because the map doesn't exist, *you'll have to make that map yourself.* Originality doesn't come in a box either. Originality is so far out of the box that you'll have to become a free-range artist to pursue it.

It's very lonely and frightening so far away from the box of familiarity out on the free-range of creativity, seeking to discover something new. It's risky and the outcome most sane people try to avoid is when the 'audience' doesn't like your pictures. Competition-within-conformity is risk-managed creativity that almost always guarantees a positive outcome — people will like your pictures because they already like all the preexisting pictures that look just like yours.

Yet I printed and used the map I found of *The Palouse* and I'll use that map I just downloaded of the obscure locations within Valley of Fire State Park; aren't I doing the same thing?

Yes and no.

Sure, when I get to *Valley of Fire* with my new map I'll find some of those locations I've not seen before. And sure, I'll probably shoot some typical stock-and-standard images (which I *won't* show as-is). But I'll shoot it my way and I'll shoot photos with an eye towards future digital composite images. For me, I'm not using these maps to shoot the same photos others have, I'm simply taking a shortcut by using someone else's research. Yeah, sure, I'm at the same place but I'm there for a different purpose and that purpose is to specifically not to make the same photo as everyone else. By using others' information and research I've saved the time and effort of *finding* the place while accepting the challenge of *photographing something different at the same place*. Finding the interesting location isn't a process of discovery, the discovery now is how to create new art from the already familiar. It's a personal challenge!

When a commercial photographer makes the same image as another he's rewarded with money, payment for services. The client is happy because they can relate to the image, the image brings the comfort of familiarity.

When an amateur or camera-clubber (and even many pros) makes the same image as another photographer they're rewarded with acceptance. The image is rewarded or 'liked' because again, it is familiar and relatable. These images require no analysis, interpretation and very little thought, they're pretty — just like all the rest. They're easy and safe.

When a 'fine-art' photographer makes an image that's similar to other 'art' images their image is also accepted because they've faithfully stayed within the box of 'fine art acceptability.' It's artistic safety within the confines of the pre-accepted.

All three of these types of photographers are rewarded with positive feedback that makes them feel good about their imagery and themselves — which are their goals. Discovery *is not* their goal.

For those of us who do wish to discover something new, to blaze a new trail or go (artistically) where no one has gone before, the path is much more difficult. Our images aren't pre-approved before we make them. We don't have a 'built-in' audience that already knows about, relates to, and likes our imagery. The newness we seek requires more thought from the viewer. Yes, the viewer must work harder with our pictures because there may not be very many preexisting similar images as reference. With truly creative art the viewer has to *decide for themselves* if the work is 'good' or 'valid.'

A lot of viewers (and alleged experts) are reluctant to express an original opinion about truly original art. They prefer the comfort of expressing their own acceptance of the already-accepted.

CHAPTER

REPORT FROM PHOTOSHOP WORLD
Originally published in Five Senses Magazine

As we enter the third decade of the digital revolution of photography, we don't have time to lament the loss of Kodachrome to the CMOS sensor, or cameras that have morphed into little more than computers with lenses or the smelly mystery of the chemical darkroom; we're too busy shooting cell phone selfies and downloading the latest junk shot from Carlos Danger. Photography has been forever changed.

One of the most profound changes in the digitalization of photography is the replacement of the darkroom by the computer. When it comes to 'development' of pictures, all roads lead to the ubiquitous program known as Adobe Photoshop. So dominant has Photoshop become that there are numerous annual conventions, workshops, schools, and trade shows devoted to it.

One of the big ones is Photoshop World, held every September at the Mandalay Bay Hotel and Casino in Las Vegas.

Each year I attend Photoshop World because it's an opportunity to see the latest gadgets and keep abreast of current trends and technologies. It's also a good excuse to go to Vegas where I can observe humans of every shape, color, and configuration gather for forced fun and hopeful debauchery. The ones carrying cameras were headed off to Photoshop World so I tagged along with Nicky Nikon, Maggie Megabyte, and Otto Focus, got my badge, and entered the exalted hall of The Trade Show.

10

Photoshop World offers workshops and lectures, where alleged great photographers, wannabes, and has-beens will show you their digital "secrets" for a fee, but I don't attend that stuff. My interest lies with the pure consumerism of new gadgetry, so I attend the (formerly free) trade show only.

The trade show was packed. Oh look, there's Johnny Jpeg, who always "wears" his Nikon over his photographer/fly-fishing vest. And he's heading towards the Nikon booth, his 500 mm lens pointing the way perched like a lighthouse on the tip of his beer gut. Why do these guys (and it's always guys) feel the need to carry extreme telephoto lenses in a crowded room where no one needs a long lens? In this context the 10-grand lens isn't useful for anything more than a penis extender. Big glass?

It's always ironic to chat up the rep in the booth and then decide to buy the thing he's showing. As soon as I say I'll buy it, he tells me, "I'm just the lens cap rep — that guy over there will take care of the transaction." Of course "that guy over there" is busy with a line of 15 people waiting for him. I'll come back later and get the thing. (I didn't.)

The Canon printer rep went on a rant about how bad Epson printers are and then, later, when I talked to the Epson printer rep he said the exact same thing about Canon printers. I laugh and tell them it's simply their jobs to trash the competition; when I asked about HP printers they really got going — and so did I, right outta their booths!

I was hoping to get my hands on some of the new LED studio lights, but all the vendors were still pushing 90s-style fluorescent lights. They did have two sets lit with umbrellas, soft boxes, and other light modifiers with huge crowds.

Why the crowds? Because on one set they had an actual girl, a pretty model, and 50 guys (including Johnny Jpeg with that silly 500 mm lens) were vying for that "fashion model" shot for their portfolios. Can't fail with pre-set-up lighting, right guys?

Inkjet printing on aluminum sheets is pretty neat. I checked out the sample prints, and I think I should do this for some of my work. If I sell prints on aluminum and someone later decides they don't like the picture, they can always re-purpose the print as building material.

I noticed a woman holding an iPad way over her head. I felt sorry for her being so farsighted she had to hold the tablet that far away, but she was actually taking a picture. Urgh, photography without using an actual camera. I hope she visits the booth showing strap-on auxiliary lenses for tablets and cell phones.

After dropping a couple hundred bucks on gadgets and a new RAW conversion program, I was about to leave when I found the most interesting booth at the trade show. It was the only nonprofit group there, and it wasn't selling anything photographic.

This was Shelter Me Photography, an outfit that photographs and publishes photos of shelter dogs. I saw a collection of good photos of good dogs, and when they shared those photos online, the dogs got adopted. Some dogs were less than 24 hours away from being euthanized and the shared photo saved the dogs' lives. How wonderful!

It was a good show, and I'll be at the next Photoshop World (so long as it's in Las Vegas). If you don't find me at the Trade Show, I'll be at the bar in the Luxor laughing at Nicky Nikon while he tries to figure out just exactly what that sexy woman meant when she asked, "Do you want to party?"

CHAPTER

THE DIGITAL PISSING CONTEST

The guy was angry. I'd insulted his precious Macintosh computer. Thank goodness I ended that conversation quickly; I couldn't stand another treatise on the greatness of the almighty Mac. Shut up about your damned computer already.

Our house frequently becomes a crash-pad for old friends or other people who suddenly become very friendly when they need a free place to stay when taking that 'once-in-a-lifetime' vacation to the Desert Southwest. And so it was when another 'old friend' invited himself to stay with us last summer. He's a college professor of photography, a serious person who teachers others how to be photographers even though he himself has never shot a photo for money. His university paid for his trip to Phoenix for some sort of conference and he spent extra time in the state photographing. That's what led another visiting landscape artist to our house.

We were sitting on the back deck one evening talking and, not unexpectedly, he started on the merits and beauty of the Macintosh computer. I shut him down. I meant it as a joke really, I borrowed a line from engineering and when he brought the conversation to his computer, I sniffed and said: "Macs, ha, toys for artists." He didn't think it was funny, he got mad.

Oh boy, that set him off. Next thing he's going on about how many megabytes of RAM it's got, and how fast the video card is, his big flat-panel monitor, terabytes of hard drives and on and on, ad nauseam. A pissing contest may have ensued, had I been willing

13

to piss back, but I don't give a damn about his computer — or mine, really.

Everybody please shut the hell up about your cameras and computers, megabytes and megapixels, and all that stuff. Shut up! We don't care!

It's an established fact that photographers are gadget-freaks. Since the computer is the ultimate photographer's gadget it's perfectly logical that gadget-discussions have a Viagra-like effect on photographers. Settle down, they're only machines. It does not matter if you have or don't have the highest-resolution camera or the speediest computer. If you think it does you've either have too much money, you're a marketing-victim, or both. Quite often the only difference between an 'ordinary' piece of equipment and some black-painted thing with the word 'professional' embossed on it is its price. Do 'amateur' cameras make only 'amateur' pictures? And for that matter, does a 'professional' camera in the hands of the untalented make better pictures? Does a 'fast' computer somehow make better pictures? Uh, no to all!

My college professor friend went on and on about computer speed, rationalizing about "not wanting to wait on filter effects and so on." Oh please, go into your darkroom (you still have one, don't you?) and make a couple of pin-registered Kodalith positive and negative masks and come back and talk to me about speed. So what if you've got to wait an extra three minutes for your computer with 'only' one megabyte of RAM to process some effect? Really, think about the time you'd spend in the darkroom to accomplish the same thing (assuming you'd even know how to do special effects, or make a simple print in the darkroom) and you ought to realize that even a 'slow' computer is 'fast.' Try to keep things in perspective.

CHAPTER

PHOTOGRAPHY AT ARM'S LENGTH

While standing behind my tripod waiting for a cloud to move from in front of the sun, I noticed that Joshua Tree National Park was crawling with "photographers." I put "photographers" in quotation marks because they weren't professional photographers but, rather, the most common type of "photographer," the amateur. It was easy to tell they were amateurs because they couldn't even hold a camera properly.

But this isn't specifically about the amateurs; it's about modern digital camera design and amateurish camera handling.

The modern, non-SLR, digital camera is a wonderful device full of hi-tech features, like face recognition and image stabilization. With the addition of these features we're unfortunately seeing one critical feature removed from many of the rangefinder/point and shoot cameras; the viewfinder. With rangefinder/P&S cameras becoming ever more miniaturized camera manufacturers are leaving off the viewfinder in favor of the live-view screen. This is not a good thing because it leads to bad form when image-making.

I don't recall where I read it, but a long time ago, in some book I studied when I was first learning the techniques of photography, there was a section called "camera handling." To paraphrase, it read something like this: For the sharpest possible image hold the camera steady when taking a picture. Stand with your feet apart, cradle the lens with your left hand and hold the camera body with your right, with the index finger on the shutter release. With the camera up to your eye, push your elbows against your body, hold your breath at the moment of exposure and gently squeeze the shutter release.

Sadly, the above (very basic) information appears to be missing from all the digital camera manuals I've read *because most of the new digital cameras do not have a viewfinder.*

Now, high technology in the form of image-stabilization, is used to compensate for poor camera design that encourages poor camera handling habits. The hand-held camera is not designed to be used at arm's length — not for optimum results anyway. You really cannot take sharp, hand-held, pictures with the camera way out away from your body with no support.

I'm not anti-technology. The live-view screen and image-stabilization are great tools that expand the capabilities of the photographer. Image-stabilization is incredibly useful in sports, wildlife or any type of action photography and I.S. allows handheld photography in lower light with lower ISOs than without it. The live-view screen is a useful secondary compositional tool, especially the fold-out types that allow for waist-level shooting. But technology is best used to expand photographic capabilities not to compensate for poor technique.

Like most people over the age of 40 I can't see up-close very well anymore. Because of 'aging-eyes' I need to hold the camera at arm's length to see that little screen — and this creates a 'stability paradox.' I need to hold the camera far away to compose the image on the live-view screen but I also know I need to hold the camera close in order to get a sharp image. I can't do both so I use a monopod a lot of the time because it allows me to use the camera further from my eye and is still stable. I am not embarrassed to put a little, 8-ounce, digital camera on a 10-pound tripod when necessary. There is no point in spending time and effort shooting photos only to delete them later when they're soft at 100 per cent enlargement. It's always better to spend a little time getting it right in the camera than spending a lot of time trying to fix it in Photoshop.

And before spending any money on image-sharpening plug-ins for Photoshop, reconsider the appropriateness of certain technologies. Image-stabilization is great when you nail that elusive 1/15th of a second panned sports shot; but it's a waste compensating for your arm's length Parkinson's-like shake shooting snapshots at 1/250th. Garbage in-garbage out. Technology is no substitute for not getting it right from the beginning.

I believe cameras are overdue for a redesign. Camera makers design digital cameras that look like film cameras because that's what the consumer recognizes as a 'camera.' But the mirror-box may be supplanted by the electronic viewfinder and the camera body no longer has to transport film. Tomorrow's camera does not have to look or handle like yesterday's camera, but until camera design does change, it's best to steady the new digital camera like an old film camera for maximum hand-held sharpness — or use a tripod.

AN EXPENSIVE CAMERA FOR YOUR EGO GRATIFICATION

"It's a 400-D." I answered.

"A 400-D is a Rebel XTi, that's an amateur camera, you're not a professional!" and that abruptly ended the conversation with the rep at the Canon booth as he walked away and wouldn't talk to me anymore.

"What the hell was that?" my wife asked.

"That's what I've been saying. These assholes don't judge a photographer by his photographs they judge photographers by what kind of cameras they use." I (again) explained. "It's like I've been telling you; he doesn't know who I am, he's never seen one of my pictures, and the work, the actual photographs, don't matter to him or all the other people like him. In their view you can't possibly take a professional photograph with an amateur camera."

"That's bullshit." She replied.

"Yes it is," I agreed, "it's all consumerist marketing crap but that's how these dumbasses and clients judge you."

"I guess you need a new camera."

"No, not really, but most clients need me to use a camera they think takes better pictures; I have to deal with their screwed-up psychology. And it serves to justify my day-rate."

And that's why I upgraded my DSLR. Not because I really need 22 megapixels, but my clients think they do — and these are the same dipshits that insisted, back in the film days, I shoot with a 4x5 view camera for a postage-stamp reproduction size.

Dipshits! They know nothing! Yet I'm compelled to kowtow to their stupid, equipment-based idea of what 'professional' is.

And how does one determine if someone is a 'professional?'

By the kind of camera you use and by the size of your studio. And this is wrong. It is ego and marketing-based bullshit that shallow, low-information people use to judge others.

The dictionary definition of the word professional says: *...engaged in a specific activity as a source of livelihood.* Notice the word 'livelihood' and not 'income.' You are a 'professional photographer' if your source of livelihood, not just a few extra bucks, comes from the production of photographs.

The dictionary definition does not mention anything about the kind of tools (camera) you use. So in other words, if you earn your entire income from making pictures with a home-made pinhole camera, you are a professional, despite what the asshole in the Canon booth thinks.

I believe there is a second component that defines what a 'professional' is, and that is acting professionally. If you don't have a clue what you're doing, you're late, miss deadlines or do dumb stuff you're just not professional. 'Professional' is a combination of livelihood-earning with attitude and behavior.

Let's carry this to an absurd level just to help that Canon rep (and the rest of the stupid people) understand. If you act with confidence and competence and earn your living from the production of photographs then you are a professional photographer — your camera equipment is irrelevant. If you're someone who takes pictures with a five-thousand dollar camera with the word 'professional' embossed on it that you purchased with the paycheck from your job in the cubicle you are not a professional — you are just someone takes pictures with a five-thousand dollar camera with the word 'professional' embossed on it. Do you understand the difference?

Photographers are judged by their cameras because it's easy. It's because of our consumerist society. People know prices, they know famous names and they know 'labels.' And they have expectations. They expect a professional photographer to a more expensive, name-brand camera that's bigger than theirs. They figure if you're using the same camera they've got, then they can take just as good a picture as you can, after all, they've got the same equipment, so why not? Of course this is stupid and shallow thinking and does not take into consideration things like photography school, or experience or even talent.

But nowadays everybody's a photographer, so everyone's a photography 'expert.' Few other professions are like this.

Most everyone uses the same word-processing programs, Word or WordPerfect, but no one assumes them to be Stephen King or J. K. Rowling. A lot of people own guitars but that makes them neither a rock star nor musician. Suzuki sells a lot of GSXR1000s but no one riding one with a license plate should mistake themselves as a World Superbike champion.

Continuing the motorcycle metaphor, I can tell you from experience that it's a lot more fun to ride a slow bike fast than to ride a fast bike slow. Similarly, making a great photo with a less than great camera is more fulfilling than making mediocre photos with a 'professional' camera.

It's not about cameras or any kind of equipment, you know this. I've never seen any photographs (if there are any) made by the guy in the Canon booth but I can infer that he's using top of the line Canon cameras because he works for Canon. Since he works for Canon he's not a professional photographer but rather, a camera sales rep who takes pictures with a 'professional' camera. I won't judge him by his camera (the way he judged me) but based on his attitude I feel confident that I can make better photos than him with my eyes tied behind my back all the while using a shitty 'amateur' 10 megapixel camera!

A thoughtful person would only find it logical to judge a photographer by his photographs. They understand that anyone can buy a certain kind of camera… anybody! And they also understand that only you make your photographs, so it only makes sense to judge a photographer by his resultant photographs and not the camera.

But most folks are not thoughtful so they'll judge you by your camera.

So that's why I bought a big, expensive, 'professional' camera. *I bought it for them.*

And it's a very nice camera, but I'm still the same photographer who shot the same great photos with an 'amateur' camera. So what's the difference?

Now they like my photos and they like my camera too.

CHAPTER

FLEEING THE TORNADO

I'd been photographing in Oregon, Washington, Montana and was on my way to North Dakota; things were not going well…

After spending the night in the unlikely-named Glasgow, Montana, it was about a 110 mile drive to the North Dakota state line. It would be an easy drive on the nearly arrow-straight state highway 2. Commercial-free jazz played on the XM satellite radio and the cruise control was set at the speed limit of 70mph. The weather had been bad for the past few days. Storms chased me across northern Washington and late May snows in central Oregon called for a mid-trip course-correction, so I was in Montana sooner than I'd planned. As I drove I scanned the skies. Although the skies were partly sunny on the high flat plains of eastern Montana I could see a thunderstorm off to the north, and two more in the southeastern distance. So far it was dry but I wondered if I'd be driving into heavy weather. As a guy who *watches The Weather* Channel and as a child lived in Kansas for a while, I know what tornado skies look like and the distant skies were angry.

As fate would have it, it wasn't long before I drove right into a Major Storm. I don't know if the road took me to the storm or the storm came to the road, but conditions got bad quickly. The windshield wipers went from intermittent to full blast. My speed dropped from 70mph to barely 30. The rains came hard, then the hail. With the hail I started to worry about the car and the windshield especially. Luckily the hailstones were small and sporadic.

Mine was the only car on a long, lonely road in a storm and I really wanted to get out of that storm. I can deal with heavy rain, but I'd prefer not to drive in a hailstorm. I searched the horizon for a tree; someplace I could park and hide until the storm passed. Yeah right, have you ever tried to find a tree on a prairie? There aren't any, there was nothing at all; just a vast plain that I assumed was still there, behind the rain and evermore darkening skies.

Somewhere near Poplar, or maybe it was Culbertson, I saw a tree on the side of the road. It was a pathetic little tree, but it would have to do. I headed for that tree and parked under it, across the highway from an abandoned building. The hail had stopped and the rain had lightened, somewhat. I scanned the fancy high-tech XM satellite radio for a weather report but the nearest station was in Minnesota. No useful information. If I just knew which way the storm was moving…

As I sat in the car wondering, should I stay or go, another car came driving up slowly from the east. It was a cop car, or more specifically, a cop SUV, one of those tricked-out heavy-duty-go-anywhere kind of rural cop vehicles. I rolled down my window and flagged down the cop. He stopped next to me in the middle of the highway — there was nobody else around for miles.

"Hey," I called out to the cop over the booming thunder, "Do you have a weather-report on that cop-computer in your car?"

"Sure do" He answered. "And there's a super cell sitting right over this area!"

"Does it indicate wind direction?" I asked, "Which way is the storm moving?"

"East." He answered.

"East! Maybe I can get out from underneath it by out running it?"

"Good idea." Answered the cop as he pointed west, straight down the highway from where I'd just come. "But first we've got to outrun that!"

I looked down the highway in the direction he was pointing and saw a funnel cloud dropping from the already low clouds. "Holy shit!"

"Follow me," Yelled the cop, "You've got a fast car, so keep up!"

With that, he whipped a U-turn, turned on his flashing red lights, and put the hammer down. The next thing I know we're hauling at 100+mph, I'm on his bumper like a NASCAR driver and checking the rear view mirror for that tornado.

Four or five miles down the road the tornado had dissipated and the rains slacked. The cop braked and motioned me to the side of the road. We pulled off; I stopped next to the cop and rolled down my passenger window.

The cop leaned out his window and said, "Tornado fell apart and didn't form, we're clear. If you continue east you'll be out in front of the storm. If you can go southward, the weather's even clearer."

"Thanks so much!" I was truly grateful. Just before I drove off the cop added one more thing: "And no more speeding without an escort!" He smiled.

"No problem." And I continued toward the state line.

By the time I got to Williston, North Dakota, it was mostly sunny. Feeling optimistic after outrunning the tornado I ignored the cop's advice and turned northward. That turned out to be a Big Mistake but for a whole 'nuther reason......

CHAPTER

My Last Five-Hundred Words
on Stock Photography

Stock photography is fantastic for picture-users. Photographs can be obtained for a little as a dollar and anyone can acquire and use a cheap photo for just about anything. We now live in a time where photos can be obtained for less than a pack of gum.

The stock photography business is totally shitty for photographers. Licensing a photograph now cost less than it costs to produce it. Any photographer who thinks they can earn significant income from stock in the 21st century is a fool.

The stock photography industry has been destroyed by corporatists and amateurs, aided and abetted by moron photographers with no business-sense and toothless 'professional organizations,' like ASMP.

Before the corporatization of stock photography, the industry was run by and for photographers. The quality of the work was much higher than it is now because stock pictures were outtakes from professional assignments. Higher fees were charged which reflected the cost of production of professional images, and clients' rights were protected. Now, mostly, images are royalty-free and can be used by anyone, for anything. Conceivably this could mean the exact same image can be used simultaneously by two clients in the same industry. And the work is of much poorer quality now because any wanker with an iPhone can upload images to a microstock website. The choices for shit stock photography is deep!

Look at the stock photography business model: The seller gets the photos for free from photographers meaning the seller has no investment in production; all production costs are borne by the photographer. Images are searched, stored and delivered electronically thereby requiring very little staffing. The seller can sell (license) the image for as little or as much as they like. And the seller can remit as much or as little as they like back to the photographer. From the sellers' side this is brilliant, from the photographers' side it's nothing but a way to work harder and earn less. I'd guess that if this business model was proposed to a Harvard Business student they'd think it was pretty cool so long as you *don't make* the pictures.

The stock picture sellers play to photographers egos; so many 'photographers' just want to be 'published.' So what? You won't get a credit-line because, if there even is one, it'll go to the picture seller and not you, the actual photographer who shot the photo. If you find the published photo you won't be able to point to your name on the tearsheet. Stock photographers are anonymous, so it'll do nothing for your career. And that dollar they paid you won't even buy you a pack of gum.

So if you're a moron who shoots a lot of photos that are meaningless and have no value, there's a place for you in stock photography. If you're smart, and don't want to devalue your work and still want to shoot 'stock' pictures, I suggest you photograph cattle, because that kind of 'stock' is certainly better than the alternative.

SELF-SABOTAGING MY SELL-OUT

"Selling-out is doing something strictly for the money that you wouldn't do otherwise." —*Tony Banks, keyboardist for the rock band Genesis, defending their evolution from Progressive to Pop music*

I screwed up on so many levels this time... Because the financial life of a freelancer is so consistently unstable I look for 'real jobs' or regular sources of income from time to time. It's kind of a stupid thing to do but I've always longed for something steady and reliable, even though that kind of security has always eluded me. After an internet search on one particularly depressing morning I found a 'job.' A company that produced real estate photography was looking for a photographer in my area so I filled out their online form, clicked 'send' and forgot about it. And forgetting about it is the proper thing to do as these 'employers' never get back to you.

Except this company got back to me. The very same day! With a personal telephone call! Shocking!! So I had a conversation with a guy on the phone and assured him that, with a degree in photography and thirty-five years' experience, I could in fact photograph the interior of a house competently. He didn't really seem to care much about my experience, or my portfolio or anything except my camera. The fact that I own an expensive, full-frame big-megapixel camera was his only concern. I found this rather off-putting, but didn't let the fact that my camera and not I had gotten the job bother me, after all it's just real estate photography. I truly didn't care, I just wanted some steady, easy money. So we set up a meeting in a week when he'd be in town.

We met at a restaurant and had another conversation. He never asked to see a portfolio, but he did ask a few more times about cameras and lenses. Again, the camera was all he cared about. No, I'm not going to buy a fifteen-hundred dollar lens to shoot interiors for seventy dollars per house. (Quick math: that's 21.5 jobs to pay for the lens.) I have a suitable wide-angle lenses, a 14mm prime lens and a 20-40mm zoom, they've served me well and they'll serve you equally well. He had a very specific workflow he wanted me to follow which involved setting a custom white-balance for each room and a seven-stop bracket per shot to be processed in his HDR software. The whole take would be sent via DropBox as unmanipulated JPEGs. OK, I'll spend the fifty dollars of the custom white-balance device, and yeah, sure, I'll shoot a test to 'prove myself.'

I left the meeting with metaphorical red flags flying. I knew I shouldn't do this, it was a bad idea from the get-go, but the lure of quick, easy and consistent money had me in its grip. I found the requirement of a big buck, full-frame camera both insulting and unnecessary. It's insulting because photographers should not be judged by their cameras, but their pictures. Stupid! It's also completely unnecessary. Since the photos will only be shown online, at 72 dpi screen resolution, small, on realtor and Zillow websites, only about two megapixels is all that's needed. I could do all the photography with one twelve megapixel micro four thirds camera and one wide-angle lens but no, I was required to carry larger and heavier equipment. I didn't much care for his 7-stop bracket and custom white-balance workflow but I did it his way despite my misgivings. I figured for 'quick and dirty' real estate photography if I could hand off unmanipulated JPEGs for him to process and then be done with it, the less time spent would be more profitable for me.

So I shot that first test and sent it to him. At first he couldn't unzip it and called me to complain. He was using Windows 8 and so was I. Just use the default WinZip to open the file, Dude! (Red flag!) When he finally unzipped the photos he didn't like the 'too warm' white balance. (Red flag!) I re-shot the test again and it again was 'too warm' but it was correct; I had difficulty convincing him that the warm, light yellow paint on the walls was actually reproduced accurately. (Red flag!)

At this point I really knew this was something I really should not do. I realized was trying to sell-out and was beginning to feel bad about what I was doing; but I'd started this thing and now I was trapped by its inertia and momentum. I'd already spent fifty bucks on a white-balance device I didn't need. And I'd shot two tests, my client wasn't especially happy and was micromanaging me. And I had to shoot his way, not mine. But, I rationalized, it's only real estate photography, who gives a shit? So I, stupidly, blundered on. Next he had me download an app to my phone (I'd only recently converted to a smartphone) so I could check-in and accept jobs. Except there were no jobs…

He wasn't having much success penetrating the local market and there wasn't any photography to do. This was OK with me, as I'd concluded that this really wasn't for me and I didn't want to do it. I secretly hoped he'd just blow me off and not call (a standard practice for so many). Eventually he sent me a job but I declined it. I located the property and it was at the end of a gnarly dirt road. Nope, I don't drive a 4WD and I'm not screwing up my car to shoot a cheap job. Pass. Then he sent another one. I guess I should do this one. The property wasn't far away and was on an actual paved road. So I agreed to do the shoot.

When I showed up at the property I figured a realtor would let me in and then leave me alone. But no, the realtor guy was in the house doing some kind of realtor stuff and he stayed for the entire shoot, getting in the way and reminding me of what I'd forgotten about realtors — which is I don't really like real estate people! No, these people will lie and bullshit and say anything to a buyer to close the deal and collect their six percent. And this guy was in full wannabe Donald Trump mode, telling me the prices of things and how rich he is... urgh, please STFU and get outta the shot!

After about three hours I'd photographed the entire house, both inside and out. I did a couple of extra shots but I noticed some wide-angle distortion on some and figured those pictures might not be used; which really didn't matter as I'd already over-shot the job. I went back to my studio, uploaded all the photos to my computer, put them all in a folder and sent them to the client via DropBox. All in all I'd spent about six hours on the job, three hours shooting and another three hours prepping and organizing files in post-production. At seventy dollars per house I was making $11.66 per hour, slightly more than a burger-flipper. And I was sore. I was sore because all the photos had to be shot at waist-level so I was continually crouching down and standing up, over and over for hours. My fifty-six year old body isn't as flexible as it once was so my leg muscles were sore the next day.

No this isn't for me. I'm sore and tired and I'm barely making more than minimum wage. The pictures are boring. Screw this! I hope the guy wouldn't call...

The next day I received an email from my client asking, "Where were all the photos?" To which I replied that I'd sent them all. "But I only have one exposure of the exteriors," the client said. That's because you don't need a seven-stop bracket for exteriors, dipshit! You only need one properly exposed photo. Why do the extra work? Apparently he ran everything through is HDR process, needed or not. Then he emailed to complain about distortion on a few shots. These were the extras I'd shot so I told him not to use them. Apparently 'editing' means 'use everything' to him! Finally he sniveled about white-balance again. Urgh! It was another of those warm, slightly yellow interiors again, which was reproduced accurately, but to his eye (which never saw the house in-person) it was 'too warm.'

The following day I received a text from the client telling my pictures had 'failed' and were unusable. The day after that I found all my 'failed' photos on the realtor's website and Zillow — and they looked just fine!

Now I was feeling crappy and conflicted.

I felt like I'd failed; the client wasn't happy, I wasn't happy, the job was no fun, uncreative, low-budget and there wasn't even enough work coming in to make it remotely worthwhile. I really did feel like I'd failed; I screwed-up the shoot. I didn't want to hear from the guy again. But I was conflicted too; although my pictures had been declared 'failed' there they were, online, used anyway, advertising a half-million dollar home. So, apparently, my photos weren't all that bad after all? In my mind it was just one huge mess, a big mistake made by me. I should have never considered doing any of it. I've now (re)learned that I can't do a good job if I don't care (and I really could care less about real estate photography). And for nearly minimum wage I'm not paid enough to give a shit. I was going to blow it off, not invoice for the 'failed' (but published anyway) pictures and just forget the whole thing.

Then he sent me a text asking for an invoice for the job.

I blew it off but he called back. "No. The pictures failed and were unusable (I didn't mention that I had seen them online), you don't pay for bad photography." I told him. But he told me the pictures had, in fact, been used (now he tells me!) and to send an invoice.

So I invoiced the job and he paid me and I thought that would be the end of it… but a month or so later he sent me another house to photograph. I blew that off for a day, hoping it would just go away. But he contacted me again (they never call when you want

them to and always call when you don't want to hear from them).
I found that I like texting with my new smartphone because I blew
him off for good with an impersonal text that said, "Sorry, too busy
with cinematography for any more real estate photography. You'll
need to get someone else." Yes, that's the chickenshit virtual
blowoff which is so easily sent by text or email with a minimum of
human involvement. This time I sent it instead of receiving it,
which is usually the case.

And that, to my relief, was the end of it, I never heard from him
again. But I still felt bad and thought about it a lot afterwards. I had
to analyze just what I'd done and came to the uncomfortable (yet
enlightening) conclusion that I'd actually self-sabotaged the whole
darn thing.

What was actually going was I was trying to 'sell-out' but my
true self wasn't having it. 'Selling out' means you're doing something just for the money that you wouldn't ordinarily do (Tony
Banks is right). And I was doing just that! Normally I would never
do real estate photography yet here I was shooting boring empty-
house interiors. For the potential of a few extra bucks I was wasting my time and talent shooting photos I didn't care about for
clients I didn't like. I absolutely didn't give a damn about the photos and because of my lack of concern, didn't try all that hard.
Maybe I should have tweaked that white balance a little more, or
used a different lens, or deleted the photos where I noticed wide-angle distortion, or… maybe I should have never answered that ad in
the first place?

I can't fake it. When I don't care, I don't try, I can't force car-
ing. Dammit, I should know better!

Actually, I do know better. I've done this before with the same
bad results, but it was a long time ago and I'd forgotten. In Western
culture 'self-reliance' and 'having a job' and 'earning' are all given
great importance and I was just trying to be 'normal' and earn
money.

Yup, I sabotaged the whole darn thing! I didn't do it purposely, but rather, subconsciously; my true self made sure I screwed-up the job because I never was supposed to do it in the first place. My soul won't let me sell-out, no matter how much my brain (and society) thinks I should.

Don't do things strictly for money that you wouldn't do otherwise!

CHAPTER

PAY THE ARTIST! ...ABOUT NOT GETTING PAID, AGAIN!

Every Christmas I give my wife a Chihuahua calendar. Twelve months of cute little dog pictures never gets old. This year I found a Chihuahua calendar at a store in the mall. I hadn't even realized that one of the calendar pictures was mine until another photographer called me.

Oh boy was he pissed! Not at me thankfully, but he was quite justifiably angry because he hadn't been paid his portion of the licensing fee from the stock photo agency that had supplied one of his pictures to the calendar publisher. He'd looked me up because his picture in the calendar had been supplied by the same stock photo agency as mine. I was easy to find because the credit line read: © 2011 Dale O'Dell/Alamy.

So he looked me up and called, which is a smart thing to do. As creative artists we tend to get isolated in our studios and taken advantage of in business and if we don't share information it just gets worse. I've made these calls myself and I always try to be as helpful as possible when I receive them. He hadn't been paid and wanted to know if I had since our pictures had both come from the same agency, Alamy, in England. To be honest, I hadn't checked. While I had the guy on the telephone I went to the Alamy website, logged-in, and went to the 'summary of images sold' link. I know that most calendars are prepared about eighteen months in advance of publication so I went back a full three years to look for the sale. Nope, no sale recorded. In fact there were no sales at all, ever, for my particular Chihuahua picture. No, I didn't get paid either. Now he's even madder. He's pissed at the calendar publisher for violating his copyright by reproducing his picture without compensation, but that's not where he should sic the lawyers. You see, when a picture is infringed upon, stolen is the more accurate term; the 'thief' does not credit the photographer and a stock agency in print — that would actually be stupider than the original image-theft. The fact that every picture in the calendar was credited indicates to me that a legitimate reproduction license was bought. That means the end client, the calendar publisher, acted in 'good faith.' They licensed the images, paid the fee, and credited the agencies and photographers in the calendar. The problem as I see it does not lie with the client, but rather with the stock agency, Alamy. They've licensed images, collected the money, and then in violation of normal business ethics and their own contract, failed to remit payment to the photographers, or even notify us of the sales. This happens more frequently than you'd think, especially with unethical stock photo agencies. They're all bad. There's no such thing as a 'good' stock photo agency any more. He wants to sue someone. I know the feeling, I've been there. I gave him the name of a lawyer in New York who's experienced in stock photography and copyright. He could sue the calendar publisher. They'd most likely respond with a copy of the license agreement with Alamy proving they've got a legitimate right to use the image. That would mean the photographer's problem is not with the publisher, but with Alamy, who's supposed to be acting on his behalf, and paying him (and me) his portion. In that case he's generally fucked (to use a business term). Good luck suing an England-based company in American court. And for what?

"What are you going to do?" He asked me.

"Nothing." I answered.

"You've, no we've, been ripped-off! Copyright law is written in our favor, there's a clear-cut case here." He ranted.

Yes, yes there is. We've both been wronged. Our works have been stolen and someone else has profited from the theft, both the publisher (who profits from calendar sales, although I suspect they did pay the license fee) and the agency, Alamy especially (who profits from the licensing fees our pictures generate, and in this case they kept one-hundred percent of the money); we've been hosed and there's really not a damn thing we can do about it. I calmly explained this to him. He was very unhappy, but he seemed to be getting my point.

To clarify my point let me say this, we're the only ones who give a shit.

This is how it works: Although copyright law is written in favor of the artist, artists stand little chance in court.

First of all most large corporations have buildings that devote entire floors to lawyers and they are paid specifically to kick the asses of pissant little 'vendors,' 'content providers,' and self-employed one-man freelance artists. They will pay tens of thousands of dollars to staff attorneys to avoid payment of photographers' invoices for a couple hundred bucks. That's how they think and operate, folks.

Secondly, this isn't a copyright-infringement case; it's a breach-of contract and conversion case against the stock photo agency, which to make matters more complex, is in a foreign country.

Thirdly, if the case made it to court (which it wouldn't), no court, judge or jury really gives a shit about some little artist who didn't get paid for some stupid dog picture. They don't get it. What they 'get' is stuff like grand theft auto, pedophilia, or murder and can't relate to 'stolen pictures.' They don't give a shit about the Chihuahua picture someone 'stole' from you, it's not important to them, it's just a picture.

The law is on our side but the court does not care. The most you can hope for is to find a lawyer who can write a good Demand

Letter and hope the recipient makes good after being threatened. In this case I'm one-hundred percent sure that Alamy would just come up with some bullshit excuse for not paying you and, using nicer terms, tell you to fuck off. That's my experience with them.

On the Alamy website there is a 'price calculator.' According to their pricing a full-page photo in a calendar, distributed in the U.S., with a press-run of 3000 copies, the photo would license for $290.00. (This is for a 'rights-managed' image, I don't do royalty-free or microstock.) But Alamy's 'price calculator' is bogus, I know of no instance where they actually charge what their 'calculator' says. I've been working with one of the larger calendar publishers in America for the past ten years and prices paid per page for images have steadily gone down. They pay $150.00 per image per page, not $290.00. Based on my experience with Alamy, if $150.00 is 'standard' then they'd license the image for $75.00. Of that $75.00 rights-managed licensing fee they remit 40% of it to me. So I'd get $30.00 of a $75.00 sale that should have been between $150.00 and $290.00. Got that?

For thirty bucks it just ain't worth it. Heck, forty percent of $290.00 is $116.00 and that's not worth a lawsuit either!

That's why I'm not concerned about it. I'm not happy about it but getting ripped-off is part of the game, and it is a 'game.' If I'd of licensed the image myself, I'd of made sure I got paid. With Alamy, I'm just one of thousands of photographers supplying millions of pictures to them for free, to license for whatever amount they feel like; they're not in business to give a shit about me (or the guy on the phone). If I were to complain to them they'd deny there was a problem and if I pushed...... they'd kick me out the door, they don't have to give a shit about individual artists. While each of us individually cares about or own incomes from licensing fees from Alamy, all they have to care about is their total bottom-line — which isn't dependent on any one photographer.

So fuck it, what's the point?

Last year I discovered another one of my pictures, licensed by Alamy, was reproduced in numerous places online by clients like Apple and other large companies. This one was a unique digital illustration and not some generic photo of a dog. I didn't get paid for that one either. And again, Alamy was the problem because they licensed the image without remitting my portion of the fee to me. When the credit line reads photo: Alamy/Dale O'Dell, I know exactly where the image was obtained. I was pissed. I wanted to do something about it. I thought about it, considered my options and then came to the depressingly inescapable conclusion, its more trouble than it's worth, what's the point?

Sad, eh?

This is just how things are kiddies. If you're a creative person working in any of the arts, you will get ripped-off. We're in a 'Rodney Dangerfield profession,' we just don't get any respect. Our 'product' isn't valued and things with no perceived value get stolen without a second thought. The thing is we expect a certain amount of theft from certain 'end users.' What we don't expect are those (like Alamy) who are supposed to be our 'partners' who have the same self-interests' as we do to rip us off, but they do.

But then 'stock photography' is a stupid business. Really, is giving pictures for free to some company to license for whatever amount they feel like and then remit whatever amount back to the photographer they feel like (or if they feel like) very smart? Uh, no! So ya just gotta figure you're gonna get hosed from time to time. Alamy is not unique. All stock photography sellers suck, from the corporate giants like Getty and Corbis to the mid-levels like SuperStock, Masterfile and all the rest of the wankers. Don't even get me started on microstock...

I'm old enough to have earned my cynicism. I just hope to be paid more frequently than ripped-off, so I end up with a positive balance sheet. I know they'll (or someone else) will do it again. I'm just so tired of fighting just to be treated fairly, but I can't fight every fight. I've given up, it's hopeless. I know my place in the economic food-chain. I lost thirty bucks on that one, the price of a dinner. I can certainly skip dinner so someone at Alamy can keep a few extra unearned bucks.

Oh, they say it was a 'mistake?' THEN PAY THE ARTIST!

Yeah, good luck with that.

But later on... There has been a change to this story! No, I've not been paid but I might be (some day).

Upon checking the Summary of Images Sold on the Alamy.com website months later I discovered (much to my surprise) that the Chihuahua image has now been listed as licensed. This does not mean I've been paid for it (I haven't) but it's at least listed as "licensed." This is good, but it's still bad too. Here's the weirdness: Given the long preproduction lead times for calendars, the image for the 2012 Chihuahua Calendar was most likely licensed in the summer of 2010. Since stock photo agencies don't let unpaid-for images out of their possession I should have been paid sometime in the autumn of 2010. I wasn't, nor was the image even listed as "licensed" at that time. The fact that Alamy licensed the image but never listed it as "licensed" on my Summary of Images Sold page I'll call unethical business practice #1. Since I work directly with some calendar publishers I know they don't pay licensing fees for images until the calendar has been on sale for about six months. So, if I were paid "on time" I should have been paid in December of 2011. I wasn't paid, so I'll call that unethical business practice #2. Now, since the calendar has been on sale since (approximately) the summer of 2011 and I bought a copy in December 2011 and only now, in April of 2012, has Alamy listed the image as "licensed" that's unethical business practice #3. Finally, since Alamy's license stipulates payment before publication and has most likely Alamy has already been paid, they're using my money for themselves because they've not paid me yet. This is unethical business practice #4.

So Alamy has done four shitty, unethical, things so far regarding this one image:

They licensed it without notifying the artists (me and that guy who called) it had been licensed.

They allowed it to be reproduced without it being paid for.

They allowed the reproduction to be distributed without paying me.

They only listed the image as licensed in April 2012 although the image had been reproduced on the calendar which had already been on sale since late 2011.

The stock photo 'agency' is behaving extremely unethically. I almost wrote, *in my opinion* but their unethical practices are in fact, FACT.

For an image licensed in 2010, reproduced and sold in 2011, which was only listed as "licensed" in the 2nd quarter of 2012.......... I hope to be paid by the summer of 2012.

At least they got the price right. They actually licensed the image for $150.00. This is a too-low rate, but it's the 'going rate' so it's as much as I can expect. Also, since a sub-agent was not involved I got 60% of the sale instead of only 40%. So I'll get $90.00. I hope. I still haven't been paid.

This whole deal stinks. I can only imagine the malfeasance that I DON'T know about. All is normal...

CHAPTER

STIFFED BY THE DONALD TRUMP TYPES
THOSE THAT GOT, GET —
THOSE THAT DON'T GOT, GET GOT

As I write, America is in the midst of the 2016 Presidential elections. It's a terrible time. The Democratic candidate, Hillary Clinton, is an experienced and competent politician. Her opponent, the Republican candidate, is billionaire blowhard Donald Trump. Trump has proven himself to not only be incompetent and uniformed, but also a racist, misogynist, and bully. And he could get elected. After all this is the country that elected George W. Bush (twice!), so stupidity may reign again.

But I don't want to get off on a political rant, politics is just so ugly, but I must comment on one particularly ugly fact about the Republican candidate, 'businessman' Trump, which affects me personally.

> *Billionaire real estate developer Donald Trump routinely stiffs and does not pay his vendors, suppliers, laborers and business associates.*

This is fact, not opinion, a great number of unpaid Trump contractors and sub-contractors who've been stiffed have come forward and Trump himself has readily admitted that he routinely breaches his own contracts and does not pay some of those who work for him. This is not *Fake News*.

During every American election cycle we hear a lot about 'small businesses.' As a one-man shop, freelance photographer, I'm a small business, and I've been stiffed more than once by Donald Trump types. There are dozens of legitimate reasons not to vote for Donald Trump (notwithstanding the fact that conservative policies are documented, universal failures) but I could never, ever, vote for the very kind of man who's put me in personal financial jeopardy. That's like voting for your torturer and I do not suffer from Stockholm syndrome!

I've written plenty about how artists are routinely screwed because artists are routinely screwed. The conventional wisdom-cliché is that 'artists are not good businesspeople' does not apply, because this is a moral issue not a business issue.

Here are the landmarks on the road to getting stiffed:

You do the dog-and-pony portfolio show for the advertising guy at Big Corp and actually get a job.

You, the one-person studio, sole-proprietor, covers the multi-million- dollar company's expenses while you do the job.

The art director from Big Corp calls you a 'creative genius' while you're shooting the job.

You wrap the shoot, process and deliver the photos. The client is happy. You deliver an invoice.

You wait to be paid, meanwhile, you pay bills for the job expenses out of your pocket.

30-days goes by, you're not paid, and you continue to wait.

At 45-days past-due you call the client. He's 'in a meeting' and doesn't call you back.

60-days goes by, you're not paid. You call the accounting department at Big Corp, they tell you they'll 'look into it.' They don't, so you call the art director, the guy who said you were a 'creative genius' while you were doing the job. He tells you to talk to accounting and then calls you an asshole after hanging up the phone.

At 90 days past due you send letters, make multiple calls to the art director, his boss, accounting, etc. You have to get mad, threaten legal action and be a general asshole to get their attention.

Meanwhile you tell one of your photographer friends what a jerk your client is. Your friend is appalled and says he'd 'never shoot for those jerks.'

About six months after the job, a check shows up in your mailbox. Better late than never.

And then your photographer friend shoots a job for the 'jerk client,' and somehow, he's surprised when they don't pay!

This isn't 'bad business practices' on the part of the photographer, this is immoral and illegal behavior from people who have more power than you. They know what they're doing.

Donald Trump knows, as a billionaire and the owner of a billion-dollar multinational corporation that you, the independent contractor, is a pissant and you have no power. Yeah, sure contract and copyright law is on your side, but that's irrelevant, he's got enough money to stiff you and get away with it. He knows you can't afford to sue him; he's not afraid, he's got more lawyers anyway.

See, those little 'entrepreneurs' like me, us small business-people, we're credited as the 'lifeblood' of the American Economy during election seasons but in actuality, we're powerless nobodies at the mercy of Giant Corporations. To be clear, they don't give a flying fuck about you or me! If a big corporation stiffs another big corporation, teams of lawyers spring into action, but no one individual is harmed. When the big corporation stiffs the little guy the little guy is always harmed.

I recall one time I called a 'Trump-type' client about four months after they'd been invoiced; I'd done my job well, had done everything our contract had stipulated, and all I needed was for the client to honor their own contract and remit the contracted $2000.00 fee for the work I'd already done (and they published).

The client literally told me to "Fuck off, we'll pay you when we feel like it." The next call I had to make was to my landlord to ask for an extension on paying my rent, and I skipped dinner that night. The company gained nothing by not paying me, the invoice was only two grand, but it harmed me greatly, it prevented me from paying my rent and buying food.

I no longer do any work without an up-front contract and front-money. Getting a contract signed isn't really a problem, The Company knows they can breach that contract so they don't care, but I get it anyway because if I do have to take legal action, I have documentation of the agreement. Getting money up front is more difficult, but I'm not in the business of providing short-term no interest loans to people with more money than me. Often, the deposit, advance or whatever you want to call the up-front money is all you're gonna get, so get it. And recognize the Red Flag that no front money often means no money at all. If they can't cover a deposit, they ain't gonna cover the final bill either.

That's just the way it is.

A contract is a legally-binding guarantee of something, usually payment for work done. If you do the work you should be paid. Period. Donald Trump likes to say he doesn't pay for bad work, which is a bullshit excuse. If a contractor truly does a bad job, they should be given the chance to make it right. When Trump or anyone of his ilk refuses to pay for work done they're simply lying and stealing. It's not just a legal issue, it's a moral issue. By stiffing anyone who's done the work well and in good faith is to cause harm. And the harm isn't just financial, it's mentally and psychologically damaging as well.

Non-payment is stealing, which is a crime. It's the violation of a covenant, agreement or contract. It's a lie. It's a violation of trust and is a moral failing. Non-payment is damaging to the stiffed parties' business. It's harmful professionally and personally. It harms families and children. It's really simple, there's no nuance or gray area here. Anyone who takes the work of others without compensation is a criminal, and an asshole.

The 2016 Republican candidate for President of the United States is Donald Trump and he is an asshole. Any 'businessman' who routinely stiffs and harms small businesspeople like me is not fit to lead. It's really that simple.

And now (as of July 2018) he's the President of the United States — we've all been stiffed!

CHAPTER

DALE'S NO-INTEREST, SHORT-TERM, SMALL LOAN BANK

On May 5, 2012 I was watching the Time Travel episode of The History Channel's, *Ancient Aliens*, when I saw one of my photos flash across the screen. It was a stock photo I'd done quite some time ago and it was a blurry photo of a 'space alien.' I figured they'd either 'borrowed' the photo from the internet (yes, I have lost control of some of my works; as hard as I try to keep control, some always seem to 'get away') or licensed it from some stock photo agency. Either way I figured I'd not be paid or paid a pittance; there was no way I'd already been paid for its use. I didn't really care, I'd either 'donated' the picture or I'd get a couple of bucks for it one day, I just thought it was cool Ancient Aliens used one of my many space alien pictures.

On June 13, 2012 I received a commission statement from the Super Stock photo agency. There was only one image licensed but it was for a film documentary. Might that be the episode of *Ancient Aliens* I saw? I plugged the image ID number into the Super Stock Photos website and sure enough, it was my alien picture.

So I'd get paid for it after all; how much?

Thirty dollars.

In six months. (To make sure the check is 'good' and clears.) What the heck, it's thirty dollars more than free, although I'll have to wait *six months* after it was used, and paid for; Super Stock doesn't let clients reproduce pictures before paying for them.

That means the agency gets to use my money, for free, with no interest paid to me, for half a year. I'm not really a no-interest, short-term, small loan bank, but that's what the agency forces me to be, I have no choice in the matter — unless I decide not to play, of course.

Considering the way 'standard business practices' are going I may be among the last photographers who actually gets paid. Picture prices have been getting lower and lower and lower over time and at this rate it won't be long before photographs are free. I hope I don't live to see the day when I have to pay someone to use my pictures. But when that day comes, you know someone will.

'Cause it'll be cool.

CHAPTER

PAY TO DISPLAY SCAMS NOW WITH MORE MATH!

From my blog:

Dear Gallerist:

Thank you for the email announcing the 'X' Galleries' second location & the Call for Art. Since 10 of my artworks are already on the 'X' gallery website and one of my artworks was featured on the cover of one of the 'X' Gallery Art Catalogs last year I was excited to submit for the new gallery.

That was until I saw the $24.00 fee merely to LOOK at my work.

Then I stopped the upload process and left the website because it's a PAY TO DISPLAY SCHEME.

Seriously!? I was going to quote back to you your own words about this from your book (yes, he wrote a book) but a quick reread shows you didn't address pay-to-display schemes. Obviously you left that bit out because you can't call-out the very thing you do! I thought you were different from the other gallerists.

When 'X' Gallery started its online gallery you charged me fees to be on your website. I paid those fees because I believed 'X' Gallery was a different and better gallery.

I also PAID to be in one of 'X' Galleries' Art Catalogs. My artwork was even featured the cover. I could have bought an ad in Art Business News for about the same cost but I believed I had a shot at [your market] via your catalog. It didn't do anything for me, but you got your catalog paid for by artists.

I've paid you enough already.

After reading your book I tried to put myself in the position of the gallerist and better understand YOUR point of view. Here's a little something from the artists' point of view YOU need to know:

Paying a gallery to LOOK at our artwork is insulting. It's really galling. And here's how it usually works:

Pay the fee.

Submit the artworks.

Wait.

Wait some more.

Assume you were rejected because you never heard back from the gallery...

...because the gallery never even looked at the artwork because...

All they wanted was your money.

You could search YOUR OWN WEBSITE & find plenty of artwork for your new space but that would eliminate an income stream of essentially, Free Money.

So, as much as I like your gallery, good business-sense tells me that paying you to view the artworks of mine you already have online is a waste of money. Seriously, if you want to be just a little bit better than the other galleries, DO NOT charge artists merely to "consider" their artworks — that's what scammers do, and you really don't want to come off like that.

Ironically, while writing this email, I received an email from your gallery bragging about the "first sale" in the new space. So, since the gallery is up & running, what are artists submitting for? And why to you need $24.00 for a look-see when you're already selling art? Do you understand that this really reeks of just another pay to (not) display art-scam?

Good luck with the new space. I was really excited to read

about it, but I won't pay you more than 50% of an art sale to be a part of it.

I know my blog has very few readers but less than 24 hours after posting the above, I received a personal email response from the actual owner of 'X Gallery.' Here's the email I received, with minor editing to protect the gallerist's privacy.

He wrote:

A friend alerted me to your blog post and I wanted to take a moment to respond. First, let me say that I understand where you are coming from with the post and you make very valid points. I do wish you would have actually sent your letter to me so that I would have a chance to respond, but I'll take that opportunity now.

There are several reasons I ask for a submission fee. The submission system we use that helps streamline the process of reviewing comes at a cost, fees help offset that cost. More importantly, however, my outreach to the artist community has put me in touch with tens of thousands of artists. Several years ago I asked for submissions with no entry fee and was overwhelmed with over 13,000 submissions. Many of the submissions weren't appropriate for our gallery, but artists from all over the world submitted because they easily could. I have found that asking for a submission fee greatly reduces the number of submissions and encourages artists to think about whether or not their work is appropriate for my gallery. I tend to get much better submissions because those who are paying a fee to submit are serious about the submission.

I hope that the value I'm providing in my many blog posts and videos at absolutely no cost to artists balances out the submission fee in the long term.

Thanks for your consideration

And my reply to his email:

Thank you for reading my blog. Obviously I've struck a chord which compelled your response. And I do appreciate your response, despite my absolute disagreement with your pay-to-view policies. Actually, I had considered emailing you directly but I really didn't want to start an argument and I figured your response wouldn't be any different than what you wrote in your email.

Please understand that I have already heard every reason, rationalization and excuse you make for the submission fee, and while you also make some valid points, I still completely and absolutely disagree with the policy. To elaborate:

First of all I view "streamlining" the review process as a cost of doing business that should not be passed on to the artist.

Secondly, if your "outreach to the artist community" has really put you in touch with "tens of thousands of artists" why don't you just contact one of those ten-thousand-plus artists to fill the walls of your new gallery space? Really, if you have contact with that many artists, simple mathematics indicates you should never, ever need to put out a call for art.

I completely agree that too many artists submit works to galleries that are inappropriate for the venue. You covered that succinctly on pp. 131-132 of your book. (I really did read his book.)

The most common complaint I've heard from virtually every gallerist I've ever met is the 'overwhelming' number of submissions they get. What do you expect?! You are in the Gallery Business, don't act surprised that artists come to you seeking exhibition opportunities, it's what you do. You guys act like Chefs that are pissed-off that the restaurant is busy during the lunch hour!

You've been in the business long enough to know that artists will beat a path to your door to get your eye for a moment. You are in the unique position to pick and choose, reject or accept, all the while basking in the economic safety of having no investment in the production of the product you sell.

This is manageable for you. Many galleries' websites have 'submission guidelines' where the words 'not accepting new submissions at this time' can be found. You could do that to lighten your 'review workload.' Or, you could set aside a month in the (traditionally slow) summer season to review portfolios. These are two "streamlining" suggestions for you.

But galleries count on two things about artists, 1.) That artists make decisions based on emotion and, 2.) Artists can't do math. Essentially, a $24.00 'review fee' is the price paid for False Hope. Here's the math:

Let's assume the gallery accepts 2% of new submissions for representation.

If 1000 artists pay $24.00 each to have their work seen, the gallery has made $24,000.00. With a 2% success rate for artists that gives the gallery 20 new artists which is many more than can be exhibited in a year (unless you're doing huge group shows). So, 980 artists have paid you $24.00 each to be REJECTED.

So, that (theoretical) 24 grand you made, which will meet your rent and payroll obligations for a while, you made on the backs of artists, while you did absolutely nothing and took no risks whatsoever. 24 grand more than compensates you for opening emails.

So yeah, I have both an economic and a moral problem with pay-to-view schemes.

In conclusion, in my case, I saw your 'artist call' as an opportunity. I like your gallery and much of the art I've seen there. Despite the decline in the [local] arts district The 'X' Gallery remains as a beacon in the [local] art scene and is, in my view, a 'prestigious' gallery. Yet I had to reconsider my submission. You can see my artworks on your own website already, I've paid for ads in your catalog, my work was featured on the cover, and none of this has done anything for me except deplete my bank account. I had to figure that paying you (again) would be little more than a reminder of what you already have online, which you have never exhibited on the gallery walls. Based on past history I had to rationally conclude that I had ZERO CHANCE of getting my works selected to hang in the new space.

I understand, but disagree with your position. I hope you now have a better understanding of the artists' position. I didn't email you directly because I didn't want this to come off as personally confrontational. I simply reject the concept. In the unlikely event I ever get the opportunity to exhibit in 'X' Gallery, we at least know where each other is coming from.

Thank you for your consideration.

I waited a full week after sending my reply email but the gallerist never responded. I suspect his lack of response is because *his position is fundamentally indefensible* based on the math I presented. I am grateful that neither my original blog, my reply and the gallerists' email to me was cordial. Often these 'debates' deteriorate to name calling quickly and that accomplishes nothing. Neither of us has swayed the others' opinion and I'm sure he won't change his policies. He doesn't have to. There are always artists who will pay to be rejected so he's got a perfectly legal free-income stream at his disposal. He's close to but not running an actual scam, but this sort of thing is often used to extract easy money-fornothing from willing artists by 'art scammers.'

Here's the easy scam that I fear and everyone should consider when paying someone to 'review' their artwork, this also applies to fees charged to submit to juried exhibitions:

1. The gallery establishes a 'pay to review,' 'pay to enter a juried show,' or, 'pay to display' system. The verbiage to watch out for which indicates this could be a scam reads something like this: "...if the gallery is interested in your artworks we will contact you..."
2. By using the above terminology, or a variation of it, what they are really saying is: If we don't like your art, you won't hear from

us OR don't call us, we'll call you. When you never hear back from the gallery you are supposed to assume that you have been rejected by blow-off. You are supposed to assume that they actually looked at your work and rejected it, but how do you know they actually viewed your submission? You don't! And you may have been scammed — they got your money and you got NOTHING.

3. A sure way to know you've NOT been scammed is to receive a communication indicating they actually saw your work. A generic rejection doesn't count, those can be sent automatically; no, you need a rejection that actually references your work. If you hear nothing back after your submission, it's possible you're a victim of a very common art-scam.

Again, mathematics tells the story. With enough paid submissions a gallery doesn't even have to sell art or mount a juried exhibition to be profitable! And here's the math:

Suppose a 'gallery' puts out a call for submissions; this could be for a juried show or a simple 'opportunity.' Let's use an average fee of $30.00 per submission. Since gallerists always complain of 'overwhelming' numbers of submissions let's use a large-ish figure of 800 submissions per month.

$30.00 x 800 = $24,000.00

Now, if you never received a communication that indicated they actually saw your work it is quite possible they never looked at it. You may or may not have been the victim of an actual scam but what we are absolutely positive of is they got your money and you got nothing.

Do you see how easy it is to perpetrate a 'pay-to-view' or 'payto- display' scam? Receiving (I don't use the word 'earn') that kind of money means the 'gallery' doesn't have to do anything to run a profitable business. They don't even have to sell art! I'm not saying that every gallery that charges a 'review fee' is a scammer. I am saying that if you send in money and make your submission and that's the end of it and you never hear a thing back it's no different from being scammed, you could accomplish the exact same thing if you never made the submission and just tossed your money in the trash.

If you pay a fee, you should get something. At the minimum you should get verification that your work was seen. Sadly, that's often too much to ask so in your own best interest STOP PAYING PEOPLE TO 'REVIEW' YOUR ARTWORK!

Imagine if we created a system where the galleries paid the artist to review their works....

Dear Gallery:

There is a $24.00 fee charged to review my artwork for the possible inclusion in your exhibition. I charge this fee to defray the cost in streamlining my presentation for you. More importantly, the fee greatly reduces the number of fruitless presentations I have to make and insures that you are serious about the submission. Thank you for your consideration. Before I open the portfolio case I must first check my PayPal account for your payment.

Does that strike you as ridiculous and outrageous? It is! Yet artists DO NOT find it ridiculous when they pay 'submission fees' to galleries.

STOP PAYING PEOPLE TO 'REVIEW' YOUR ARTWORK!

One final thought of a philosophical nature:

Whenever an artist pays someone MONEY merely to look at, consider or review their artwork the artist gives the other party tremendous POWER over them. The artist is conveying a message that their work requires a bribe to be seen, that, somehow, the artists' work is isn't worthy of being seen without some form of remuneration first. The very word remuneration means 'to pay for services provided,' yet artists again and again are content to receive no services in return aside from the hope that some self-proclaimed expert has had a look at their work. This system is like a RELIGION where the artist must make a tithe to The Church of the Gatekeeper in order to buy a chance to potentially reach the audience for their work!

A gallery is nothing without the artist. An artist without a gallery is still an artist. Think about this carefully. A gallery is a gathering place where art is displayed. It's a building with walls. A gallery can be anywhere; it is not a unique thing. Art, IS a unique thing, it is the creative expression of one soul. Art can exist without the gallery, but a gallery cannot exist without art, it's just an empty room. Certainly a gallery can be more. A gallery can be a partner, an advocate, a marketer and a promoter. These are the services galleries should supply at no charge to the artist. These things should be a part of the 50% commission the gallery receives for the sale of a piece of art. This is the cost of doing business the same as an artist absorbs the cost of materials, time and presentation of their artworks. So long as a gallery can extract money from artists for doing nothing or next-to-nothing then they will remain empowered. But, alas, there will always be more artists than galleries so this system will remain in place, aided and abetted by dumbass artists who willfully throw money at false hope. Use your power! Keep your money!

Final, final note: Upon further consideration, that gallerist IS a scammer.

CHAPTER

REJECTED, BUT NOT QUITE…

I get it from time to time, rejection but with a back-handed compliment, and I'm never quite sure if I should be pissed-off, complimented, or both. I grew up in a passive-aggressive family so I should be used to it, but I never could figure out how to react; the slap still hurts even when it's followed by a kiss.

It was another juried group show submission. I don't do a lot of these anymore because the ego never benefits from the expense but this one had decent award money and it was an online exhibition. The nice thing about online art shows is your picture frames aren't returned damaged because all you have to exhibit is a JPEG.

But, as happens all too often, I got the "…jury was impressed with the quality of works submitted, unfortunately yours was not…" bulk email and I'd been rejected. BFD, it happens. The very same works have won awards at other venues in the past so I know they're good and I don't get too depressed when rejected. I don't get too excited when I do get in the show either. In or out, the end result is usually the same.

But the day after I received the rejection email I got another email from the same online gallery, this one wasn't a bulk email but personal, and it was from the organizer, not the jury. He was very complimentary of my artworks, said I'd been 'robbed' by the jury and my works should have been included in the show. How nice! (Too bad he's the organizer and not the jury.) He said he felt so bad about it that if I submitted for their next exhibition he'd waive the fee. That's very nice and it does ease the pain of rejection a little. I would take him up on his offer and told him I'd be sure to submit to the next online exhibition. Then the next day he sent me another email. He'd visited my website and seen my portfolios and now he wanted to interview me for his photography blog. I love talking about art and photography and readily agreed to the interview. He emailed me the questions and I took a long time to write lengthy, cogent and honest answers to all the questions. For a day or so after the interview was posted I got complimentary emails and was quoted on social media. Again, nice!

So, although my work was deemed by the jury not good enough to exhibit, I made an online friend, got interviewed for a photography blog and got a free entry for the next exhibition. Then it got… something else.

He emailed again and asked that I not submit imagery for the next exhibition but instead he wanted me to be one of the jurors for that show. Of course I accepted!

It was a little hard to wrap my head around: I'd paid the fee, submitted my artworks and they were rejected. Then I got a complimentary email with an offer of a free submission for the next show. Then came the online interview. Ultimately I get asked to be a juror — that is, to judge others' artwork-for an online gallery that judged my own work as not good enough! That's definitely unusual!

What occurred is the exact definition of irony: *incongruity between what might be expected and what actually occurs.*

Ultimately I did serve on the panel of jurors for their next online exhibition, but my presence wasn't especially influential, in fact, none of my choices made the final cut. What happened?

When it comes to 'juried exhibitions' it's important to remember that there is no 'standard' for selecting artwork, everyone's got their own system. In my case I was one of a number of jurors whose selections were averaged to come up with 'winners.' If I'd had a better understanding of their jurying process I would have scored the artworks I selected higher to compensate for the other jurors' choices. But I didn't, I scored images based on my own aesthetic and my scores were overwhelmed by the other juror's scores when averaged with mine, which had the effect of negating my scores. Therefore, I actually had no influence whatsoever on which images were selected as 'winners.' In other words, don't thank me if you got in the exhibition, I actually had nothing to do with it!

One might think that selections made by a single juror, as opposed to a panel, might be a better process but it isn't always that way. If the juror is objective and open-minded then the chances of a stronger, more interesting exhibition are possible. However, and all too often, a single juror can be narrow-minded and won't select works outside their own personal comfort zone. I was once in a juried exhibition where my image was literally the only one on the wall that was sharply-focused; every other image was soft and blurry. It was a really bad exhibition and I was actually embarrassed to be in it. Believing that good photography is good photography I had not researched the (single) juror before submitting. Only when I saw the juror's selections in the exhibition did I Google the juror. As soon as I found the juror's website I understood the reason for all the blurry, out-of-focus pictures in the exhibition — the juror had selected images that looked just like theirs! The selection of my tack-sharp image must have been a mistake!

As mentioned a few paragraphs back, the best thing to remember about juried exhibitions is to not get excited if your work is juried in and do not feel bad if you are rejected. Decisions made by committees are seldom meaningful and selections made by single jurors are merely one individual's opinion.

I have learned this because I have been both entrant and juror. The perspective from both sides is very helpful.

And again, I don't submit to a lot of juried exhibitions anymore, the expense is seldom worth the reward. However, from time to time, there are legitimate exhibitions that provide the potential for awards and broader viewership. Choose carefully.

I never did take the guy up on his offer of a free submission — I know too much about their jurying process.

THE UNCOMFORTABLE CIRCUMSTANCE
OF HAVING TO SUCK-UP TO YOUR LESSORS

The position I now find myself in is uncomfortable and possibly untenable. An unforeseen confluence of my age and lack of success places me here. Because I could be described by some as a 'failed artist,' and now I am 'old,' I have to question if I can carry on in this business of art. The combination of my age and my lifelong inability to cultivate any long-term relationships with the 'powers that be' in the world of galleries and gatekeepers of art puts me where I am. I don't like it, it's highly discomforting, and I take full responsibility for it. Naively I put 'the art' first and now, after thirty-five years of hammering a nail that just won't budge, I've learned that 'the art' is nowhere near the top of the list of what's necessary to succeed in the arts; I find it's nearer the bottom than I ever imagined.

In the autumn of 2013 I made a trip to Phoenix (about eighty miles from where I live) to attend a lecture. Whenever I go to Phoenix it pretty much kills an entire day, so I always try to do more than one thing. On this visit I not only attended the lecture; I did some shopping and I visited a gallery. I'd found this particular gallery online and liked what I'd seen on their website. It was a gallery specializing in photography that I thought might be a 'good fit' for my work. It was also located on Marshall Way, the epicenter of Scottsdale art galleries. Unfortunately it was a Monday and I'd forgotten that most galleries are closed that day, so all I could do was look through the window, but I liked what I saw and felt that this was a gallery where I should show a portfolio. During the two-hour drive home I remembered it had been quite a long while since I'd done an in-person 'sales pitch/portfolio show' and also recalled how reticent most galleries are when it comes to meeting artists and viewing portfolios. During the following weeks I talked myself in and out of 'making that call' and attempting to set up a meeting. I wasn't sure I had the heart for another probable rejection. One day, while visiting the gallery's website once again I saw they were having a juried show. Oh wonderful, another 'contest,' another chance to 'compete' for a spot on the wall and another opportunity to pay to be rejected. Knowing my chances of getting my work seen in person was nearly nil, I opted to enter the competition with the knowledge that by paying the fee and submitting the JPEGs might be the only chance I had in getting my works in front of the eyes of the gallery. So I submitted and, lo and behold, I got one piece in the show. This was good. My work had been seen and deemed acceptable for display.

Upon receiving my acceptance email I was informed of a size limitation. This was not mentioned in the 'call for entries' and I'd hoped on displaying an impressive, large-scale print. So I called the gallery to discuss the size requirement and got the owner. We had a pleasant enough conversation; although my 30x40 inch print was deemed 'too big' we compromised on a mid-sized piece framed 20x24 inches. I got my opportunity to meet the gallerist and check out the gallery when I delivered my artwork a few weeks later. The gallery met my expectations and the gallerist-owner, well... the guy was young. I found him 'hard to read' (not that I'm especially skilled at personal-interaction), kind of abrupt (in a non-offensive, stick-to-business way) and not terribly 'enthusiastic' (for lack of a better description). I wisely stuck to the business at hand and refrained from making any overt pitches like, 'you should see more of my work.' I kept my role to delivery-boy and not salesman.

When the time came for the exhibition itself I again drove down to Scottsdale for the opening. I waited in my car so as not to be 'too early' (or eager) and made my entrance socially-late, and dressed as one would expect a 'surrealist' to appear. Although it was 'Art Walk' night, the gallery wasn't especially crowded. I spent an inordinate amount of time viewing the artworks on display while noting little more than a mere nod of recognition from the gallerist. After making something like my tenth unnoticed lap through the gallery I began to realize that among the hip young-sters and expensively dressed collectors I was most likely per-ceived as an 'old guy' — that is if I was noticed at all. As a nottoo-ugly yet graying and balding middle-aged man I'm beginning to realize that the Romulan Cloaking Device really kicks in at this point in life — I'm essentially invisible. I am no longer hip or cool. Despite being one of the featured artists and my Dali-esque appear-ance, I am no longer noticed by the women in the Little Black Dresses and probably not thought of as an artist at all.

I don't do 'small talk' very well I actually considered leaving but I hung around anyway. Announcement of the 'winner' would be made later in the evening and I held out a slim hope that it might be me. (After all this time I still find the concept of 'winning' and 'best of show' vaguely insulting, after all this is art and not base-ball. Everything's a damn competition!) After a while a group of well-dressed people actually noticed me, and one of the women asked if 'I was one of the artists?' I replied in the affirmative and pointed to my artwork when she asked which was mine. Fortunately she seemed interested and began asking questions about it. This broke the ice and I was then included in the group's (of mostly artists) conversation. My comfort-level improved and we engaged in a lively discussion of each other's works for the next hour. We had (at last!) in an interesting and intellectual conversa-tion that concluded with the gallerist's announcement of 'the win-ner.' Of course it wasn't my piece. Actually the artwork selected was one of the weakest in the show and didn't come close to my 'I wish I'd shot that' standard. That's the way it always goes and I was not surprised.

The announcement finally got the gallerist talking about the different artworks and when he got to mine he mentioned how 'controversial' it was. I snickered to myself, controversial? The image doesn't even have any naked tits in it, what's the controversy? The 'controversy,' it turned out was whether it was 'a photograph' at all, given the amount of digital work I'd done to it. Ah, now this is a conversation I want to have because I don't consider my work to be photographs any more specifically because they wouldn't look the way they do without extensive computer-manipulation. But, just as I thought I might be making some intelligent conversational inroads with the gallerist, he pronounced my work 'photography' and that was the end of discussion.

As I said farewell to the group I mentioned to the gallerist that, 'this is from a larger body of work,' but my soft-sell comment was met with indifference and I left. It was already 9pm and I had a two-hour drive ahead of me — and the Great Surrealist's stomach needed a stop at McDonalds on the way home. When I got home my wife asked, 'how it went?' and I replied, 'meh.' That was that. After living in Arizona for twenty years and being completely shutout of the Scottsdale gallery scene for as long, my first and only opportunity to exhibit in the Big Time of Scottsdale was anticlimactic.

I thought; perhaps, when the show was over and I had to go pick up my artwork I'd simply ambush the gallerist. I'd bring a portfolio of pictures and just force the dude into looking at them simply because I was there and put him on the spot.

As it turned out I didn't have to go pick up my artwork because it sold; a few weeks after the opening I received a check in the mail (for the usual fifty percent of retail) and was thrilled. Seldom do pieces in juried group shows sell but mine had, and quickly. This meant a number of things to me, one, a sale is a sign of acceptance, any time someone forks over hard-earned cash to acquire a piece of art it's a validation of the art itself. Secondly, it would mean to the gallerist that there's a market for my imagery and as a business-man he might be amenable to showing more 'saleable' artwork. I sent off a 'thank you' email and included a line that said, 'this is from a larger body of work and if you'd like to see more I'd be happy to come by and show you more.' My email was met with the typical response of no reply at all. Once the show ended and was uninstalled I finally got up the nerve to call the guy on the phone and make my 'since my piece sold, would you like to see more?' pitch. To my surprise he agreed and we set up a meeting for the fol-lowing week. The meeting itself brings me to the sucking up to your lesser point.

Experience told me I wouldn't get much of the guy's time or attention so I only brought ten pieces and copies of my books. Just in case, I did bring three framed, ready-to-hang prints of my most popular works but, as usual, I ended up taking those right back home with me. I arrived perfectly ten minutes late (it's a 110 mile drive from my studio to the gallery so travel-time estimation is tricky, but ten minutes late was perfect). We got right to business. I handed him copies of three of my books to have a look at while I retrieved my prints from the car. The meeting lasted about an hour, which in my view is just about right. Although he 'didn't have the wall space' for the framed prints he kept three matted pieces for 'the bin' and asked for prints of four of my newest works. This was fine. Although I had held out hope for a 'representation' offer my main low-goal of achieving something other than being completely blown-off was met. I would have seven pieces available for viewing in a legitimate Scottsdale gallery and that was good enough for now. Hopefully, if something else sells, he'll get the idea that, in the pur-suit of money, I ought to have a show. I'm taking a very soft-sell approach and proceeding in small, baby-step increments.

I left him with digital copies of my books, the three prints, and apromise to return in two weeks with the other selections. If thiswere sex, it would be considered foreplay.

Since Scottsdale Fashion Mall was just down the road I decided to go shopping after the gallery meeting (might as well, a four-hour round-trip drive for a one-hour meeting is a lot of work) and while I was eating a Five Guy's burger in the Food Court a number of disconcerting things struck me. Again there was that invisibility thing. In tennis shoes, jeans, a sport coat and gray hair I was still unnoticed by the dressed-to-the-nines fashionistas at the mall. Nope, none of the mini-skirted pixies looked up from their phones and I was cheaply dressed in comparison to my jewelry-dripping contemporaries. Well, Scottsdale is a bastion of the wealthy and I was certainly out-of-place. Perhaps I've 'gone native' as a resident of a small town of forty-thousand? Maybe I've 'lost my edge'— assuming I ever had 'an edge?' But then in my mind I began reviewing the meeting and it's a good thing I've got firm control of my ego because I realized that I ate some shit.

First of all the guy is young, I'm pretty sure I've been a working artist longer than he's been alive. So I'm in this weird rolereversal situation where me, as the 'old' experienced guy is sucking up to the younger, less experienced guy. It's my fault for not establishing long-term relationships with those in his position when I was younger -but it's not from a lack of trying. Although he's in the position of 'power' he's clearly not done as much as I have and is far less experienced and it's galling to have to 'impress' someone lesser. On the other hand he is running a seemingly successful gallery in the High Rent District so I've got to give him a lot of credit for that. But still I cannot escape the nagging feeling that he finds me somehow… pathetic. He left me with the impression that he thinks he's really smart despite the fact that he asked no questions whatsoever, made no art or photography history references and felt comfortable telling me how I should print my works. I graciously listened because I knew it was pointless to debate him, besides, any disagreement on my part could have tainted what little I was hoping to accomplish. At the end of the meeting, I learned he was doing infrared photography himself (something I have experience with going back to the 1970s) and I tried to engage him in a conversation about something we have in common. Yes, I attempted to play to his ego because everybody loves talking about themselves. But he came off as a cocky 'expert' telling me how things were and weren't and presented his opinion as fact. OK fine, kid, again you'll get no debate from me. I will show him a couple of my silver-gelatin infrared prints when I drop off the other works, and I'll let my work speak for itself — and prove some of his presumptions wrong. I decided not to mention I published a book of infrared photography way back in 1997 (after all I was there to show color, digital, surrealism; I do know that too much diversity in a portfolio only causes confusion).

The thing that really got me was his lack of enthusiasm, there was no 'spark,' no questions, no back-and-forth and worst of all, no excitement. I don't understand. Maybe it's just the fellow's personality (god knows I'm a lousy judge of character) but what the hell, man? We're doing this because we love it, and I didn't feel the love. I've met more enthusiastic insurance salesmen.

So I'm weirded-out. Maybe I'm an anachronism, my mold has been broken, I'm the end of the line and my model has been discontinued ...or something else I can't quite put my finger on? A few years ago I subjected myself to a series of paid Portfolio Reviews with gallerists, curators, art directors and other so-called 'experts' and didn't get much more enthusiasm from them either. Maybe that's how it is nowadays but damn, doesn't anyone get excited about anything other than sports? I'm not expecting cartwheels or lightning to fly out of anyone's ass, but a little engagement would be nice. Oh well, I'm grateful he didn't stare at his phone the whole time like those pixies at the mall.

It had been a long time since I'd done an in-person portfolio show so maybe I'm out of touch? It was nice to actually get the meeting since so much rejection is done by online blow-off nowadays. At least I got more information than I would have via email by being able to read his expressions and watch the body language — we do get a lot of nonverbal information when we actually meet. Maybe I'm just getting too old for this game, the rules have certainly changed and it is a game. But this game is my life and I have dedicated myself to it. I know I've failed in many respects but I have done the hard work by actually making the art and not quitting. Or maybe I should have quit a long time ago? I feel like a teacher begging his student for a grade and it's just awkward and uncomfortable.

THE THREE STAGES OF AN ARTIST'S DEVELOPMENT: IMITATION, EMULATION AND INNOVATION

As a full-time artist, occasional art teacher, and ex-art student, I've noticed that most artists seem to travel the same developmental path. It's a three-part journey and many artists never leave the first or second stage, but it's the third part of the journey that history remembers.

The young or 'immature' artist begins with the first stage, imitation. The young artist, unsure of their technique and style usually begins by imitating other artists. As a photography student I recall many of my classmates' desires to be 'the next Ansel Adams' or 'the next Edward Weston.' They would dutifully reproduce Adams' landscapes as best they could while learning the craft of the black and white darkroom. Others would bring hairy-legged models to the studio and copy as precisely as they could Weston's nudes from the 1920s and 30s. Aesthetically they weren't travelling new ground, they were copying what's already been done while working on their technique. These are 'accepted' images, already recognized by the monoculture as 'great art' and thus of little risk to make. Young artists copy established artists' work while they perfect their technique; much like the still life is used by painting students to practice their technical skills. Being able to reproduce others' art is a good way to hone one's skills, but it is no way to express one's individual creativity.

The second stage is emulation. Although very similar to imitation, emulation isn't blatant copying, but rather, working in the style of. Some artists move very quickly from the imitation stage to emulation and I watched some of my photographer friends who wanted to be 'the next Ansel Adams'working very hard in the style of Adams to became successful. They didn't become 'the next Ansel Adams' but instead they joined the ranks of all the other Ansel Adams. Emulation means your art is yours, but it's like someone else's. For those landscape photographers working in black and white that meant not shooting exactly what Ansel Adams shot, but something very similar. Essentially, Adams himself chose the subject for them, the time-tested and accepted landscape, but they didn't shoot the same landscapes Adams did, they shot different-ent scenes and presented them with impeccable Adams-like black and white prints. There will always be a market for emulation, for Adams-ish black and white landscapes and for those who can't afford an original Adams; there are plenty of lower-priced emula-tors making pictures. Some artists never leave the emulation stage. To leave the emulation stage the major requirement is having something new to express.

Imitation is like singing someone else's song in their voice. Emulation is singing someone else's song, in your voice. Innovation is singing your song in your voice. The last stage, inno-vation, is where the artist uses their technical abilities in concert with a fully developed 'style' and expresses something truly new and innovative. This can be a rough road. It's easy to continue in someone else's footsteps as they've blazed the trail for you and this makes the emulation stage a comfortable place to remain. There are many, many artists who never leave the emulation stage. Emulation is comfortable and one's imagery is so pre-approved by the marketplace they can easily obtain exhibitions. When the gallery asks, "What kind of photographer are you?" the emulator can say, "My pictures look like Ansel Adams'," and the gallery immediately knows what to expect. And, since you're not Ansel

Adams (you're only like him) your works should be a cheaper alternative to the Adams works they can't afford to exhibit.

Using Ansel Adams is an intentionally easy example. Prior to Adams, there was no one producing photography quite like him; after Adams there were many imitators and emulators. How do clichés get started? Someone does something first, that thing becomes accepted and safe, and then others make their versions of it. A comfortable familiarity breeds clichés.

Art innovators are the ones who do things differently and do them first. Art innovators learned technique while imitating others, they further developed their technical abilities while emulating the imagery of their forebears and when they took their technique and used it to express their own unique and personal ideas, they innovated. Today an innovator cannot use the term "looks like" when presenting their works to galleries and publishers. Because of the lack of easy reference, innovative artists have greater difficulties getting exhibitions because they're different.

Those artists who have something to say, some mental concept to make real, bring to fruition, and express tangibly are the ones who will follow all three stages of the artist's developmental path and arrive somewhere new. These are the ones who are truly original. And they've been on the path the longest, all the way to the end — and found themselves. They've followed the hardest course and although they may have crashed a few times they've gotten back on track and continued on.

Innovation is the destination, don't stop short.

THE GALLERY'S ONLINE PRESENCE IS MUCH MORE IMPRESSIVE THAN THE ACTUAL GALLERY

Way back in 2007 I had a solo exhibition in a gallery in Las Vegas, Nevada. It was a successful exhibition that was well promoted, with strong attendance at the opening, and we sold enough artwork to make it profitable for both artist and gallery. The gallery was located near downtown, in an area being re-developed as an 'Arts District.' But, as it so often goes, the gallery didn't last long as the owners moved onto other ventures and closed the gallery. My presence in the Vegas art scene was positive, but shortlived. Despite my successful sales record and good reviews, no other gallery 'picked me up' and I was out of the Las Vegas market.

Although I go to Las Vegas at least once a year I didn't seek out another gallery until seven years later. In the spring of 2014 I had a business trip scheduled for Las Vegas and decided I'd recheck the Vegas art scene, so prior to my trip I did some online research. While surfing the web I discovered that the Vegas downtown 'Arts District' had been further developed. The 'Arts Factory' which was under development back in 2007 was now fully-occupied and there were a number of new galleries and studios in the area. Some of the galleries' websites were quite impressive and one in particular stood out. Their website featured some interesting art and was run by two people with impressive credentials. One co-curator had run a software design studio for nearly 20 years. His stated goals were to "…re-invent the gallery experience and show works that are bold and relevant... memorable... powerful and stimulating... they must be shared!" The other co-curator was a "former creative director... heavily involved in branding... [and] the gallery is not your stuffy fine arts gallery." Impressive sounding and right for me, I thought. So I decided I'd check out the entire district and pay extra special attention to that gallery with the impressive website.

After finishing my scheduled business in Las Vegas I headed downtown to the 'Arts District.' First I noticed that, with the exception of Fremont Street, the downtown area is still seedy and run-down looking. Not a good impression. Since my former gallery from 2007 was located on the fringe of the developing 'Arts District' I drove past it. Expecting to see a different gallery in that space I was dismayed to find a tattoo parlor in its place — with a bail bonds office next door. Not good, and I wasn't even in the official 'Arts District' yet. Rounding the corner onto Charleston Boulevard I found the 'Arts District' and immediately wondered if any Mercedes-driving, discretionary-income-type art collectors would be paranoid parking their cars there on Gallery Opening Night. Maybe the area looked less seedy at night? Parking my car I waited for the drunken homeless man to pass before exiting the car and setting the alarm (which I rarely use) and headed into the 'Arts Factory,' a place that, seven years ago was just cranking up and was full of artist-run bohemian energy. Not much energy this time and, aside from me, there were no patrons, no 'lookers' or anyone shopping for art. Although the building was filled with small galleries, studios and a restaurant there was nothing going on. I met one very friendly (and I suspect, lonely) artist who was very chatty but aside from him, nobody. Some of the galleries were closed. I wandered through one gallery but the girl behind the counter didn't look up. There was one tiny photography gallery but I didn't go in for fear of interrupting the two people clicking away on laptop computers, I didn't want to intrude on their Facebook time.

There was another arts building across the street so I went there next. I wandered into the not-yet-open-for-business Polaroid museum and had a nice chat with a fellow dedicated to instant photography but moved on as I was seeking galleries and not camera museums. Things weren't right when I found the building's main door locked during business hours! Walking around the side of the building I discovered that gallery with the impressive website, and discovered its doors locked too. Continuing a lap around the building I finally found an open door and entered the dark space. Perhaps an interior door will open into the impressive-website gallery? No, that door was locked too. The gallery was closed and dark. Peering through the windows I saw framed photographs on the walls of a rather small and mundane white-cube type of gallery. I don't recall the subject matter of the photographs although I might have had they been "memorable, powerful or stimulating." The impressive website was nothing but a front for another same-old art gallery, which was closed during business hours indicating that its "co-curators" must have been at their day jobs. No sign with business hours or, 'by appointment' was visible. The buildings' other galleries were closed as well, 'by appointment' signs on their doors. Briefly I considered having lunch at the 'Arts Factory' restaurant, but since it was empty (never a good sign at mealtime) I opted to go back to the hotel, where the food was of known quality.

So that was it, a brief mid-week, mid-day bust. Move along, there's nothing to see here despite the big sign that says 'Arts District.' I didn't meet a single gallerist or show a portfolio or even talk to a gallery person. I slid my business card under the door of the gallery with the impressive website — it's probably stuck to the bottom of some 'co-curator's' shoe — assuming anyone even came to the gallery since then.

I'm not dead, or a market-savvy producer of lame commercial art like Thomas Kinkade or Peter Lik, so going to any uptown galleries was pointless. It was time for lunch and a drink, and perhaps another drink. I'm not going to be exhibiting in Las Vegas in the foreseeable future, nosiree.

There is no easy-to-find mid-level art in Las Vegas. Sure, there are Peter Lik's vanity galleries full of overblown, oversized and overpriced stock-and-standard landscape photographs. And there's the High Art found in the gallery/museum at The Bellagio but, aside from that kind of flash there's little left but the bohemian art that nobody buys. The 'Arts District' was a nice idea — for the real estate developers, but it's just a way to 'art up' an area until it's acceptable to go there, raise the rents, kick out the artists and covert the place to trendy 'lofts.' I think the downtown Vegas Arts District will remain low-rent bohemian artists' studios/galleries for a long time. I really don't see Rich Folk parking expensive cars in an area that reeks of High Theft and slumming it among the paintsplattered 'art spaces.' No 'art acquisition manager' is going there seeking art for hotels, offices, public spaces or private residences. If there are any discoveries to be made I don't think they'll be discovered there. It's just another low-rent, funky, bohemian arts district populated and visited mainly by artists. And mainly they just show their own and each other's stuff.

And that gallery with the impressive web presence? Well, *anybody* can look good in cyberspace but in actual space... not so much, although I would like to meet their web-designer.

Your Photos look better on my Phone

The images were intriguing and caught my attention. I'd been seeing them on social media for a few days announcing an upcoming exhibition. I clicked through the Facebook post and even surfed over to the artist's website. Nice stuff, I may have to check out the show.

In 'Yoda-speak,' checked out the show I did, disappointed I was. The imagery was heavily-manipulated digital photography and the Gicleé prints were in the 11x14 inch to 16x20 inch size range. Unfortunately the large prints on the wall didn't hold up to the small images displayed on my phone, tablet and computer monitor. It's dissatisfying — and I'm finding myself more and more dissatisfied in these 'small screen display' days. I doubt I would buy art online based on monitor-display unless there was a firm money-back return policy. The visual differences can be too great and too variable.

The obvious difference between print vs. monitor-display is size. My SmartPhone has a display area of about 10.5 square inches; my Android tablet is about 43 square inches, and my laptop computer is 108 square inches. A 16x20 inch print has 320 square inches of viewing space. Image size, and thereby viewing distance, is usually larger with prints than monitors. Larger size makes prints easier to see — especially at a distance. Another major difference between print display and monitor display is *backlighting*. Images on screens/monitors are viewed by *transmitted* light whereas prints are viewed by *reflected light*. When light strikes a print and is then reflected back into your eyes there is some scattering of the light which makes the image just a little less contrasty and less color-saturated than an image viewed on a monitor by transmitted light.

Simply put, an image viewed on a screen generally looks 'better' than a print. Now, a great print image most always looks good when displayed on a screen. But the thing is average, mediocre or even bad imagery looks pretty good on a screen — especially a small one, like a phone. This is what I ran up against when I attended the exhibition of disappointing prints. What looked good on a screen didn't hold up in the larger prints. Small screen display can hide bad technique and obscure subtleties and other details.

This begs the question, "What are we shooting for? How will the image be displayed, screen or print?" Nowadays the answer is usually both, or monitor-display only. Very little photography these days exists in print-only form. If there's a print, there's a digital file of it, and it's probably online.

In digital imaging it's always better to downscale than to upscale. Here's a practical example: I frequently produce CD covers for bands releasing new music albums. A CD cover is about 5x5 inches, which is pretty small. But I do not create the CD art at five by five inches, I work larger, usually about 20x20 inches. This is much more data than my client needs and when we upload artwork to the record label or publisher I downscale the image to the printable size and I archive the large-scale file. If the CD is a hit (it could happen!) and the musicians come back and ask for a larger version of their CD art for the vinyl release, or t-shirt, or poster or whatever, I've got the hi-res data. A poster made from an up-sized 5x5 inch file is going to look pretty poor next to one made from a large-scale file. This is 'resolution 101' and should be obvious to anyone working in digital-imaging.

But the images in the exhibition weren't low-resolution. They were 'digital paintings' and (in my opinion) many of the paintbrush effects were out-of-scale in the large prints. This produced an arti-ficial 'softness' which created the illusion of low-resolution. I'm sure this was not at all obvious on the photographer's computer-monitor and shouldn't be considered a 'flaw' or 'mistake' — they just look better smaller than larger. Sometimes it's wise to make a full-resolution 'work print' (like we used to make in the darkroom) to test the size-viability of some effects.

I guess I'm an 'old timer' in that I value prints and print-qual-ity above all else. It is true that if the image looks good printed it likely looks good on a monitor but the inverse is not *necessarily true* that if it looks good on a monitor the print will look good too. I won't even get into the other, non-visual, aspects of prints like texture, weight, and having an actual physical artifact instead of just data that requires software to display.

This is why actual, physical display in brick-and-mortar gal-leries (or other physical venues) is so important. What I saw at that exhibition was the real thing, actual physical prints; but what origi-nally caught my attention was *data*. That data just happened to dis-played in a way that exceeded the quality of the real thing. Remember this especially if you shop for art online because what you see may not be what you get.

CHAPTER

APPROPRIATION
ABOUT PHOTOGRAPHING OTHERS' ARTWORKS

When we talk about photographing other's artwork we're not talking about *copywork*, when the photographer photographs another artists' artwork *for that artist as client*. That's providing a noncreative photographic service so the artist will have a copy of their artwork, either for archiving or reproduction. What we're discussing here is appropriation or, photographing other's artworks and including those artworks as a part of our own creative expression. In most instances appropriation/re-appropriation is simply *stealing* — with a lot of bullshit justification from art historians talking about fakes vs. originals, but mostly it's just stealing from others.

But it's not always stealing and we need to know the difference. When you make an unaltered photograph of someone else's artwork and claim the thing itself as yours, that's stealing. That's obvious (or should be) but co-opting someone else's art gets tricky in a hurry. Avoiding photographing other's artwork is a good personal policy but isn't always entirely possible. As an art student, we argued about this during many late-night, alcohol-fueled debates; as a working artist I've confronted the issue many times. Based on education, personal ethics and experience here are some guidelines and thoughts about them:

Cemetery headstones/mortuary sculptures was the subject we obsessed about as art students. Every semester way too many freshman Photo One students invaded cemeteries and made

79

'spooky' or 'goth' photos of gravestones. Yawn. Yeah, they still do this, get smacked-down in critique and then they get it out of their systems — or should. I know of one 'famous name' fine-art photographer who shot a whole series of gravestones. He merely documented the sculptors' works and add nothing creative himself. He did nothing original yet he claimed the photographs as 'his own art.' He was nothing but an 'art thief.' I doubt any of the mortuary sculptors knew or cared, but if any had sued for copyright infringement they'd of won. Instead he got a museum exhibition of his photos of *somebody else's sculptures*. He should not have been rewarded for stealing.

While that's blatant stealing, merely including a headstone or mortuary sculpture in a photo isn't. The Photo One students that photographed in the cemetery and used it as a *backdrop* to stage their own set-up scenes used the existing mortuary art to create their own unique creative expression and are *not thieves*. They may be purveyors of cemetery-clichés but they're not stealing anyone's art.

I confronted this very thing once when shooting for a client. My assignment was to illustrate a 'ghost story' for a magazine. Since the story's setting was a cemetery I photographed a cemetery as a background (like a 'plate' in cinematography) and then in post-production I digitally added 'orbs' and 'smoky ectoplasm' and some 'ghosts.' The sculptures and headstones were not subject but *setting* for my digitally-added tableau. Had I photographed a headstone and done nothing to the image *then* I would merely be photographing someone else's art and violating their copyright. That would also make me creatively lazy artist, like the schmuck who got the museum show.

Public Art is similar, but a bit trickier than photographing the sculptures in the cemetery. *Public Art* is most often found in the form of large-scale, 3-D, installations of sculptural art. The most commonplace 2-D public art is the Mural, which I will address separately. Whereas the sculptor of the cemetery statue is mainly anonymous, the sculptor or installation artist responsible for a piece of contemporary public art is definitely not anonymous. Usually the artist's name is attached to these pieces or is publically documented. Technically, photographing *public* art without the artists' permission is illegal, however, since the art is public there are exceptions. Public art is usually associated with a place or a building. When photographing a *scene* which may include the public art, architecture and other things is not a legal or ethical issue when the public art piece is *part of a larger contextual scene.* Using that public art as a backdrop for a portrait, for instance, isn't a copyright violation or unethical either. Only when a photograph is made of the art itself and is *claimed by the photographer* as theirs do we run into a legal and ethical conundrum.

Architecture can be considered 'public art' itself. If you can make a photograph of a building without going on the property you are free to do so. You can also claim copyright of the photograph. As long as you don't claim the building itself as your creative expression, you're good.

Murals are another form of 'public art' and are almost always associated with architecture. Fortunately it's easy to perceive a mural as art as they're often found on walls which are easily imagined as 'giant canvases,' and murals are usually signed by the artist. Murals are obviously art. Photograph a mural and claim it as your own makes you a liar and a thief. Photographing the mural in the context of the building and location is fine. Using the mural as a background is OK too.

Graffiti isn't really any different than a mural, except that graffiti is applied illegally and murals are commissioned from painters. So, yeah, graffiti is unsigned and anonymous — the 'artist' isn't going to come after you for copyright infringement if you photograph it and claim it as your own. You're still an unoriginal, uncreative asshole if you do that, but you won't get sued. If you're documenting graffiti then you're permitted to photograph it as-is.

Graffiti-covered locations make great backgrounds for Urban Fashion photography.

'Land art' installations must be dealt with individually. Some are on private property and require the usual landowner permission to photograph but most are installed with the knowledge they will be photographed and are quite accommodating of the photographer. Whenever I photograph a 'land art installation' I try to be creative and 'make it my own' but I always credit the 'installation artist' as a professional courtesy. Some of the installations I've photographed are: *Carhenge, Cadillac Ranch, The International Car Forest of the Last Church, The Goldwell Open Air Museum, Stonehenge (Texas and Washington), Prada Marfa, Janet Echelman's Her Secret is Patience, The Cabazon Dinosaurs, Ricardo Breceda's Borrego Springs metal sculptures,* and dozens of 'found' *folk art* installations.

Again, most land art installations are erected with the knowledge that they will be photographed. After all, if you put an unusual thing in an unusual place people with cameras will show up to take pictures. At the entrance to *International Car Forest of the Last Church* there is even a sign that reads, 'photographer's playground.' Ricardo Breceda's giant metal sculptures in the Mojave Desert of Borrego Springs are so popular they are the subject/destination for Night Photography workshops! If you photograph these objects just remember to do two things: credit the installation artist and do not claim the subject of your photos as yours. Do that and you're cool.

I briefly mentioned **folk art**. Folk art or *outsider art* installations are not unlike other land art installations except they're usually created by non-artists, for free. I see a lot of this stuff in my travels and I call it 'roadside art.' Often folk art is found on private property, so you'll need permission to go on the property to photograph. Since much of this is visible from the road, it can be photographed from the road too. Most *folk artists* don't mind having their artworks photographed but just remember you're photographing *someone else's* art so don't claim it as your own creation. Your photo is yours, but the artwork you photographed is not.

Finally, there is **ancient art**. Pyramids, ruins, hieroglyphics, petroglyphs, pictographs, geoglyphs and all those mysterious ancient structures and artworks created during the early Common Era or Before the Common Era. Obviously the ancient artists are no longer with us nor was there anything like copyright laws during their times that a modern photographer could violate today. Basically any of these things can be photographed without concern of violating anyone's rights and the resultant photographs would clearly be copyrightable in the photographer's name. Nobody will look at your Mayan Pyramid photo and think you built the thing, so the image is yours without debate. Nonetheless, I believe that the ancients should be credited in some way. I've photographed many ancient petroglyphs and pictographs at Indian rock art sites scattered throughout the American Southwest and I provide references to the peoples who've created them. Unless I'm specifically omitting information (to prevent vandalism) I will provide information about the time of creation, location, style and associated tribes along with my own copyright protection. Usually something like: *Nine Mile Canyon, Archaic Style, 700-1250 AD, Ute & Fremont,* © *Dale O'Dell 2018.*

Respect the ancient artist and credit them as much as possible. If your own artworks are re-discovered 500 years from now you'd want the same.

CHAPTER

THE CEL-PHONE VIDEO CAMERA
TECHNOLOGY FOR SOCIAL CHANGE

"You push the button, we do the rest."
—Eastman Kodak advertising
the first Kodak Box camera, 1888.

Barely sixty years after photography was invented the original Kodak Box Camera brought photography to the masses. With a Kodak Box Camera anyone could take a photograph simply, without specialized equipment or the chemical knowledge required by early glass plate photographic image-making. With the invention of photography, and especially after George Eastman brought photography to everyone, people everywhere began documenting their lives. A rich, detailed, visual history of humanity was begun in the late 1800s because photography became easy and affordable. The ability of the everyman to document his life changed the world. And the world changed in profound ways. It became more visual, distant places were brought near thanks to the photographic print, and things unseen, or seen by very few, could now be seen by many.

The invention of photography was one of the most important, zeitgeist-changing technological advances ever. Visual communication changed forever with the Kodak Box Camera and even more so by 1900 with the even more user-friendly roll-film Kodak Brownie Camera. But today, nearly a century and a quarter after the Kodak Box Camera, it is the lightweight and simple-to-use cell-phone video camera that may prove to be an even more important technological invention leading to widespread social change.

To put things in context, here is a very brief history of photography, video, and cellular phones:

1827 Nicéphore Niépce makes the first photograph, which took days to expose.

1839 Louis Daguerre develops the daguerreotype process, which took hours to expose.

1839 The glass plate negative is invented.

1840 William Henry Fox Talbot invents the Calotype paper negative process.

1888 Kodak Box Camera introduced.

1900 Kodak Brownie, roll-film camera introduced.

1935 Kodachrome color transparency invented.

1983 Sony released the first consumer video camcorder.

1983 First commercial cellular phone.

1986 Kodak scientists develop the Bayer-pattern sens for digital cameras.

1995 First consumer digital video cameras released.

2000 First cell-phone still camera, Samsung, .35 megapixels.

2006 650 million camera phones sold.

2007 Video capabilities added to cell-phone cameras.

2010 The worldwide number of camera phones totals more than a billion.

In terms of easy and inexpensive image-making, photography has made many profound technological advances in the past two centuries. But some other things, such as violent human nature and abuse of authority have not changed at all.

With still and video capabilities available on a device that's relatively inexpensive, fits in a shirt pocket, and with such simplified operation that virtually anyone can shoot a still photo or video I'm a little disheartened that the narcissistic 'selfie' has become the commonplace photograph of our time. With cameras in everyone's pocket, at the ready, I'd hoped to see some photos of such elusive subjects like:

Bigfoot
UFOs
Space Aliens
Ghosts
The Loch Ness Monster
Any kind of Cryptid or paranormal activity…

But we're not seeing those photos. Maybe those things don't exist? Or perhaps 'phone photographers' are missing the shots? Maybe the UFOs and aliens really can disable electronic devices? We're not seeing new discoveries captured on cell-phone video, but we are seeing more videos of what's been going on for a long time, but rarely filmed until 2007:

Police, abusing their authority and murdering or beating the shit out of innocent people.

Personally I'd rather see a high-resolution image of a UFO, but society needs to see authority figures behaving badly. And let's face facts here, unless you're Caucasian/white, you know the police can beat the hell out of you or even kill you with impunity. Most white people know this too, but won't admit it because they are the beneficiaries of 'white privilege' and aren't as effected by police brutality as non-whites. But although I'm a gringo even I've known since I was a little kid that the police are not really our 'friends' and they can get away with pretty much any type of bad (and illegal for the rest of us) behavior.

Even as a never-arrested, law-abiding, 'privileged' white guy, I've had my share of run-ins with Bad Cops:

The first time I saw my mother cry was when a cop was leaning into the car, pointing his finger in her face, and screaming at her. I think I was about 5 or 6 years old and scared to death. I blame my fear of, and life-long lack of respect for authority figures on this incident. This happened in Kansas.

In high school I worked at a burger joint and I rode a small, licensed, 90cc motorcycle. After closing one night I rode home at about 1am. When I pulled into my driveway, the place lit up with blue and red lights and the next thing I knew I was being pulled off the bike and thrown against my parents' house. Two cops, with guns pointed at my face, were arresting me for 'stealing' my own motorcycle! They had no interest in my protestations and nothing I said got their attention. What did get their attention was the pump of 12-gauge shotgun held by my father, standing behind them. Only upon staring down the barrel of a weapon held by my Dad did they choose to listen to reason. My family should have sued, but instead the cops apologized to my Dad (but not to me) and left. This happened in Texas. And yes, I had my motorcycle license and my Dad had the title to the bike.

At the age of about 35 I got pulled over by a traffic cop for allegedly speeding. Before I could even get off the motorcycle he began berating and screaming at me. I feared for my life; I'd pulled over immediately and complied with his orders, except for one. I refused to remove my helmet because I really did fear I'd be killed or beaten. (There is no law that requires a motorcyclist to remove a helmet and I didn't need a head injury at the hands of a cop.) At that point I was handcuffed and tossed into the back of the police car. The cop actually screamed at me: "I can blow your fucking head off and toss your body off that cliff, nobody will find your body, you piece of shit." This kind of verbal abuse and intimidation went on for over half an hour. Finally, something came over the cops' radio and he dragged me out of his car, un-handcuffed me and drove off in a big hurry. I was not ticketed. This happened in Arizona.

Post 9/11, a rent-a-cop pointed a gun at me when I aimed my camera at a public building. I was not detained or shot but I didn't get my client's photo either. This has happened a lot to photographers after the terrorism of 9/11. Photographers are easy marks for police harassment because we're unarmed. I was standing on a public sidewalk. Photography is not an illegal activity and there were no 'no photography' signs.

I thought police harassing photographers was confined to the city until I was harassed, asked for I.D. and subjected to a lengthy and intimidating lecture while I was photographing a cactus in the desert. I was fifty miles from the nearest city and completely alone! The officer's excuse for detaining and questioning me was because, according to him, "...a number of dead bodies have been found along this road." The next day I checked the local news and verified that the policeman was lying, no bodies had ever been found along that road. It's really annoying to have to show a cop your identification when taking a picture of a cactus in the middle of nowhere!

At the 'mature' age of 'well over fifty' I was pulled over by a traffic cop with my wife in the car with me. For over half an hour I had to listen to an idiot cop lecture. It was intimidating, emasculating and was extremely frightening. I told the officer that he was causing both me and my wife to fear for our lives. Was he going to kill us? That prompted another twenty-minute tirade about the second amendment. All the while I'm sitting in the car trying to shut up and be calm and just stay alive. I noticed the cop was wearing a bullet-proof vest, I could see the bulge of a weapon in an ankle holster under his pant leg, he had a 9mm Glock in his belt holster, he had a Taser, and he had a fire-extinguisher sized pepper spray. I was unarmed and wearing a t-shirt! We were not ticketed. My wife was so frightened she begged me to go home, we never made the event we were going to attend. This happened in Arizona.

That's just a half-dozen of the incidents that I have been involved in personally. I list these incidents to illustrate just how bad the police can be. None of these incidents were of major importance nor involved any criminal act or endangerment to anyone (except me, at the hands of the police). And to restate, I'm a Caucasian, male, I've never been arrested and I do not have a criminal record. I'm a good boy and a law-abiding citizen, but I'm sure if I were non-white I wouldn't be alive to write this. As a result of these incidents I am convinced of two things: 1) 'white privilege' saved my life, and 2) all cops are assholes.

Of course that's just my opinion... Based on personal experience...

(In that respect I'm no different than the average African-American man.) Yes, I've had a few encounters with 'nice' cops but in my view, about ninety-nine percent of them are assholes and liars. Unfortunately the problem with cops is you can't tell the good ones from the bad ones until it's too late, or you're dead. For one's own safety one must assume that all cops are killers. Cops do the same thing, they assume all black men are criminals — which is exactly why so many innocent, unarmed black men are murdered by cops. As far as I'm concerned all cops are potential murderers until they prove themselves to me that they're not. The cops' reputation precedes them and currently that reputation is that of a killer, not a friend.

The only thing that can stop a 'bad guy with a gun' who's also got a badge and bad attitude is someone with a video camera. Video cameras scare the hell out of cops because they know they can't lie their way out of their own criminal acts caught on tape — although they do try and often their lies still allow them to get away with murder in our corrupt system.

Now let's look at an abbreviated history of photography, video, civil rights and police killing or beating the shit out of unarmed Black Men:

1704 The colony of Carolina developed the nation's first slave patrol. The institution of slavery and the control of minorities, however, were two of the more formidable historic features of American society shaping early policing. Slave patrols and Night Watches, which later became modern police departments, were both designed to control the behaviors of minorities.

1751 First American Police Force, Philadelphia.

1807 First American Police Force, Richmond, Virginia.

1838 First American Police Force formed in Boston.

1845 First American Police Force, New York.

1861 United States Civil War begins.

1865 United States Civil War ends. The 13th Amendment to the United States Constitution frees the slaves.

1948-1972 Gordon Parks (an African-American) serves as photographer for *Life* Magazine documenting the civil rights movement.

1970 Kent State and Jackson State. In May 1970, the collective student body of the United States erupted in protest over President Richard Nixon's invasion of Cambodia. On May 4th, students at Kent State were shot at by Ohio National Guard. Nine were wounded and four were killed. On May 15th, in Mississippi, at Jackson State, a large group of students had protested throughout the day. That night, police fired over 140 shotgun blasts at the group of students, killing two and injuring twelve. This was extensively covered by television and print media.

1983 Sony released the first consumer video camcorder.

1991 Rodney King beating is videotaped. Era of 'Citizen Journalism' begins.

1992 L.A. Riots as a result of police acquittal for the Rodney King beating.

2005 Robert Davis, a black man and retired elementary school teacher from New Orleans, was arrested and brutally beaten by police on suspicion of public intoxication. The beatings were videotaped by an Associated Press producer, who was also assaulted by police that night. The officers were either fired or suspended for their involvement, but many of the charges against them were cleared.

2007 Video capabilities added to cell-phone cameras.

2009 Christopher Harris was outside Seattle's Cinerama Theater when an officer charged at him and slammed his head into a wall, leaving him in a coma. Police were looking for a convenience store stabbing suspect when two witnesses mistakenly identified Harris. The King County sheriff's office investigated of the incident and says that it appears to have been a "tragic accident." This was recorded by surveillance video.

2014 Michael Brown, an 18-year old black man in Ferguson, Missouri, was fatally shot by Darren Wilson, 28, a white police officer.

2014 Kajieme Powell was reportedly carrying a knife, seemingly no larger than a steak knife, when police shot him down. We learned later that a bystander had videotaped the entire incident on his cell phone from before the cop car pulled up to the scene until Powell lay motionless on the ground as officers cuffed him. The video has put on full, unadulterated display what it looks like for cops to shoot a man down just seconds after arriving on the scene, without trying any other mitigating measures first.

2014 Eric Garner. Garner was killed after a New York police officer used a banned chokehold technique to restrain him, despite being unarmed. He was wrestled to the ground by several police officers after a complaint he was illegally selling loose cigarettes. In a video that went viral, the black 43-year-old said: "I can't breathe" which was soon adopted by protesters after Daniel Pantaleo, the only officer that was investigated by a grand jury, was not charged.

2014 Tamir Rice. Twelve-year-old Rice was shot by Ohio police in a public park as he was playing with a BB gun. It was reported at the time that a man called police saying someone was brandishing a pistol but added it was "probably fake." The police claimed Rice reached into his waistband for the toy gun when the two officers ordered him to raise his hands. Cleveland city claimed Rice's injuries — and subsequent death — "were directly and proximately caused by their own acts, not this defendant" in response to the family's lawsuit. In the lawsuit, the family accuses officers Frank Garmback and Timothy Loehmann of acting recklessly and failing to provide first aid and also name the city of Cleveland as a defendant.

2015 Sureshbhai Patel. Mr. Patel was left partially paralyzed, his family says, after being beaten by police in Alabama. The FBI has launched an investigation into what happened to the Indian grandfather after his encounter with police. A police officer has been arrested accused of badly injuring the man. In a video released by police, it shows an officer throwing Mr. Patel to the ground after officers stopped the man. He had been walking when police said officers tried talking to the man who spoke little English. Larry Muncey, Madison Police chief, announced last month that officer Eric Parker would be fired and he has pleaded not guilty to assault.

I have to conclude the list here in its woefully incomplete form. This shit just goes on and on and on, these are some of the 'low-lights.'

We can see it almost every week on television news; 'authorities' and 'leaders' like police and politicians behave in aggressively stupid ways and try to lie their way out of their own illegal, immoral, unethical and abusive acts all the while their hideous deeds exist on video for all to see. Why do they lie knowing there is video that contradicts their stories? Because for so long there had been no record of their wrongdoing and they knew their positions of authority granted them immunity from penetrating questions. For decades every cop knew that merely being a cop made them instantly credible. For decades no one would question a cop's word, all the while disbelieving the black man — no matter how credible 'the black man' might be. And the police also knew that their cop-buddies would cover for them. Lying liars who support other liars while noncriminal minorities lie dead on the ground. They ignored the visual facts of video because for so long there was no video, no visual record of their misdeeds, so they continue to lie today. They're simply used to lying and getting away with murder as standard operating procedure. Although this won't last forever in the new age of 'citizen journalism,' change is going to take quite some time; perhaps a decade or a generation. And no one changes their behavior until they first change the way they think; and cops still think they're above the very laws they're tasked to enforce.

Today the 'bad guys in blue' use lame, weak and fallacious arguments when their illegal acts are caught on video, like the videos being 'edited,' 'faked,' or 'taken out of context.' But video, unlike human perception, is easily analyzed and proven (or dis-proven) authentic and those who abuse their authority are begin-ning to have their lies exposed. Many police cars use dash-cams that mysteriously fail or point in the wrong direction when the police are busy abusing, beating and murdering their victims. The call for 'body-cams' is a good idea that will easily be defeated when the cop 'accidently' shuts off or disables the camera. I sus-pect the all-too-typical refrain of 'he's trying to get my gun!' will be augmented with 'the bad guy smashed my body camera — if he hadn't done that you'd see I was justified.'

Meanwhile the police act as if photography is an illegal activ-ity. It isn't. The police want to make photographing and videotap-ing them a criminal act with the knowledge that without video of their own criminal acts, they get away with it. I've been a victim of cop-photographer intimidation on more than one occasion and to be completely honest, knowing that the law was on my side was in no way helpful in the face of knowing the cop could kill me on the spot. And the cop who'd kill me? He'd get a paid vacation while a farcical 'internal investigation' took place while the police department trashed my reputation!

Again I reassert my whiteness. I'm lucky! If I were black I'd be dead at the hands of a policeman by now. And this is normal, but none of my white friends get it. One of my (seemingly more intelligent) white friends was amazed that the black guy on the TV news tried to run away, "Why doesn't he obey the policeman's commands?" he asked. Because, my clueless white friend, that black man knows he's got no chance with that white cop. He knows, guilty or innocent, he's probably going to die, so by running away he's at least got a chance to survive his cop-encounter. This seems perfectly logical to me. Avoid the bad guy! But my dear dumbass white friend has been a beneficiary of 'white privilege' his entire life and cannot comprehend that certain groups of people have a generations-long legitimate fear of the police.

I'm sorry to say, but my white friend is part of the problem. He's part of the problem because he doesn't recognize there is a problem because it's not affected him personally. He lives in a white neighborhood, his kids went to white schools, he votes for white conservative pro-law enforcement politicians who share his point of view and just doesn't get it that different demographic groups (re: dark-skinned people) might have a different experience. He thinks (without much effort, critical thought or analysis) that if the cops detain someone then that person must have done something to deserve it. And my dear white friend has a smartphone; I wonder if he'd video a cop abusing a minority? I hope he would because if he doesn't, he could be a racist. (My now former friend has exposed himself as a racist by voting for KKK-endorsed candidate Donald Trump.)

If we look at history, policing doesn't have a good reputation in the black community and never has. The very first police forces, going back to the 1700s were founded specifically to round up escaped slaves, who, by the way, were black! A three-hundred year-old institutional mindset isn't going to change overnight but, thanks to easily photographed and shared cellphone video, it will.

The name Philippe Kahn should be remembered by history — and loathed by police because Mr. Kahn was the inventor of the cell-phone camera. In 1997 Mr. Kahn wired his cellphone, laptop and a digital camera together to document and share the birth of his daughter. This began the era of cellphone photography. A decade later, in 2007, video capabilities were added and now, just short of a decade of cellphone video later the 'home movie' isn't what it used to be!

The social impact of cell-phone camera still and video photography has been amplified tenfold thanks to the ease of sharing the imagery. Social media and free video websites like YouTube allow for huge, instant-audiences for all kinds of imagery — including videos of 'authorities behaving badly.' No longer are non-photojournalist images ignored and unpublished. Prior to the age of 'citizen journalism' a photographer, videographer or filmmaker had to have a client, a publisher, to get the images in front of the public's eyes, but that's not true anymore. Anyone with a cell-phone camera can upload their pictures to the internet where they can be seen, shared, copied and disseminated with democratic equality. In our modern era, where just a few companies control all our news media outlets and cannot be trusted it's best to go around them, straight to the public, unfiltered. One person with a cell-phone video is as powerful as CNN! The camera plus internet sharing equals widespread awareness and only with widespread awareness does society change. The ACLU even has a free cellphone app called Mobile Justice which allows the cellphone-videographer-witness-victim to record their police interactions and immediately upload the video to the state office of the ACLU. The immediate-upload feature is especially useful when police (illegally) confiscate people's cellphones. When police confiscate cell-phones they've effectively suppressed evidence against them — nobody ever gets their phones back. Civil rights-era photojournalist Gordon Parks (a black man) said, "I saw the camera could be a weapon against poverty, against racism, against all sorts of social wrongs." A gun is a weapon that can kill while the camera is a weapon that can expose the bad guy and change society for the better. In 1961 Dr. Martin Luther King, Jr. recognized that, "The world seldom believes the horror stories of history until they are documented via the mass media." What Dr. King could not foresee in 1961 is that by the early 2000s the people are the mass media.

"The fact is that photography is power," says Jay Stanley, a senior policy analyst at the American Civil Liberties Union (ACLU) and creator of the organization's guide to photographers' rights.* "People are loathe to give up power, including police officers."

Americans thought they'd made progress on civil rights and racism after the Civil Rights Act of 1964 made discrimination based on race, color, religion, sex, or national origin illegal. Although the act made institutional racism illegal it did nothing to alleviate the visceral racism that still remained in the hearts and minds of many white people. So, even with the 'whites only' and 'no Negroes' signs removed, racism still exists in full force, quietly, subtly in the hearts and minds of too many white Americans. Racism and discrimination never went away, it was merely expressed less frequently, publicly.

Sexual discrimination never went away either and Americans were unable to pass a simple, clearly worded Equal Rights Amendment to the U. S. Constitution. Today, on average, a female worker earns twenty-five percent less than her male counterpart doing the same job. In 2016 a Republican presidential candidate routinely calls women 'pigs' and no one cares. America has made zero progress with issues of sexual discrimination and the progress made in civil rights is illusory.

The terrorist attacks of September 11, 2001 exposed ignorant

*The ACLU Guide to Photographers' Rights

racist Americans at their worst. Fear and 'terrorism' now excuses discrimination and hatred based on religion (Muslims), national origin (Mexicans, Syrians, Iranians, etc.), race and skin color (all non-Caucasians).

The election of Barack Obama, the first African-American President has laid bare the closeted racism of America. I'm sorry to have to point it out, but Americans (as a group) are more racist than ever. We have one horrible political party that has held 300 million Americans hostage as they spent eight years obstructing virtually everything 'President Blackula' has done. I can't say that all Republicans are racists but the Republican Party does provide shelter for racists. (Author's note: with the election of the clearly racist Donald Trump in 2016, the Republican Party is now the official party of the racist.)

When racism, misogyny, and unchecked hatred are combined with authorities with weapons we end up where we are today, with fully militarized police forces terrorizing those they swore to protect.

Technology has always 'evolved' at a faster pace than man's intellect, morals and ethics. In medicine we have technology to keep a body alive, but few ethical guidelines on when not to. Listen to our 'fearless leaders' (especially conservatives) who talk, willynilly, about 'nuking' this and 'bombing' that while ignoring the veracity of negotiation. In the society we've created for ourselves, force beats finesse and competition is valued over cooperation.

Although I live in a state with 'open carry' laws which allow any dingbat to strap a gun to his or her belt and go to the shopping mall, I won't carry a gun. As a civilized person, I don't need a gun because my life is routinely not in danger. The only time I've ever felt absolute fear for my life has been in interactions with police, the authorities, and I know, even if I were armed, I'd have no chance whatsoever if the cop felt like killing me, I'd be outgunned anyhow. And I'm supposed to do whatever he says, right? If I don't, he can just kill me for not following his orders. All I can do is kiss his ass, hope he's not in a killing mood, and thank god I'm Caucasian. This is no way to live and I can completely relate to how minorities feel when interacting with police. When dealing with cops I'm just as scared shitless as any black person would be.

The cops aren't scared of me, but they are scared of my camera!

The camera doesn't lie. But cops lie — routinely. Most cops with whom I've interacted care greatly about the second amendment (despite the inherent danger to their own lives) but don't give a damn about the first amendment. The first amendment protects journalists and 'citizen journalists' alike. But the era of police lying to cover their own abuse of authority and bad behavior is coming to an end thanks to the cell-phone video camera.

Yes, the objective, dispassionate, accurate, apolitical technology of the pocket-sized video camera will eventually force the police and other 'authorities' to do the right thing because when their crimes are laid bare for all to see they will no longer get away with murder. Gordon Parks was right, the camera is a weapon. It's the best weapon to use when fighting for The Truth. No one has ever been murdered by a camera. A camera is not a dangerous thing. A camera is not a tool used to intimidate. While the police are armed with guns which too often are used against us, we are now armed with cameras — technology for truth! If officer Obie has a problem being photographed then he's afraid of the truth and your life may very well be at risk. If the NSA can rationalize eavesdropping on our cellphone calls by saying, "If you're not doing anything wrong, you have nothing to be afraid of," then we can use the same logic on the police. "Officer, sir, if you're following the rules, why fear video?" The common police argument that videotaping somehow 'interferes with police duties' is complete bullshit.

The momentum of change is upon us thanks to integrated circuits, miniaturization of technology, Philippe Kahn, Bill Gates,

Steve Jobs and Samsung. Human nature, ethics and the abuse of authority has not changed on its own, but it is being forced to change as a result of cell-phone video technology. For now, to preserve our own safety we must assume all cops are bad (the same as they assume all black men are criminals) until they prove themselves otherwise. For centuries we've given the police respect and they've abused it; now they must earn it. In combination with a healthy wariness of police we must use the video camera — and we've all got them in our pockets now. The cell-phone video camera is a dispassionate machine with no opinion or agenda, it's a device for recording pictures and sound — what it records is up the policeman. He can behave professionally, with respect (so can you) or he can be an unprofessional, disrespectful criminal, either way, 'the tape tells the tale.'

We are at an epoch where video technology can change human nature for the better. People do behave differently when they know others are watching. Continual videotaping of police will ultimately force them to be accountable. Average citizens are filmed by surveillance cameras every day for 'our own safety' on sidewalks, in parking garages, office buildings and many public spaces; we can film the police for the same reason, personal safety. Photography is not illegal — and it may save your life. The cellphone video, a democratization of communication and documentation is the unblinking lens of objectivity which will change society and eventually make us all better persons.

But until video forces police to change their behavior...

...this murder may be videotaped for training purposes...

The ACLU Guide to Photographer's Rights

Taking photographs of things that are plainly visible from public spaces is a constitutional right — and that includes federal buildings, transportation facilities, and police and other government officials carrying out their duties. Unfortunately, there is a widespread, continuing pattern of law enforcement officers ordering people to stop taking photographs from public places, and harassing, detaining and arresting those who fail to comply.

When you are on private property, the property owner may set rules about the taking of photographs. If you disobey the property owner's rules, they can order you off their property (and have you arrested for trespassing if you do not comply).Police officers may not confiscate or demand to view your digital photographs or video without a warrant. The Supreme Court has ruled that police may not search your cell phone when they arrest you, unless they get a warrant. Although the court did not specifically rule on whether law enforcement may search other electronic devices such as a standalone camera, the ACLU believes that the constitution broadly prevents warrantless searches of your digital data. It is possible that courts may approve the temporary warrantless seizure of a camera in certain extreme "exigent" circumstances such as where necessary to save a life, or where police have a reasonable, good-faith belief that doing so is necessary to prevent the destruction of evidence of a crime while they seek a warrant.

Police may not delete your photographs or video under any circumstances. Officers have faced felony charges of evidence tampering as well as obstruction and theft for taking a photographer's memory card.

Police officers may legitimately order citizens to cease activities that are truly interfering with legitimate law enforcement operations. Professional officers, however, realize that such operations are subject to public scrutiny, including by citizens photographing them.

Note that the right to photograph does not give you a right to break any other laws. For example, if you are trespassing to take photographs, you may still be charged with trespass.

If you are stopped or detained for taking photographs:

Always remain polite and never physically resist a police officer. If stopped for photography, the right question to ask is, "am I free to go?" If the officer says no, then you are being detained, something that under the law an officer cannot do without reasonable suspicion that you have or are about to commit a crime or are in the process of doing so. Until you ask to leave, your being stopped is considered voluntary under the law and is legal. If you are detained, politely ask what crime you are suspected of committing, and remind the officer that taking photographs is your right under the First Amendment and does not constitute reasonable suspicion of criminal activity.

Special considerations when videotaping:

With regards to videotaping, there is an important legal distinction between a visual photographic record (fully protected) and the audio portion of a videotape, which some states have tried to regulate under state wiretapping laws.

Such laws are generally intended to accomplish the important privacy-protecting goal of prohibiting audio "bugging" of private conversations. However, in nearly all cases audio recording the police is legal.

In states that allow recording with the consent of just one party to the conversation, you can tape your own interactions with officers without violating wiretap statutes (since you are one of the parties). In situations where you are an observer but not a part of the conversation, or in states where all parties to a conversation must consent to taping, the legality of taping will depend on whether the state's prohibition on taping applies only when there is a reasonable expectation of privacy. But no state court has held that police officers performing their job in public have a reasonable expectation.

The ACLU believes that laws that ban the taping of public officials' public statements without their consent violate the First Amendment.

Photography at the airport:

Photography has also served as an important check on government power in the airline security context. The Transportation Security Administration (TSA) acknowledges that photography is permitted in and around airline security checkpoints as long as you're not interfering with the screening process. The TSA does ask that its security monitors not be photographed, though it is not clear whether they have any legal basis for such a restriction when the monitors are plainly viewable by the traveling public.

The TSA also warns that local or airport regulations may impose restrictions that the TSA does not. It is difficult to determine if any localities or airport authorities actually have such rules. If you are told you cannot take photographs in an airport you should ask what the legal authority for that rule is.

The ACLU does not believe that restrictions on photography in the public areas of publicly operated airports are constitutional.

CHAPTER

SEXY MACHINES

Just when I thought I'd acquired every kind of camera I'd ever need, photography changed so fundamentally that my cameras became obsolete nearly overnight. Suddenly the dozens of film cameras I owned metamorphosed into expensive metal paper-weights and had to be replaced with digital cameras. Although I was not an early adopter of the digital camera I bought one when it was becoming clear that film's lifespan was becoming limited. I really didn't have a choice if I were to continue working as a professional photographer, the industry was *going digital*.

My first digital camera was a little 3.3 megapixel Canon G1. It was a little silver box and clearly un-sexy; I've got another old box of a camera in my collection, a 1948 Argus C3. Back in the day the Argus C3 was nicknamed 'the brick,' my year 2000 Canon G1 is also a brick, a lightweight and even less sexy brick. Both cameras are ugly, utilitarian devices but the half-century old Argus is slightly sexier!

What exactly is a 'sexy' camera?

In my view, a 'sexy' machine is a device that's well designed and engineered. A sexy machine has some heft, some weight, because it's made to last. Sexy machines are complex with many gears and other mechanical parts that fit together and move smoothly. Some examples of 'sexy' machines are: steam locomotives, mechanical clocks and watches, Ducati motorcycles, old typewriters, hand-operated printing presses, telescopes, record-players, analog synthesizers, the enlargers (which I no longer use) in my darkroom, and pretty much all old mechanical cameras, especially those from Germany. Simply put, sexy machines are those with clever engineering and have a 'solid' feel to them.

Digital cameras are decidedly *not* sexy!

There's very little going on mechanically inside a digital camera. Although cameras still look like what we expect cameras to look like, they've become little more than *processors with lenses*.

Converting light into a silver-halide latent image on film was a very different process than converting light to ones and zeros that can only be expressed after *processing* with *firmware*. All that camera-back space that used to be filled with film, motors and film transport gears is now taken up by batteries and processors, tiny computers that 'do math.' They're little more than black boxes inside a larger black box shaped like what we expect a camera to look like. Digital cameras are certainly amazing devices, but 'sexy' they're not!

Good industrial design is what makes cameras 'sexy.' There is something about the human interaction with a well-designed machine that's natural, pleasant or even exciting which is wholly missing from interacting with strictly utilitarian devices.

Steampunk art is today's ultimate expression of 'sexy' machinery.

A follow-up to 'Wide Awake at Dreamland' from
'Photographic Memories,' (2009)

Everybody knows about the 'secret' air-base in central Nevada, Area 51. It hasn't been secret for a long time, in fact Area 51 is so well-known that it's become part of the UFO Folklore. But unless you're some kind of super-secret, deep-back, military contractor, X-Files type who's signed an 'upon pain of death' security oath/nondisclosure document, you have not been to Area 51. Any 'normal person' including Ufologists, ancient-astronaut theorists, conspiracy-theorists or the general 'paranormal tourist' who says they've been to Area 51 hasn't, they've actually been to Rachel, Nevada. Rachel is a tiny town-oasis located along highway 375, aka, 'The Extraterrestrial Highway.' It's the nearest 'town' to Area 51. The hub of all human activity in Rachel is The Little A 'Le Inn, a combo motel-restaurant-bar where the true believers gather. If you've watched any kind of UFO program on TV during the past two decades, you've probably seen some 'expert' standing in front of The Little A 'Le Inn espousing some theory about 'back-engineered' alien spacecraft or captured alien pilots held at Area 51. These stories are garden-variety UFO folklore.

It was the UFO folklore that motivated me to visit Rachel way back in 1996. You can read all about that adventure in my book,

Photographic Memories in a chapter called 'Wide Awake at Dreamland.' Without repeating myself too much, that 1996 visit was interesting; I met some 'true believers,' and I visited the infamous 'Black Mailbox' when it was still actually black. In Rachel, aside from The Little A 'Le Inn there was the Quick-Pik convenience store with a gas station and there was the bright yellow trailer that housed The Area 51 Research Center. In short, Rachel was the Mecca for Ufology, and it was kind of a Big Deal just to get there, it was off the beaten path.

I returned to Rachel a couple more times after 1996. I shot some background photographs that I used to create some UFO illustrations. Another time I went with a 'UFO hunter' and we spent the night scanning the skies with night vision equipment. We did our surveillance from 'The Black Mailbox' which by then had been painted white (fooling no one). Aside from Rachel and The Little A 'Le Inn, the black (white) mailbox is one of only a few manmade objects in the otherwise desolate desert. It's just a 'UFO landmark' twenty miles south of Rachel where UFO 'enthusiasts' meet. Insofar as penetrating the base, I was never fool enough to try and never felt the need to drive the dirt road from The Black Mailbox to the sign that says if you pass it deadly force is authorized for trespassers. There was no need for me to mess with the white SUV-driving 'cammo dudes' Area 51 security forces; they'd probably ID me from the highway anyway.

During the late 1990s there was a seriousness to UFO 're-search.' You really could meet an 'aviation expert' at the bar at The Little A 'Le Inn and the 'Ufologists' and 'researchers' were actually collecting data. The people who went to Rachel, to the edge of Area 51, meant to be there. They weren't lookie-loo tourons screwing around.

Twenty years later, in 2016, I returned to Area 51, or Rachel more specifically, and things were a lot different.

My 2016 visit to Rachel was a side-trip and not my ultimate

destination. I'd been photographing in east-central Nevada and was on my way to Las Vegas, so the excursion to Rachel was just for fun, and lunch at The Little A 'Le Inn. Driving up the 'extra-terrestrial highway,' 375, I wanted to shoot another photo of the infamous Black (or white) mailbox but didn't see it. I wonder what happened to it? I'll bet there's someone at The Little A 'Le Inn who knows.

Arriving at the sparkling metropolis that is Rachel, Nevada I first noticed that the 'Area 51 Research Center' was gone. The Quick-Pik was also gone along with the gas station, I suppose the few Rachel residents must have to drive forty miles to the nearest gas station now. The parking lot at The Little A 'Le Inn was oddly full. When I'd been there before there was never more than a beat-up work truck and car or two in the parking lot. This day the parking lot was packed with cars, many of them rentals with Enterprise stickers on their back windows, and there were SUVs and minivans and, of course, beat-up work trucks. My entry into The Little A 'Le Inn was as dramatic as it was twenty years ago. Upon opening the door of the restaurant the harsh desert light floods the interior of the dining room and everyone inside (and there were a lot of every-ones this day) turns to the light to check out the new arrival. Hi, hello, yes it is about ten f-stops brighter outside, shade your eyes, let me stop-down the aperture by closing the door.

Holy crap! The place was packed! Every table was full! There was a lot of activity for an out-of-the-way restaurant. I headed straight to the 'gift shop corner' and picked out a few must-have souvenirs. My souvenir shopping was restrained and I spent about eighty percent less than I had last time. While paying for my UFO trinkets the lady at the cash register asked if I was staying for lunch to which I replied, "Yes." She asked if I wouldn't mind sitting at the counter since the restaurant was full; I slid over to the counter and she slid over and immediately took my order.

"Alien-burger with secretion (cheese), a soda and chips, please."

I surreptitiously shot a few photos of the restaurant and patrons with my little mirrorless camera and checked out the other diners. All tourists. There were a few gringos like me but we were outnumbered by Japanese, Mexicans and Australians. I was trying to read a sign by the door when one of the Australians thought I was staring at him and struck up a conversation, every other sentence ending in 'aye mate.' He was enjoying his 'adventure tour' and looking forward to his next tour-stop at the 'black mailbox.'

"And what's the deal with the black mailbox?" I asked the waitress. "I've seen it before but I missed it on the drive up."

"It's gone." She said.

"Gone? Really?" I was surprised. "It's probably the most famous mailbox in the world, definitely the most photographed."

"The rancher painted it white many years ago." She went on.

"I know that, but it didn't fool anybody."

"Yeah." She laughed. "It's the only mailbox within twenty miles, so if it's black or white, ya gotta figure it's probably the one. Now it's a shrine to the old mailbox."

"Uh, a shrine?"

"Yeah." She continued. "People were stealing the old mailbox. They'd either dig it up including the concrete it was set in, or they'd show up with portable cutting torches and just cut the pole at the ground and steal the whole darn thing! The rancher finally gave up and stuck a fake mailbox in its place."

"Wow!" I said, thinking the real mailbox is probably enshrined in some UFO-geek's basement. "I guess the rancher has to drive to town to get his mail now?"

"Ya know, I have no idea." She laughed. "His ranch is right on the edge of Area 51, he probably gets his mail delivered by drone!"

"I'll keep my eye open for a 'mailbox shrine' twenty miles down the road." I said and finished my (pretty darned good) alien-burger.

I paid the tab, left a healthy tip, and went outside to shoot a few phots of the signage and stuff. This didn't even merit shooting with a 'real camera' so I shot a few selfies with my phone and posted them on Facebook just to make my Mulder and Scully wannabe friends jealous. There was such a line of selfie-shooters at The Little A 'Le Inn sign I actually had to wait to take my picture! It was becoming apparent to me that Rachel and The Little A 'Le Inn was no longer a Mecca for true believers, but rather, a destination for UFO tourists who really knew very little about the actual UFO phenomena. They just want to visit 'Area 51' and get their picture taken outside The Little A 'Le Inn.

Actually, it's kind of sad.

I walked across the bright and hot parking lot back to my black car, started it up, and found my best friend, Max, which is the air-conditioning highest setting, and headed back southward the way I'd come. I noted the odometer reading because in plus-twenty miles I should see that mailbox 'shrine.'

Sure enough, almost exactly twenty miles south of Rachel, on the west side of the Extraterrestrial Highway I found the 'shrine to the Black Mailbox.' Oh, now this has gone from sad to pathetic…

In cop-parlance, I 'exited the vehicle' with camera in hand to examine… what the heck, I'm not quite sure. There was a rinky-dink little mailbox that looked more like a children's toy posted atop a bent and twisted pole. It was surrounded by rocks, organized by…. someone. On the rock were arrangements, 'offerings' of coins and pictures and a handwritten note that said 'I want to believe.' Seemingly the whole 'shrine area' was treated as if it were some mystical spot, a place of UFO-worship, and a place of reverence.

In fact it's nothing more than a wide spot on a desolate highway were one lonely rancher couldn't even keep a rural mailbox from being stolen! This is really sad. All this means so much to those who know so little.

Then a white SUV pulled up next to my car. Well probe my

ass and call me an abductee, I thought, it's the Area 51 'cammo dude' security forces! But no, it wasn't security, it was worse, they were 'UFO Tourists!'

A group of tourists (including the Australians) got out of the white SUV, cameras in hand, and began extensive photography of the 'mailbox shrine.' The SUV driver/tour-guide lectured the group, in low and serious tones, about the 'history' of the black mailbox, telling them essentially the same thing the waitress at The Little A 'Le Inn had told me a half-hour earlier. Someone made an 'offering' at the mailbox shrine and then the group piled back into the SUV. There was a big 'Sightseeing Adventures' sticker on the side of the SUV so I asked the driver if he had a brochure. He happily gave me a brochure (obviously hoping I'd become another tour-sucker in the future) and then he and his 'UFO sightseers' were off in a cloud of dust to take a picture of the sign on the border of the no longer secret base.

The dust settled and I found myself standing in the hot sun, alone by the shrine, reading the 'Sightseeing Adventures' brochure. The 'Sightseeing Adventures' brochure advertised all sorts of daily tours out of Las Vegas. Most were the typical 'Vegas daytrip' fare; Hoover Dam, Colorado River, Valley of Fire State Park, the Grand Canyon and, Area 51 — Top Secret Military Facility. Seriously? Twenty years ago, after doing a minimal amount of research, UFO 'enthusiasts' would just gas up the car in Vegas and head north to Rachel for their own personal 'UFO adventure.' Now they're running tours out of Vegas! For two-hundred bucks a person! Again, seriously? Hmm, what does a $200 tour get you? According to the brochure: A trip to the Vegas airport to see the unmarked planes that fly employees to Area 51. You get to see this through a chain-link fence (been there). There's a stop at the 'Extraterrestrial Highway' sign (seen that). You also get lunch at The Little A 'Le Inn, and a visit to 'The Black Mailbox' (shot that). Two hundred bucks for this? Oh, that includes the lunch and 'bottled water and snacks.' At least you get to ride in a 'luxury 4x4' with other like-minded UFO tourists.

This has all become commercialized in the cheesiest way!

If there's a way to make a buck on something, people will find it. Driving into Las Vegas from 'Area 51' a couple of notions popped into my tiny mind. First is that the current state of 'UFO folklore' is stale, there's not a lot of new things going on. A lack of 'newness' is what leads things like 'the black mailbox' and The Little A 'Le Inn to mainstream commercialization. There's nothing remotely 'secret' about a tour-bus destination! UFO culture has been normalized (although the giggle-factor remains high).

My other observation comes back around to photography, and it's what I'll call the 'Selfie-Factor.' It seemed the most important thing on the minds of the 'UFO tourists'were getting their pictures taken in front of the 'famous UFO sites' like the mailbox shrine and The Little A 'Le Inn. It's as if they signed on for a no-risk 'adventure,' got on the bus, and shot pictures of themselves to prove to their friends back home that they'd personally 'been to the UFO promised land.'

Yeah, well, I did the same thing myself this time; I shot a self-ie in front of The Little A 'Le Inn sign, so I'm no better than the 'UFO tourists' except I did it for only fifty bucks. Fifteen dollars for a half-tank of gas, another fifteen for lunch and twenty bucks on souvenirs I really don't need. I'll take the $150 I saved and put it towards a 'UFO adventure' to another UFO hot-spot, Dulce, New Mexico. What? You haven't heard about the alien base at Dulce? Don't worry, you will; it won't be long before someone starts running tours there too, you know, so tourists can shoot selfies in front of a sign.

CHAPTER

TEN QUESTIONS

I was asked to answer the ten questions below by an art gallery where I was exhibiting. I hope this is helpful, especially for young artists.

From the gallery: In an effort to have each of our artists connect with their audience we have designed 10 questions for each artist to complete if they wish. This will help our efforts to encourage more artistic creation in all its unique forms while also encouraging more people to connect with art in general. People need to feel connected to something to feel inspired to get involved in it and especially spend their money on it so this is another avenue we can make each artist more relatable to the public.

What would you say was the first thing or moment that got you inspired to start creating?

I got started very young. As a kid my parents enrolled me in a lot of after-school art classes. I wasn't a very good painter or too good at drawing but I did learn all the fundamentals. In the 7th grade I was introduced to photography and discovered that photography was the medium for me. Photography is a blend of both art and science and I took to it. I enjoyed both the creative time behind the camera and the scientific aspect of the darkroom. I didn't choose art, art chose me.

What inspires and motivates you now?

Curiosity. I'm interested in things I have not seen before so

I'm motivated to push the limits of photography and digital art. I'm also motivated by the classical surrealists and have closely studied the works and writings of Salvador Dali, Rene Magritte and others. Today, as a result of the 'digital revolution' of photography I find more inspiration from the history of painting than photography. Technology allows me to use photography in ways that go far beyond the traditional photograph. The 'photograph' is no longer my final destination creatively.

What do you feel or experience when you are creating?

Joy, discovery, and a lot of hard work.

Are there certain things or people that influence your creative flow or process?

Photographic influences are Pete Turner, Mitchell Funk, Jerry Uelsmann, Man Ray and the classic American Western photographers, f-64 group, etc. From painting, influences are Dali, Magritte, Jacek Yerka, and Picasso. Science-fiction literature is also an influence including authors such as Frank Herbert, Robert Charles Wilson and Robert J. Sawyer. I like surrealist writers like Jeff Noon. Another influence is progressive rock music. This is the music that's not heard much on the radio. Just as I seek novelty and innovation visually, I appreciate musicians that continually push boundaries to create something truly new; musicians and bands such as Steve Hackett, 1970's Genesis, King Crimson, Pink Floyd, Yes, The Watch, Pendragon, Marillion, Marc Dwane, Erik Wollo, The Flower Kings, etc. Freud and Jung are influential. Those who don't follow formula are my primary influences. As diverse as this list is, all of it somehow gets into my brain, is processed, and comes out in my work.

What is your favorite atmosphere or environment in which you like to create?

When photographing I prefer to work alone, both in the studio and on-location. Also when working at the computer in my studio I prefer to be left alone, frequently for hours or days, and I require time for quiet contemplation. I work out many concepts during that time (the hypnogogic state) between fading wakefulness and sleep. *What would you say would be the one thing you would like someone to take with them when viewing your work, if anything?*

The joy of discovery and the impetus to THINK.

What other professions, interests, or hobbies do you have?

I ride motorcycles which brings me great joy and freedom. Motorcycling exercises different parts of my brain, is physically demanding and serves to 'reset' my creative thinking. I play classical guitar, not very well, but I work at it specifically because it's HARD to do. I'm also tangentially involved in paranormal research including UFOlogy, Cryptozoology, ghost-hunting, psychic- functioning and remote-viewing. Quantum physics interests me a lot.

Give an example of a difficulty you have had to overcome.

Extreme introversion.

Where do you see yourself in five years?

Hopefully as a more recognized and collected artist and not living under a bridge!

What advice would you give someone just wanting to start out with their art career?

Success is the result of not quitting.

THE QUESTION REMAINS

The question popped up on Facebook and it led me to a blog. The blog was titled, *Does Photography Need This?* It had a graphic of the letter 'F' with a diagonal line through it, indicating 'not fake.' The author was a photography instructor somewhere and his concern was his inability to tell the difference between a digitally manipulated photograph and a straight one. He felt that some sort of indicator, like the 'not fake' symbol mentioned above, should be used to label an image as un-manipulated, thereby making the image 'authentic' and differentiating it from manipulated or 'Photoshopped' images.

I rarely comment on blogs or Facebook postings (it just encourages the trolls) but this one merited a response. After all I tackled the subject over two decades ago in an article entitled Seeing is not Believing published in *LensWork* magazine (#10, Summer 1995). I wrote a second piece about the subject for *LensWork* in the Fall of 1997 entitled *Computer Manipulated Imagery*, is it Photography? Both of these articles were reprinted in my 2009 book, *Photographic Memories*.

Back in '95 I had hoped to initiate a dialog that would eventually lead to a definition of both exactly what a photograph is and what digital art is. But no dialog ensued. Nobody seemed to care (or *LensWork* didn't have much of a readership). 'Digital Photo-graphy' since became a dumping-ground term for 'Photoshopped' imagery; but the question remains: How much digital manipulation can be done to a photograph before the result becomes something other than a "photograph?"

I posted the above question on the blog. The few responses it garnered missed the point. Most of the responses mentioned that 'everything is manipulated,' and 'depends on how you define manipulated.' No one tackled the basic question, where is the line? When one crosses the still undefined digital-manipulation line, is the result still a photograph? Or, by crossing that line does the resultant artwork become something that's no longer a photograph? (Re-read Chapter One for the answer.)

As this was an academic blog, that is, a photography teachers,' one might think that this is a subject for deep thought. After all (I think) it's extremely important that we have a clear definition of what a 'photograph' actually is. And it's equally important that 'Digital Art' be clearly defined, as it is a new medium without precedent. The blogger just kind of threw the question up, and the respondents weren't really contemplating the issue, instead answering the question with more questions. Heck, I brought this up over *twenty years ago* and it's only now hit some academic's radar? (Professors rarely listen to Professionals.) But does it matter?

Perhaps it does not matter? Maybe it's just too late? When 'digital'was in its infancy (1995?) that would have been the appropriate time to draw a line between 'straight' photographs and 'digitally-manipulated' photographs but now we're all cynical. 'Photoshop' is now noun and verb. We pretty much assume all photography is manipulated in some way and is therefore 'inauthentic.' (Intellectual laziness.) In 1995 I suggested it might have been the right time then. Now it's just one big mess-o-imagery as we've rushed headlong to digital, giving little thought to definitions and not recognizing the birth of a new medium (digital art).

In the opening paragraph of my 1995 article, *Seeing is not Believing*, I wrote: there has been a call for some designation or symbol, like the circle C copyright symbol, denoting photographs as altered or manipulated. No one answered that call. I also expressed misgivings about it because that symbol would probably not be attached to the image, but rather, buried on some copyright/credit-line page that no one reads. In the article I also mentioned context: Print a photograph inside TIME Magazine and it might be believable. Print the same photograph inside THE NATIONAL INQUIRER and it might not be believable. I believe we judge 'authenticity' by context as well as content. We expect sources like TIME or National Geographic to be truthful, and conversely we're automatically suspect of images appearing in tabloids. (This was all prior to the 'fake news' nonsense of 2016.)

After receiving zero response in 1995, I revisited the subject in 1997 with an article entitled, Computer-manipulated imagery, is it photography? In that piece I proposed this definition for digital art: *Any still image that owes its existence to digital generation or manipulation that could not be realized in any other way without the use of a computer is considered digital art.*

(This became my Digital Manifesto, again see Chapter One.) That seemed pretty simple to me, but again, I think I'm the only one who was thinking along those lines at the time — or now!

So, here we are twenty-plus years after I first asked the question and almost three decades into the 'digital revolution' and now one person in academia is finally contemplating the issue! But you're way too late, professor, the digital cow is out of the barn and it doesn't matter. Not only does photography have little credibility anymore but amateur photography is considered more 'real' than professional photography which is often thought of as nothing more than the set-up photo-op. Add to that, that people just really don't want to know what's going on and don't really care about 'authentic' photography. Nowadays what passes for 'news' is opinion presented as facts that reconfirm the viewers' preconceived notions (confirmation bias). Photographs, or more accurately 'images,' that conform to preconceived notions are more likely to be 'accepted' than imagery that is challenging or different from the expected.

It's a big mess in my view. All sorts of photographic, digitally-manipulated photographs and computer-graphics are all lumped together as 'digital photography,' which is a very broad and inaccurate term. I don't think academics or those in the high echelons of the museums and art galleries really want to tackle the subject. They'd have to clearly define what is a photograph, what is not a photograph and what's digital art, and one thing I've noticed these folks fear most is clarity (read any art review and you'll see what I mean).

Photographs have been manipulated since photography was invented, but darkroom skills were required; now it's easy with Photoshop. Don't question the integrity of the image until you question the integrity of the photographer first.

ART OR OCD?
IS ART-MAKING AN OBSESSIVE-COMPULSIVE DISORDER?

My girlfriend came back from the kitchen shocked and appalled, "All you have in your refrigerator is a half-jar of mayonnaise, a can of Pepsi, and sixty rolls of Kodachrome, you don't even have food, how can you live like this?"

"I've got film," I answered, "what's the problem?"

That's the way I thought, I was obsessed, so long as I had the materials to make art I had all I needed and food was an afterthought. More than anything else I had to make art. Making art was numero uno on my personal 'to do' list, it ranked above acquiring wealth, getting laid, and even eating. And it's been like this my entire life. I've gladly made the sacrifices and I've happily gone without in order to make art. I've gone without new clothes, health insurance, driven old clunky cars, have no savings account, no retirement plan or many of the things considered 'must haves' by those non-artists who live 'normal,' conventional, consensus-reality lifestyles.

Then thirty years went by I looked back and thought, "Oops, I really screwed-up my life! I've got nothing to show for my work except my work. What will I do if I get old and sick? I can't afford to retire and kick back and wait for death. What have I done? All I have to show for my life is a large series of incredible pictures that are ignored by the museums. My god, I've wasted my life in pursuit of art."

Of course the other side of that coin is the fact that I have, indeed, done the work. I've pushed the boundaries of photography and digital art, I've explored new themes, techniques and territories; I've picked up the torch lit by the classical surrealists and continued their work into the 21st century. I've happily lived my life and have made a contribution to the culture of my time.

I could not have accomplished this if I were 'normal.' Sometimes I think I've got an obsessive-compulsive disorder because I must make art. Most of my artist-contemporaries feel the same. We're in our mid-fifties and past life's halfway point. We see some of our acquaintances of similar age looking towards 'early retirement' and meeting with their 'wealth management teams' and we laugh about how we have no wealth to manage but it would be helpful if we managed our portfolios (not the money kind), licensing, and exhibitions better. We must be crazy, we laugh, who would spend their whole life making things no one needs and very few want? And we do it to the detriment of our security and sometimes our health. Are we obsessed? It must be some kind of character flaw, disorder or disease. We should be good subservient employees like everyone else, right?

I think, to some degree, there is an obsessive-compulsive aspect to art-making. This isn't recognized by the medical community thank goodness, if it were art students would probably be medicated until they were 'cured' and enrolled in accounting classes.

Here is the detailed medical definition of Obsessive-Compulsive Disorder from the Brain and Behavior Research Foundation (www.bbrfoundation.org) website:

Obsessive-Compulsive Disorder (OCD) is a brain and behavior disorder that is categorized as an anxiety disorder in the Diagnostic and Statistical Manual of Mental Disorders, Fourth Edition (DSM-IV). OCD causes severe anxiety in those affected and involves both obsessions and compulsions that interfere with daily life. Research suggests that OCD involves problems in communication between the front part of the brain and deeper structures. These brain structures use a chemical messenger called serotonin. Pictures of the brain at work also show that in some people, the brain circuits involved in OCD become normalized with either serotonin medicines or cognitive behavioral therapy (CBT).

What are the symptoms of OCD?

OCD causes severe anxiety in those affected and involves both obsessions and compulsions that interfere with daily life. Obsessions are persistent ideas, thoughts, impulses or images that are experienced as intrusive and inappropriate and cause marked anxiety or distress. The most common obsessions are repeated thoughts about contamination, repeated doubts, a need to have things in a particular order, aggressive or horrific impulses, and sexual imagery. Compulsions are the individuals attempt to suppress such thoughts or impulses or to neutralize them with some other thought or action. These can include repetitive behaviors, such as hand washing, ordering or checking on things; or mental acts, such as praying, counting, or repeating words silently.

At what age does OCD begin?

OCD can start at any time beginning as early as preschool and continuing to adulthood. Age at onset tends to be earlier in males that in females: between ages 6 and 15 years for males and between ages 20 and 29 years for females.

Is OCD inherited?

Research shows that OCD does run in families and that genes likely play a role in the development of the disorder. Genes appear to be only partly responsible for causing the disorder though and it is thought that it is more likely a combination of genetic susceptibility and environmental influences.

How is OCD diagnosed?

There are no laboratory or brain imaging tests to diagnose OCD. The diagnosis is made based on the observation and assessment of the person's symptoms by a mental health professional.

How effective are treatments for OCD?

Currently, there is only one type of medication that has been shown to be effective in treating Obsessive-Compulsive Disorder (OCD). Serotonin Reuptake Inhibitors (SRIs), including clomipramine, have been shown to reduce symptoms in 40% - 60% of patients with OCD. Cognitive Behavioral Therapy (CBT) has also been shown to be effective. Patients who respond to medication usually show a 40 to 60% reduction in OCD symptoms, while those who respond to CBT often report a 60 to 80% reduction in OCD symptoms.

An actual diagnosis of obsessive-compulsive disorder is a very bad thing and is debilitating, but I think, sometimes, it requires some degree of obsessive-compulsion to create art.

Just as Asperser's Syndrome describes a functional person with just a 'touch' of autism, perhaps 'artist' describes a person who manages their 'touch' of OCD?

The OCD symptoms I think are most applicable to artists are:

...obsessions and compulsions that interfere with daily life...

...persistent ideas, thoughts, impulses or images that are experienced as intrusive...

The most common obsessions are...repeated doubts, a need to have things in a particular order...

Compulsions are the individuals' attempt to suppress such thoughts or impulses or to neutralize them with some other thought or action.

The first of the 'artist-applicable' symptoms are the *obsessions and compulsions that interfere with daily life*. If we use the conformist's consensus-reality definition of daily life we find the lifestyles of many artists are far outside the standard Americanworker definition of what constitutes 'normal' daily life.

Now, many of these artists are merely enjoying an alternative lifestyle in that they don't have 'real' or 'regular' jobs. That doesn't mean there's anything wrong with them, but in the eyes of 'Joe Average' they're weird. Joe Average defines everyone by his own narrow standard, so in Joe Average's view (and the majority of the population is 'Joe Average') the artist is somehow, abnormal. But this is society's view and society is often wrong (especially in our present disinfo-thick/propaganda 'journalism' culture). But the obsessions and compulsions listed in the OCD definition are in the mind of the OCD sufferer and not external. So if the person, or in this instance The Artist, has an internal obsession with art-making and it interferes (like staying up all night painting and then being late for their 'real job' the next day) with their so-called daily life they might be described as having a 'touch' of OCD. But I wonder if their 'daily life' might be the thing that's interfering with their art-making? After all, most artists with 'real jobs' work jobs that aren't in the field of art, and therefore are an unsatisfying means to an end — which is to generate enough money to continue making art. But if we define 'art-making' as the artists' daily life then it's the 'normal' kind of daily life that's interfering with their art-making.

A different definition could be: *an obsession with art-making that interferes with what society agrees is a normal 'daily life' could be a symptom of OCD*. Although art-making is one of the purest expressions of individuality, the individual does not define what 'normal' is. Society at large and the medical-pharmaceutical-hospital- industrial complex decides what's 'normal' and an obsessive desire to make art is 'abnormal' by their standards.

The next symptom *...persistent ideas, thoughts, impulses or images that are experienced as intrusive...* is the very 'drive' that drives artists to create. I can attest from personal experience that persistent ideas are motivating and their very persistence is the thing that sets me to work. For me the 'image in my head' must get out and the only way to get it out of my head is to make the image!

Only when the image is 'realized' on paper or pixels (or is at least begun, meaning it will be completed) does the persistent idea abate — usually to be replaced by another in short time!

If I'm driving down the road in my car and the persistent image of some picture is stuck in my mind, that's inappropriate, but not debilitating. But if it's a really good idea (how I determine 'good' is not quite known to me) then I do feel some 'anxiety' until I can at least write it down, sketch it or shoot the photo. I think one difference between artists and 'normal' people is although we all have intrusive creative thoughts from time to time, artists act on those thoughts. The same thoughts had by non-artists are not acted upon and dissipate (or debilitate). Of course the full-blown, diagnosed, OCD sufferer has similar intrusive, persistent ideas too; the difference between the OCD patient and the artist is much of the time the OCD patients' ideas and thoughts are *unproductive*. Repeated hand-washing, for instance, isn't particularly productive but sculpting that thing you visualized is productive because *an artist acting on the persistent idea produces a product, art.*

The third OCD 'artist-symptom,' is the most common one *...repeated doubts, a need to have things in a particular order...* doesn't strike me as especially symptomatic of OCD. After all the arrangement of graphic elements and colors in a particular order are what artists do when they produce art. Only when that's externalized and it becomes intrusive does it become debilitating and 'anal-retentive.' I don't find *repeated doubts* to be especially problematic unless your doubts become paralyzing. Doubt, to a manageable degree, is good, in my view. Heck, I have doubts about every image I make! Who knows? It is those who are cocksure of themselves beyond any doubt that scare me!

The details of the definition get scary though: thoughts about contamination...aggressive or horrific impulses, and sexual imagery. These things, when acted upon inappropriately can be dangerous. The 'germ phobia' thing is too common to get into.

But the aggressive or horrific impulses and sexual imagery could lead the OCD sufferer to murder, violence or rape. Less horrible outcomes of this might be nude or 'dark' art. An artist is a person with an appropriate outlet for these thoughts. Perhaps it is creativity itself that provides the means to 'manage' some lesser forms of OCD?

Finally, *compulsions are the individuals' attempt to suppress such thoughts or impulses or to neutralize them with some other thought or action.* I'd call art-making a 'positive compulsion' because it is the very compulsive nature that drives the artist to work. An artist must have a degree of compulsion otherwise he might not create at all. Who would willfully struggle with both art-making and the business of art if they weren't somewhat compulsive (especially when you have more film than food in the fridge)? Without a level of compulsion the call of the couch and TV would overwhelm the desire to create art. But the medical definition speaks of *negative, nonproductive compulsions.* And again this means to me that the artist has 'managed' the compulsion to produce something tangible and positive through art instead of wasting time with nonproductive rituals.

Perhaps there's a fine line between art-making and obsessive-compulsion? Perhaps art-making is the result of the person *managing* their (slight) OCD? I've either done it myself or know people who:

Work night and day making art.

Will buy art supplies instead of food if their budget only allows for one.

Forgo a steady income to make art.

Won't leave home without sketchbook, notebook or camera.

Live in their studios.

Have a great Art Portfolio but no Investment Portfolio.

Don't use this as a diagnostic tool to label your artist friends obsessive-compulsive wackos. I'm not your doctor. I'm simply pointing out a correlation between generalized obsessive behavior and the specific obsessive-like behaviors of artists. This may be only correlation without causation, I don't know. My conclusions (or more accurately, suggestions) are the result of thirty-plus years of observation of myself and other artists. I've lived among them for my whole life, so I've learned something about how they (we) think. The OCD aspects of art-making would be an easy thing to quantify if any credentialed researchers had interest. Until legitimate research is conducted, my conclusions are strictly anecdotal.

Postscript: I never did have much more than condiments and leftovers in my fridge until I married that girl. Then she got me a separate freezer for film. Then we stopped using film altogether. Eventually I sold all the frozen Kodachrome and now there's more space for popsicles in the freezer. I'm still obsessed with making pictures, but now I've got plenty of memory-cards, *and plenty of actual food in the fridge too.*

CHAPTER

COMFORT, FEAR AND ACCEPTABILITY

As a culture at this point in our collective history we seem to be comfortable only with things we already know. Showing familiarity in a new way is the limit of acceptability. As a society we seem unwilling to consider things outside our everyday comfort-zone, a comfort-zone overly determined by the media. When I look at the 'art' photography produced in the first decade of the 21st century I'm not seeing much innovation (at the moment in history anyway, this is cyclical). From my perspective, photography seems to be at a plateau. I'm seeing familiar subjects shown in new, digitallyenhanced ways, but that's about it.

In my view, some forms of photography are 'criticism proof.' Wildlife, landscape and astronomical photography come to mind. There will always be a market for the beautiful wildlife and landscape photo and getting the shot (assuming no technical flaws) is often enough. 'Art photography' does not fit this 'criticism proof' category and this is the specific area where I see a lack of innovation.

Perhaps it's now time for 'photography' and 'digital art' to diverge and become recognized as separate art forms? If 'digital art' were defined as an art form separate from photography it may eliminate a lot of confusion.

At the beginning of the 'digital revolution' of photography we were just happy to get an image out of the computer. In the 1980s, and 1990s especially, we saw a lot of 'digital noise' coming forth.

The computer and image-processing software were so new, so innovative and so different that virtually anything 'digital' was fresh and got noticed. The technical innovation of 'digital' opened many new aesthetic doors and it's taken nearly two decades for some artists to peek behind those doors. A few artists have kicked those doors in, embraced digital for what it is, and are innovating. However, far too many are using new tools to express the same old things.

Early on (and 'early' wasn't that long ago) 'digital artists,' who at the time were merely photographers with computers, used digital imaging to emulate older art forms. I saw many photographs 'digitally painted' to imitate expressionist paintings. These weren't abstract-expressionist artists creating abstract-expressionist works, but rather photographers 'polishing turds' to make their images appear to be something they were not. This was nothing but technical innovation being used to create 'aesthetic imitation,' in my view. I recall a national ad for software that used a digitally altered photograph to create a portrait of a woman with both eyes on the same side of her head, as if the software would make one into some sort of 'digital Picasso.' I found the image profoundly creepy; a photorealistic image of woman with weird eyes; a pretend Picasso. Picasso did it better, and he did it first. To me it was a misuse of technology, a powerful new machine useful in creating an image *already accepted by the zeitgeist.* Early on, the razzle-dazzle of digital trumped subject and yes, meaning too. It was all 'style' and very little 'substance.' A mile wide but only an inch deep.

As a result of 'digital,' photography seems to be splitting into two camps, the 'straight or analog photographer' and the 'digital photographer.' Some of the 'analog photographers' have almost entirely rejected digital, preferring to shoot film and use the darkroom in traditional ways. These are our modern traditionalists, carrying the torch of Analog Photography. There will always be a market for their works, albeit a shrinking one. And I've always believed, and still do today, that as a result of the digitalization of photography, the silver-gelatin, handmade, darkroom print will only increase in value as they become more rare as fewer and fewer practitioners of the 'darkroom arts' continue working. More than likely, these photographers will continue to produce familiar 'straight' subjects by purely photographic means, leaving overt retouching and trickery to the 'digital photographers.' I foresee Analog Photography as a limited, yet viable 'traditional' art-form. I'd guess that of all the photographers working today the 'Analog Photographer' represents less than ten percent of the total. The market doesn't really care that these photographers use film and chemistry, *but the analog photographers do.*

The 'digital photographer' is the mainstream these days. The mere speed of digital is necessary to compete in today's evermore time-compressed world of commercial photography. These are the folks who have embraced 'digital' as the new darkroom, a darkroom with far more speed and flexibility than ever before. They are producing the works we see in print and on the web every day. Their works range from heavily retouched (portraits, advertising imagery), to composite imagery (adding/removing objects, headswaps, chroma-key photos), to 'photo-illustration' such as HDR effects and digital infrared, to name a few. Although not all of their photographs look like 'photographs' they are labeled 'digital photographs.' We seem to be developing a 'digital acceptance standard' for the digital manipulation of the photograph and 'digital photographers' are mostly remaining inside that box of acceptability. Technique seems to supplant 'meaning' in much of todays' digital photography. I'd estimate that the number of 'digital photographers' exceeds eighty percent of the total.

I believe the expanded capabilities of Adobe Photoshop has ushered in a new era of 'Post-Surrealism.' Art History gives the year 1924 as the approximate beginning of the Surrealist Movement. I have not found an official 'end date' of the Surrealist

Movement in my Art History studies so I'm going to date the 'end' of the 'traditional' Surrealist Movement at 1989, the year of Salvador Dalí's death. Art historian Sarane Alexandrian stated, *"The death of André Breton in 1966 marked the end of Surrealism as an organized movement."* There have also been attempts to tie the obituary of the movement to the 1989 death of Salvador Dalí. (Wikipedia). I place the beginning of the 'Post-Surrealist Movement' at 1990 because it's the year Adobe Photoshop 1.0 brought digital-imaging to the masses and changed photography forever. It's also one year after the death of Dali. I'm sure the next generation of Art Historians will determine this for us — and it's unlikely they'll use my timeline, but it will suffice for now.

So, here we are, barely a quarter century into the 'Post-Surrealist Era,' thanks mostly to digital imaging technology, and where are we? As I see it, we are at a point where the discussion is irrelevant in terms of commercial photography. Commercial photography has always been about the single image and it doesn't really matter to the viewer how that image came to be. Commercial art is, by and large, temporary and disposable (although there are well-known examples of commercial imagery transcending its original intent and recognized as 'fine art'). The subject of the commercial photograph is determined by the client not the artist, thereby limiting the artists' contribution to mostly the technical (especially in advertising). If there is one thing 'digital' (the technique and not the aesthetic) has done for photography, and commercial photography especially, is that it's made photography even easier, and has taken jobs away from the traditional commercial photographer. The sheer volume of digital images produced now (as a result of the no-longer-necessary darkroom or photo-lab combined with the ease and economy of the digital camera) has devalued the photograph. Nowhere is this more obvious than in Stock Photography, where one can license a stock photo from a Microstock website for a dollar — less than the cost to produce the photo! Looking towards art photography, I see digital has made inroads in the creation of *decorative images*, images that have been enhanced and altered in acceptable ways (high color-saturation and the addition of textures comes to mind). And, obviously, the digital printer has made it easier and cheaper for the artists themselves to produce posters or large-scale prints without the necessity of outside services. But, as these things go, the discussion often dwindles to the technology and not the *aesthetic*. And it's still hard to separate the technical from the aesthetic when computers are part of the discussion.

In terms of aesthetics, if about ten percent of photographers are Analog Photographers, continuing to work with traditional photographic methods and eighty-plus percent are 'digital photographers,' that leaves less than ten percent who have embraced 'digital' for what it is and are true 'digital artists.' Most of these 'digital artists' came from photography (certainly artists from other mediums have embraced digital, but by far photographers lead the pack) and it is clear many of them are pursuing a 'Post-Surreal' aesthetic. These are the few (although highly productive) who are really pushing aesthetic and creative boundaries to create something new — and they're the ones having the most difficulties finding acceptance in a culture that fears change and the unknown. They are mislabeled 'digital photographers' or 'digital painters' when, in fact, they are 'digital artists,' practitioners of a new art form.

There is no category yet for the 'digital artist' so they're lumped in with photographers. They are producing a lot of imagery and much of it is very good; it's different, it's innovative and it's unlike much that has come before. These artists are finding it difficult to find an audience for this in traditional art venues. When I do a Google image-search using the terms 'photo+digital+surrealism' I get pages and pages of artwork, and much of it is very exciting. But why am I seeing so little of this work in the galleries or in print? My guess it's fear, a cultural and institutional fear of the new and unknown, a fear of an aesthetic so new that it doesn't easily fit into the preconceived notion of what's acceptable. 'Different' always scares the shit out of the intellectually complacent conformist. But I don't believe it's fair to lay all the blame at the feet of the viewer because there is an audience for these new works. I know this from my own gallery exhibitions of my digital art. At my exhibitions, I witness patrons actually having *fun*; they're engaged by the artwork and enjoy the act of discovery. They have no fear of things they haven't seen before, and, as my digital-surreal imagery is based on the landscape, they have a known reference-point to begin their contemplation of the art. Often, gallery patrons at my exhibitions tell me how "creative" my work is. I kind of find that comment silly; isn't the *point* of art to be *creative*? But when I consider the comment, I have to conclude they've seen a lot of familiar art-works, things they already know about but when they come to my exhibition they see something a little different, and thus the "creative" comment. And collectors do buy my work; but it's hard to get a gallery show, and nobody buys what they can't see.

I feel that much of the blame for the 'non-acceptance' of much of the Digital Post Surrealist works (as well as the difficulty in getting a show) can be laid at the feet of the gatekeeper-gallerists. Gallerists who feel they 'know their market' and automatically reject anything that's outside their pre-acknowledged zone of acceptability. They are fearful to be 'alone,' 'out on a limb' showing artworks that haven't been pre-approved by the monoculture. The galleries' fear of things too far from the easily-relatable is actually an impediment, and is a barrier between artist and audience. As a result, the 'Post-Surrealist Digital Artist' has gone around the gallery, direct to the viewer, via the internet. For the moment, the galleries seem to be very risk-adverse. I'm sure they'll get on-board when all this is declared 'safe.' Yes, yes some galleries specialize in specific mediums or styles. The 'photography gallery' is where we find the most digital art, but that's not really the appropriate venue because 'digital art' doesn't always look much like 'photographs.' There are a few 'digital art galleries' (many more online) but we need more. 'Digital Art' should not be the poor stepchild of photography.

When I see all of the incredible photo-digital-surrealistic works online, sometimes I lament how easy this stuff is to make ('easy' is a relative term, largely dependent on one's depth of knowledge of Photoshop). I've *always* made photographically-based 'special-effect' or 'conceptual' imagery. In the pre-digital days of photography, in order to create the kind of 'surreal' or 'conceptual' imagery that's so digitally-plentiful today, a photographer had to be *clever*. It was a highly-technical process that few photographers had the patience for. It required a backwards-and-forwards and inside-and-out knowledge of photographic processes. It required both aesthetic and technical creativity. It was *hard* to do, and that's precisely why so few of us did it 'back in the day.' It was easy for me to stand out when so few photographers were extending the creative process past the point of exposure, now it's hard to get noticed at all. It's hard *to* be noticed because the computer and Adobe Photoshop have made it easier and the easier a thing is to do, the more people do it. As a result digital artists have circumvented the gallery and have gone direct to the viewer on the Internet where at least their works have a chance to be *seen*. But the bleeding-edge of the cutting-edge sword cuts both ways. *Anyone* can put a gallery up on the internet and internet lacks the 'art-legitimizing' force of the 'Brick-and-Mortar' Art Gallery. In my view, many of the (nonvirtual) galleries need to catch up to the viewer, a viewer who has a wider acceptance of the 'unknown' than the so-called 'experts.' This fear of the new and unknown isn't new at all. Here's something Salvador Dali wrote about the subject in 1939:

Any authentically original idea, presenting itself without "known antecedents" is systematically rejected, toned down, mauled,

*chewed, rechewed, spewed forth, destroyed, yes, and even worse —
reduced to the most monstrous of mediocrities. The excuse offered
is always the vulgarity of the vast majority of the public. I insist
that this is absolutely false. The public is infinitely superior to the
rubbish that is fed to it daily. The masses have always known where
to find true poetry. The misunderstanding has come about entirely
through those "middle-men of culture" who, with their lofty airs
and superior quacking, come between the creator and the public.
(From "The Persistence of Memory: A Biography of Dali."
Meredith Etheriington-Smith, Random House 1992.)*

So, there's really nothing new seventy-plus years hence. We
continue to fight the battle against fear of the new and unknown.

Because of the 'density' of art available online, I wonder if
anything can really stand out, no matter how good or innovative it
is. There's just so much. Are the days of the Iconic Image in past?
When we think of Surrealism we automatically recall Dali's 'soft
clocks' or Magritte's man in the Derby hat; Rothko's color-washed
canvases and Pollock's paint-splatters automatically come to mind
when considering Abstract-Expressionism. And who doesn't asso-
ciate Ansel Adams with black and white landscape photos of the
Sierras? These are Iconic Images that are burned into our collec-
tive- consciousness and you don't even have to know anything
about art to know those images. These images are recognized
because there were very few images like them reproduced at the
time. Publishers deemed this imagery acceptable (and profitable)
and the public dissemination of those images brought them into the
cultural awareness and ultimate widespread acceptance. I fear that
in an endless sea of online 'content' no imagery will be contemplated long enough to become 'Iconic.'

Our societies' belief in 'what's acceptable' is largely determined
by the media. People believe what they're told. It must be a good
book because it's a 'best seller,' it must be a good song because 'it's

a number one hit,' and that sort of mentality. Most people don't seek innovation, but they accept what they've been told is innovative by 'experts.' But the 'experts' aren't really experts, more often they're just people who managed to get themselves on TV, and TV automatically makes one a perceived expert. Humans have too much of a pack mentality and fear getting too far from the pack, aka, the 'mainstream.' Too far outside the mainstream gets one labeled as 'difficult' or 'weird' or 'different' and we're living in a society that rewards conformity and condemns 'different.' I think this is especially true for groups of people. Get people together in a group and you often get 'group-think.' But tear one individual away from the group, where alone they lose their fear of ridicule, and quite often the *individual* is open to newness or the unknown. Once that newness or unknown becomes acceptable, usually from pronouncement by the media-monoculture, then it has become 'mainstream.' Liking a thing that society says is OK to like, is not a risk. Here's a personal example: At one time the music of the Rolling Stones was considered scandalous or even 'satanic.' But Mick and Keith and the boys kept at it (mainly by virtue of making huge amounts of money for their record label, which continued to 'disseminate' their music to the masses) and their music became more and more acceptable by mainstream culture — familiarity breeds approval. Now, after making music for over fifty years they've reaped widespread acceptance. The music is not only good, thereby making it valid, but it's widely available (a further validation) and is now so ubiquitous that you're considered 'weird' if you don't like the Rolling Stones. Among my contemporaries I'm considered 'weird' because I'm not a Rolling Stones fan. "What's wrong with you, Dale; you don't like the 'Stones?!" I don't consider myself weird at all; I'm just not a Rolling Stones fan. Not liking a thing doesn't make it 'bad' it merely means you don't like it. But as the 'Stones are completely mainstream now, I'm out-of-the-mainstream as a non-fan. It's riskier not liking the 'Stones now!

Most people just accept what's acceptable by those who tell them it's safe to accept it. This is why really, really innovative artworks are marginalized by their lack of art-gallery acceptance and thus, legitimization. Again, it's the mentality of "if it's in an art gallery it must be good art." The art gallery is perceived as 'expert' and most people are more than willing to believe the 'expert.' A lot of art galleries exhibit crap in my opinion, but often 'crap' is what society has been told is 'acceptable' and instead of questioning 'conventional wisdom' it's simply accepted and unquestioned. Acceptance of what you're told by the marketing-media requires no critical thought, is always safe, and you'll never get criticized for 'going along.'

Call it 'societal peer-pressure.' Going along with the marketing-flow. Believing what you're told instead of what you could *think*; being afraid to disagree with the monoculture. Not knowing *how* to say, "I'm not so sure about that," when everyone else is cocksure despite a complete lack of contemplation.

I'm just not satisfied with a lot of contemporary photography these days. (Yes, I'm old and jaded and have seen a lot of stuff, I'm hard to impress — but I want to be impressed.) A lot of contemporary photography seems to be engaged in self-reference. 'Art' photographers are traveling old ground with new cameras. 'Documentary' photography is in vogue in the more influential galleries. Perhaps this is good for photographers? Perhaps photography, in order to remain 'photography' must concern itself with documentation of 'what is?' Perhaps 'digital' will lead to a diversion of aesthetics, with photography concerning itself with the 'real' and 'digital art' defining an image 'beyond photography?' Perhaps individuals (and art galleries) need to become more self-assured in their aesthetic choices and not concern themselves with what 'everybody' likes and not fear expressing a 'lone opinion?'

Perhaps I'm full of shit? It's not unfamiliar territory.

'Conventional wisdom' requires no thought, contemplation or

study, only blind acceptance. Conventional wisdom means the statement "everybody knows..." is actually true. Conventional wisdom told Galileo the Earth was flat but his observation told him otherwise. He was 'difficult' and we know what that got him. You're not going to be imprisoned for disagreeing with what you're told about art so really, make your own choices. Fight the monoculture! In art there really is something for everybody, and you don't have to like what you've been told to like. It's OK to declare the Emperor Has No Clothes.

As artists we take aesthetic risks, that's what we do, and that's why some art is declared 'ahead of its time.' (Think Van Gogh.) What we ask of the viewer (and moreover, the galleries that stand between us and the viewer) is to take a moment and contemplate the aesthetic risk we took and come to your own conclusion on the arts' success or failure. It's a bigger risk for me to exhibit the art than it is for you to form an honest opinion about it. Don't let 'the culture' determine your opinion.

Now I'm going to read a book by Jeff Noon, while sitting under a painting by Zdzislaw Beksinski and listen to a CD by The Weed Brothers. Ever heard of these guys? I didn't think so. The monoculture hasn't told you about them. You've got to do a little searching to find the really cool stuff.

FUN FACTS:

Of all the photos shot in 2017
85%
Were shot with SmartPhones
4.7%
Were shot with Tablets
10.3%
Were shot with actual Cameras

SOME STATISTICS TO CONTEMPLATE

It is estimated that 1.2 trillion photos were made in 2017.
To break it down, that's about:
100 billion photos per month.
3.3 billion Photos per day.
136.9 million Photos per hour.
2.3 million Photos per minute.
38,333 photos per second!
Of those 3.3 billion photos made per day, let's assume that ninety-nine percent of them are selfies and other crap that won't be seen more than once and are basically disposable.
Let's also assume that one percent of those photos
are actual art.
That's 33 million new pieces of photographic art
created every day!
With so much to see it's no wonder so little is seen.

CHAPTER

I AM VINTAGE!

I knew this would happen one day…

Before I answered the phone I checked the caller ID and instead of some telemarketer's 'blocked number' I saw a name I had not seen in over a decade. It was the owner of the gallery where I had my first 'real' New York City exhibition. In the intervening years between then and now she had closed the gallery in New York, relocated to Colorado, and now had opened a new gallery in Denver. During those same years I relocated from Texas to Arizona and have transitioned from black and white analog photography to color digital art. The years have brought many changes for us both but fundamentally we're doing the same things: she's still selling art and I'm still creating it.

She was preparing for a group exhibition featuring the nude as subject and remembered my work from the 1980s which had been exhibited in New York and wanted it for her new gallery in Denver. I still had the remaining prints stored in portfolio cases in my studio so it was easy enough to find the images she wanted. Locating the photographs was one thing but actually looking at them was something else entirely. Basically, I had put the entire subject of the nude, and straight black and white photography, behind me a few years after publication of my photography book, *Human/Nature*, in 1997. My goal then had been to create a series of photographs of the nude that were not male-oriented and were as different as possible from what had already been done. I'd done the work, exhibited it, sold enough prints to prove it was viable imagery, and ultimately got it published in book form. I accomplished that goal and moved on. By this time photography was becoming more and more digital and I was transitioning away from analog photography to digital art (not digital photography). By the 1990s I was mostly done with nude.

As the 21st century progressed so did my development as a digital artist. None of the galleries I'd been associated with as a 'black and white nude photographer' was interested in the new digital works I was producing. I was once told that it is 'artistic suicide' to make such a fundamental change in both subject and process and I'd best keep doing what I was known for. Known for? I guess the few people who'd bought my prints know who I am but when the subject of nude photography comes up I'm pretty sure my name is not mentioned in a list including Weston, Newton, Bernard, Mapplethorpe, et al. There was tremendous pressure from the galleries to keep making the same picture. I suppose if I had achieved a significant degree of fame and fortune for my nude photography I may have been compelled, or gotten greedy enough, to continue on. But I figured I can be poor and keep doing the same old thing or be poor doing something new so I tried the new thing. I have no regrets. In fact, I've probably received more recognition as a digital artist now than I ever did as a photographer of the nude back then. Still, the black and white nude photography is good work. I ultimately ended all my old gallery affiliations as a 'photographer' and struck new deals with new galleries who only know me as a 'digital artist.' I've noticed that most gallery people can only conceive of an artist doing only one thing. When they have to contemplate the possibility of an artist working in multiple mediums or with multiple subjects their heads just explode and they reject the unfamiliar.

The gallery owner in Denver has no interest in my newest digital work but she really believes in the black and white nudes and doesn't care that I do other works in other mediums with other subjects. She's a rarity in that respect and I appreciate her openness. Because of her invitation to exhibit I've had a reason to look at photographs that I really had not seen or thought of for a very long time. And it's strangely nice to revisit my own history. I'm pleased to see that the work holds up. It doesn't look dated or stuck in some historic or artistic time-frame. Naked bodies do have a timeless quality; the fashion of flesh never goes out of style. What has gone out of style, replaced by digital information or metadata, is the rubber stamp on the back of the print that has the copyright information and the date the print was made. As I was pulling out the prints to ship to Denver I checked all the print dates which ranged from 1982 to 1989. All the prints are between 19 and 26 years old! I taught a photography last fall and the realization that the prints in my studio are older than my students is downright frightening!

Photographic art historians define a 'vintage' print as one made near the same time as the negative and are over twenty years old. Prints made later are considered 'modern' prints. This means that my (dare I say, *early*) work is now vintage! Having works of my own considered vintage leads to another alarming observation, I am vintage too! Twenty years ago I had more hair on the top of my head; fortunately my 'vintage' prints are more archival than my follicles.

About a decade ago when I was becoming less involved with developer dilutions, cold lights and selenium toner and becoming more concerned with processor speed, random access memory and output resolution, I did figure that someday, someone, somewhere would want to exhibit the black and white darkroom prints. Sure enough, over a decade later, that day has come. To conclude this exhibition of my 'vintage' photography the gallery is putting on a panel discussion one evening on the topic of 'nudity and eroticism in the arts' and I've been asked to be one of the panelists. Now I've got to try to recall and articulate all the stuff I was thinking twenty-odd years ago when I was making the images. I have not thought about this in a long, long time. One thing is for sure, the photography is the same, only the psychology, the artists' relationship with his work, has changed. My relationship with the imagery, process and subject has evolved considerably from the time the photographs were made when I was in my twenties to now at the age of fiftyish. Honestly, I don't really care what people think about it anymore. It's a subject from my past that has withstood the test of time. I'm done with it and whatever someone has to say today won't affect how I approach the subject tomorrow because, to quote a camera shop T-shirt, "been there, shot that." The gallery discussion will be interesting. Because I'm not involved with the subject on a daily basis I can approach it with some objective distance without the impediment of cognitive dissonance.

Despite the 'old age' aspect rearing its ugly head the great thing about vintage photography is that it commands vintage prices. We've tripled my prices. This time, when we sell a print I'll earn enough to go back in the darkroom and make another — yeah, right, like I'm going back in the darkroom. This edition is closed!

CHAPTER

THE MASTER

At the newsstand I picked up a couple of magazines dedicated to two of my favorite subjects, photography and music. Returning home I tossed the magazines on the kitchen table and they both fell open to interesting pages. The photography magazine hit the table open to a full-page ad screaming about an upcoming seminar led on by some 'master of photography' I've never heard of. The music magazine dropped onto the table open to the very article I wanted to read. Interesting! This is the very sort of random event or coincidence that we should learn to notice. I'm convinced that odd coincidences like this serve to direct our consciousness in unconventional ways — if we pay attention. Since the music magazine was already open to the article I bought the magazine for, I read that one first. It was an interview with guitarist Allan Holdsworth, a musician whose position in the pantheon of contemporary guitarists is secure. He's a true master and doesn't need to say so, others say it for him. Despite Holdsworth's technical and compositional accomplishments, and the respect other guitarists have for him, I was surprised and pleased to read the following quote from him:

"I resigned myself to a few things a long, long time ago. For example, I knew that no matter how long I was fortunate to stay alive, I would never know anything about music. And once I realized that, I didn't worry about it ever again. And even though I

constantly keep learning new things, I'm okay with the fact that I'll never know anything." *

Read that quote again substituting the word 'photography' for 'music' and try to imagine a photographer saying it. I hope some photographer (other than me) has uttered a similar sentiment, but I've never heard it. Actually, when I listen to most photographers talk, I find most of them aggressively egocentric. In my experience, musicians, especially rock guitarists, have huge egos. But no matter how big a guitarist's ego grows, his or her ego seems downright tiny compared to the ego of the most imminently average photographer!

Here are a couple of true scenarios that illustrate the above point: I was at a gallery opening and got into a conversation with an award-winning photographer. He hardly stopped talking. He went on and on about this and that piece of equipment and finally wound up telling me he'd won the Blue Ribbon for Best in Show photo at the County Fair. After he finally stopped complimenting himself he asked me what I do. I said that I too am a photographer. Then he asked what kind of work I did. I pointed to the gallery wall where my work was displayed and said, "This is my work." I got a sheepish look in return and I'm pretty sure he was thinking, "What an asshole," but hey, he started the conversation about his work and it would have been rude of me to interrupt.

Another photo-ego-incident occurred when I was on location in New Mexico photographing birds. The Big Time Wildlife photographer standing next to me felt the necessity to tell me how his big-dick 600mm lens was so much better than my 'little' 400mm lens was. And his carbon-fiber tripod is so much more 'professional' than my beat-up 20-year old aluminum tripod is. "Nice gear," I said and then asked, "So where can I see your work exhibited or

* "In search of the uncommon chord." Interview with Allan Holdsworth, *Guitar Player Magazine*, April 2008, Vol. 42, #4, pp.74-88.

published?" He replied he didn't exhibit or publish but always wins the ribbons awarded by his camera club. He then turned the question back to me and asked where my work was published or exhibited. I mentioned the name of a photography magazine that had one of my images on its cover that very month. He gave me the same look as the guy in the gallery and suddenly got real busy with whatever he was seeing through that big 600mm lens.

The thing is, if you are good at something it'll show in the thing you do, be it photography or music or whatever. And if your artistry is noticed, recognized or receives any kind of acclaim, others will say nice things about you or maybe even call you a 'master.'

Getting back to the full page ad for the 'master' in the photography magazine, I carefully read the whole ad and found no actual accreditation for the claim of 'master.' I've never heard of the guy either but that's not a barometer for fame as I don't know everybody. I do try to stay well-informed but the 'master' was not on my radar. I Googled the master's name and got less than ten hits. When I Googled "Allan Holdsworth" the search returned over a half million hits. That in itself tells you something about each ones' status. I also noticed the picture of the 'master' in the ad showed a guy who might be thirty years old. Holdsworth is 62. Isn't it interesting that the older guy 'knows nothing' while the youngster is a 'master?'

There is only one legitimate path to the attainment of respect, recognition and fame and that is to earn it. But now, in the time-compressed, ADD world we've created, there is another path to fame and it is through declaration.

Once I was doing an interview for a magazine article about my digital art and photography. I mentioned to the interviewer that I first used computers for image-making in 1982 and the first wholly- computer generated image ever published in advertising was one of mine. The interviewer (who was probably in diapers in 1982) paused and said, "1982! You're a digital guru!" I stopped him right there and made it clear that I am in no way any sort of 'guru.' Although I appreciated his compliment (guru is a declaration of reverence) it's not a title I claim for myself.

Beware of unearned proclamations.

CHAPTER

THOMAS KINKADE RECONSIDERED

Thomas Kinkade may be one of the few 'renowned' artists whose art will not increase in value after his death. There's a ton of it out there already and it's more 'commodity' than 'art' anyway. Kinkade's legacy will be debated for years to come despite his *persona non grata* status among 'art experts.'

Once I was a participant on a panel discussion at CopperCon, the annual science-fiction convention in Phoenix. I was the 'digital surrealist' on a panel of sci-fi/fantasy illustrators and during Q&A time the subject of Thomas Kinkade came up. As expected, pretty much everybody in the room from the panelists to the audience had a litany of disparaging things to say about the 'Painter of Light' and his cheesy paintings. He's an easy target. I agreed with most of what everyone was saying; that his paintings are cheesy and commercial, they're market-driven and generally eye-candy with little depth. My view was that he'd basically painted one painting over and over and over. After a while things started getting vicious and I had to intercede.

I stopped the Kinkade-flogging when I reminded the audience (consisting of young wannabe sci-fi/fantasy/surrealist artists) that despite Kinkade's cheesy imagery he'd accomplished something everyone in the audience, and including us on the Panel of Pros, wishes they could — that is, Thomas Kinkade was Rich and Famous. And who doesn't want to be rich and famous? Thomas

147

Kinkade's fame was the kind that few artists' attain, which is being famous *outside* the world of art. I told the audience that while it may be fair for us to criticize Kinkade's style and subject matter, his marketing skills exceeded his artistry. Simply put, Kinkade was a brilliant marketer (and perhaps fraudulent in the case of certain limited-editions) and it was his marketing ability above and beyond his artistry that convinced one in twenty Americans that they needed to own a Kinkade reproduction.

There's nothing at all wrong with being Rich and Famous and Thomas Kinkade was both. I believe his religiosity was hypocritical and more marketing tool than belief, but that didn't stop his fans from buying his art. The fact that he caused his own death by overdosing on drugs and alcohol doesn't square with his religious, family-oriented, 'clean' seeming lifestyle doesn't matter to me. I know from art history that many artists have demons in the form of sex-drugs-etc. and it's almost expected for an artist to be a little screwed-up. Most artists are forgiven for this and Kinkade should be too (except perhaps by those religious types who take this more seriously than the rest of us).

Thomas Kinkade died an unhappy man. Despite his great wealth and international fame he was bothered by critical negativity. Kinkade's works will never hang in The Louve. So what? Thomas Kinkade's works, according to reports, hang in one of twenty American homes — that's about fifteen million homes! That is more exposure than any single painting in The Louve ever gets! (Except for the Mona Lisa.) But Kinkade made a choice and he went for the bucks before recognition, so he got what he bargained for and he should have gotten comfortable with it. With millions of dollars in the bank as well as millions of paintings in millions of homes, Thomas Kinkade had earned the right to tell his critics to fuck-off! But he still wanted what all artists' crave, which is peer recognition.

Let's take a brief look at Thomas Kinkade's most important accomplishments:

He was able to earn a living as a full-time artist without the need of a 'real job.'

He did what he loved.

He earned a shitload of money for it!

His work was widely collected by millions of people.

He was famous outside the arts community.

His works made millions of people happy.

That's quite an accomplishment for a guy who essentially painted one painting — over and over again!

Only three artists come to mind when I think of the 'artistic integrity + brilliant marketing' scenario.

Ansel Adams was known outside of the art community and his works have both merit as art and commodity. But Adams didn't make any real money with his art until late in life so he was fortunate to have been independently wealthy. Adams was born rich and died rich.

Salvador Dali proved himself to be a Great Painter before becoming a master self-promoter. So he, like Adams, is in the Great Museums. Unfortunately during his later years, Dali's self-promotion exceeded the positive perceptions of his art thereby 'tainting' his later works in the eyes of 'art experts.' Dali died broke.

Peter Max took the opposite path of Dali. Whereas Dali was recognized as a 'fine artist who sold out.' Peter Max began as more of a 'commercial artist' with brilliant marketing and only later found acceptance in the Great Museums. Peter Max is still with us and still working.

Perhaps if Thomas Kinkade had lived longer he might have found himself on a path more like Peter Max's? We'll never know.

What we do know is, despite what anyone might say about his art, Thomas Kinkade's art made a lot of people happy.

Despite the Fame and Fortune, what's more important for me as an artist is that people possess my works and it makes them happy. Kinkade accomplished both and more.

I call him a Successful Artist — even if I don't like his paintings.

CHAPTER

THE COMMUNITY OF NIGHT PHOTOGRAPHERS

If you think rock and roll guitarists have big egos you might be right. But rock music isn't the sole domain of the Big Ego, there is at least one group of people who can rival, and often exceed, the inflated ego of the Rock Star, they are: *photographers*. I don't mean to pick on rock guitarists but they're easy. We expect them to have big egos — the fame, bright lights, glitz, glamor and, of course, the groupies. But photographers? It took me by surprise, but as it turns out, there are a *lot* of big ego photographers who act like they invented light or something, and think their pictures will change the world. And damn, they're an annoying bunch. Many of the Big Ego Photographers I've met are these types:

Commercial photographers who incessantly talk about big budget jobs and exotic locations. They name-drop 'famous' art directors, and their client, and the bigtime ad agency... urgh!

Gadget freaks who brag about how much they spend on cameras and lenses. Don't get these guys started on computers because you'll just end up with RAM-envy, they have more! Their discussions rarely leave the realm of consumerism; they never talk about art. They're camera-collectors who never show their pictures.

Fine-Art Photographers who think they're going to change the world with their pictures. Everything they shoot is oh-so profound and, ugh, *meaningful*. They're complimented when you don't like or 'get' their pictures because that *proves* just how much smarter than you they are.

Wedding 'Photojournalists' who somehow believe shooting the same picture every Saturday is 'innovation.'

But I've found one group of photographers that don't have giant egos, are genuinely friendly, will actually help out another photographer, and are hardly recognizable in the daylight. They are the *Night Photographers*, and in my experience they're a community of friendly folk.

I first encountered the *community of night photographers* while shooting (at night, of course) at Mono Lake, California. It's about a mile walk from the parking area to the famous surrealistic *tufa spires* and just as I'd located the first place I wanted to photograph a light flashed in my eyes.

"Is that another photographer?" I called out into the darkness.

"Yeah, over here." A man's voice replied.

"OK," I called back, "I'm gonna be over here, opposite where you are, shooting to the northwest. I don't want to screw up your exposures, so give me a heads-up if my light gets in your shot."

"No problem," he answered, "As a matter of fact, when you were walking up, your light shone on that tall spire over there, would you mind pointing a light over there again for half a minute?"

"Sure thing." I answered as I illuminated the tufa spire for him. And so it went for the rest of the night. We were respectful of each other and didn't get in each other's way. We talked in the dark, him over there and me over here, never actually seeing each other. During the night we'd help each other out; I'd shine a light over here for him and he'd shine a light over there for me. Helpful, respectful and without ego or competitiveness. There had to be at least a half-dozen photographers out that night and nobody got in anybody's way or messed-up anyone's picture with a stray flashlight. Nobody got a good look at each other either!

It was kind of funny, we were all doing our own things at the same place and time. Every photographer out there had to know that their pictures wouldn't look much different from the other guys' but that didn't matter, we all wanted the same thing — good pictures — and nobody prevented anyone from getting the best possible shot, heck, the other photographers were actually helpful. What a nice surprise! It kind of reminded me of the camaraderie of sports photographers from my newspaper days, all working the sidelines and yelling "Watch out!" when a tackle was about to take down another photographer.

The next time I found myself in the company of the *community of night photographers* was at Palouse Falls State Park in Washington. I'd arrived mid-afternoon and was a little underwhelmed. The Falls were small and basically down in a hole. The park itself was small and the campground tiny, with only about a dozen campsites. I'd seen one very cool photo of Palouse Falls online and I really wanted to get a shot like it, or preferably, better. That photo I'd seen online was pretty much the photo of the waterfall; The Hero Shot. Did I really want to spend the night out there for just one shot? Not so much, but I was tired so I took a campsite, set up my tent, and took a nap.

When I awoke the campground was nearly full, all twelve sites occupied. I got to chatting with the other campers. There was the Canadian guy, traveling alone (like me) and hoping to find someone else in the campground with a guitar who'd play with him. There was the Indian man who 'had the kids for the summer' and took them camping. There was the hippie couple traveling and living out of their VW van. There was a couple of college boys with cameras who were going to try to 'get that night shot like they saw online.' There were a couple of families and one guy, probably homeless, on a permanent 'campout.'

As I talked with my fellow campers the college boys said they'd be out shooting after 11pm, the Canadian had a crop-sensor DSLR and asked if I'd show him how to photograph at night, and the Indian guy said his kids had never seen the Milky Way and could he and his kids hang out and see how night photos were done?

Sure, sure, no problem at all! Come join me at the overlook at 11 that night and I'll show you how to shoot a night photo, I'll show you where the Milky Way rises and name as many constellations as I can.

So we all met at eleven o'clock that night and I gave an impromptu 'night photography lesson.' The Canadian man got some nice photos of the stars *with his own camera*, the Indian kids had a great time looking at the Milky Way — in the sky and on the back of my camera. I helped out the college boys when they had technical difficulties. And we all had a nice time, talking, laughing, and just hanging out in the dark taking pictures. At the end of the night *nobody* got the starry-sky shot of the falls like we'd seen online. We all decided that we really *couldn't* get that shot because it was probably a composite. Yeah, that photographer online must have cheated!

The irony is I really didn't care at all about not getting that shot. I had more fun hanging out and talking with the night photographers! Nope, I didn't get that one shot but I'd made some new friends — which is way more fun than listening to 'professional' photographers trying to out bullshit each other at some ASMP meeting.

The summer is the best time for night photography in North America. The Milky Way rises early and the nights are warm. One of the best 'dark sky' locations is the Mojave Desert and I went to Borrego Springs, California to photograph Ricardo Breceda's giant metal sculptures. There are about a hundred metal sculptures of dinosaurs, eagles, elephants, camels, scorpions and a serpent scattered in the desert all around Borrego Springs. I'd envisioned lighting them with colored LED lights and photographing them at night with the stars of the Milky Way in the background. So, I scouted locations and decided that I would photograph the coolest sculpture first, The Serpent.

Driving down the highway at about 10:30 at night I was all set to photograph The Serpent except for one thing — I couldn't find it! When planning for night photography one thing that's not wanted is moonlight, so I always time my outings during the New Moon. But in the pitch black of no moonlight combined with no artificial light, like streetlights, it's pretty darned difficult to find objects that are located about a quarter mile off the highway! So there I was driving slowly in the dark with the window down pointing a flashlight off the side of the road like a cop looking to spoil some kids' make-out session, and I can not find that damn giant Serpent!

I'm scanning the roadside with my flashlight when another light shines in my direction, "Is that a photographer?" I asked the darkness.

"Yeah, we're over here, behind the Serpent," came a voice from the dark.

"Do you mind if I join you?" I asked.

"Sure, pull in from where you are, just don't hit my car, it's black and to the right of The Serpent."

"No problem," I answered, "My car is also black, but I've got my lights on."

I pulled about an eighth of a mile off the road, parked and killed the lights. Then I got out to meet the other photographers.

There was a guy and a girl with DSLRs and fast lenses and they were photographing that serpent. I told them I wanted to light the thing and would they mind if I lit it up? That was no problem whatsoever, so long as they could get a few shots using my lighting. OK with me, I didn't care. So we (they helped) set up gelled lights and shot. And then we moved the lights and cameras and shot some more. They were friendly and helpful and we all worked together for over an hour and got some great shots of The Serpent.

Then the guy asked me, "Have you seen The Scorpion?"

"No! I have not been able to find that one. Do you know where it is?"

"Yeah, it's not far down this road, but it's a little over a mile off the highway, so it's harder to find. Follow us, we're going there next."

Wow! How nice. I've known photographers to be super-secret about this kind of thing, but again, *The Community of Night Photographers* isn't competitive.

With cameras back in their bags we were hauling ass down the road after midnight; I'm following the guy as he heads off-road, rooster-tails of dirt and dust blowing, my GPS showing *no roads whatsoever*, just a little icon of a car in a vast, empty space, and in the headlights of the car in front of me was The Scorpion — and two more photographers!

We parked a discreet distance away and then immediately apologized to the other photographers for messing up their exposures with our headlights.

"Ah, no worry, it's digital, just delete the overexposures." They said, which was cool, I've seen other photographers throw fits over similar things.

There were two Japanese guys with the latest, greatest, big megapixel Sony mirrorless cameras. We weren't in a hurry, after all it was the middle of the night and we were not chasing the light, so for a while everyone stood around talking, swapping stories and talking about night photography. Although night photography with digital cameras is somewhat new, none of us on location at The Scorpion were inexperienced and the next thing I see is everyone sharing their portfolios… on Instagram… on their phones… in the middle of the night!

I had to laugh! There I was, standing out in the middle of the Mojave Desert at about one in the morning with a group of geeks, their faces lit by the glow of cel-phones, sharing their Instagram pages. I had only one thought:

Now I've got to get on Instagram, dammit!

The five of us photographed the scorpion. We shot it as a

silhouette, we lit it, we shot a lot of pictures and tried a lot of variations. We all worked together like a team! After another hour or so we all felt we'd all gotten the shots we'd come for and it was time to go. But how do we get out of here? Which way did we come from? "Follow us!" The Japanese guys yelled from their car. So we wagon-trained it outta there all following the bright lights of their rental car. Back on the highway we all waved a happy and tired good-bye and I was off to my motel for half a nights' sleep.

I got a lot of nice photos that night (and the next) at Borrego Springs, and I'd met another group of friendly photographers. The funny thing about the Japanese guys is they knew *everything* about their cameras. I mean they knew their operations inside and out, backwards and forwards. Impressive. What was less impressive is they knew absolutely nothing about astronomy! While we were shooting I'd mentioned that it was ironic that we were photographing a *scorpion* just as the constellation Scorpious (the scorpion) was rising behind it. Ha! They knew they were getting great photos, but of exactly what, they had no idea!

Most recently (as of this writing) I was shooting at Great Basin National Park in Nevada. The main feature of Great Basin is Wheeler Peak which is 13,000 feet. The campground is at 10,000 feet elevation which is *two miles* closer to the stars than the justbelow- sea-level Borrego Springs. I was looking forward to the night's photography but the weather was looking iffy while I was scouting locations.

There is a grove of Bristlecone Pine trees at Great Basin which I'd considered using in the foreground of my night photos but decided against it. First of all, despite the 'newness' of digital night photography, Bristlecone Pines are already becoming somewhat of a cliché in night photos. But, secondly and most importantly, the hike to the Bristlecone Pines would be six miles roundtrip. A six mile hike in total darkness (new moon) carrying equipment seemed like a recipe for trouble and I didn't need my name in some tiny local paper as 'the bonehead who got lost and had to be found by search-and-rescue.' Nope. I wisely chose to photograph the night sky from two easy-to-drive-to overlooks.

I was waiting for the *blue hour* at the first overlook when a guy on a motorcycle rode up. I'd noticed a 1000cc Suzuki V-Strom bike in the campground earlier and this was that guy. As I'm also a rider, he and I immediately struck up a conversation about motorcycles (you can always talk to anyone, anywhere, about motorcycles or dogs) as I made a few exposures of the still-blue night sky. After a while I decided the second overlook would be a better vantage point and decided I'd drive there. The biker, Dillon, asked if I cared if he tagged along.

"Sure. Follow me. When we turn into the overlook it's about an eighth of a mile dirt road, veer to the right to avoid the potholes on the streetbike." I always try to help out a fellow rider.

When we arrived at the overlook, sure enough there was one other photographer and a couple of 'stargazers.' Right after parking the car and bike Dillon and I apologized to the photographer for ruining her photo with headlights, but she was as cool as night photographers are and said, "No worry."

We chatted with her for a while and she was helpful with weather information and which direction the storms might come. She mentioned there were a good number of shooting stars that night. Next I set up my tripod and camera and got to work.

My new friend Dillon was from Portland where it's cloudy much of the time and had *never seen* the Milky Way. He'd just ridden from Utah where his friends had told him you've got to go to Great Basin to see the stars! He took their advice and, standing there next to me in the middle of the night, continually gasped in amazement at the incredible beauty of the night sky. I named all the constellations I could, which was quite a few actually. When I began my adventure into night photography I studied up on astronomy so I knew what I was looking at, and I recommend anyone who photographs at night to do the same. The more you know, you know?

The sky is really, *really* clear two miles up and I got a lot of good photos — until the storms came. Around midnight the skies began to cloud-up and the storms blew in from exactly the direction the other photographer had predicted. It had already been a good night so calling it a wrap at that point meant a little more sleep.

"Oh man, I hope it doesn't rain tonight." Dillon said as I was folding-up my tripod.

"You don't have a tent?" I asked.

"Nope."

"What? You're sleeping under the stars in a sleeping bag?

"Nope. No sleeping bag, but my jacket has a back-pad." (A back-pad is a protective device that's built into a lot of modern motorcycle jackets. It's designed to protect the rider's back in the event of a 'high-side.' A 'high-side' is when the rider gets thrown off, over the handlebars, and a back-pad is really useful in that unfortunate event — believe me, I've done it — but they're not designed to sleep on!) Oh, to be 24 years old again!

"Dude!" I said, "If it rains just come down to campsite number 21. I've got a tent set-up but I'm not using it because I sleep in the back of the car. Just crawl in my tent and stay dry if it rains — just don't go to campsite 22, the woman in that site may not want the company!"

"Oh, thanks, man." He smiled. "But if the weather holds you won't see me."

But I did see him. He rode down to my campsite the next morning, fresh and dry, and we had coffee together. This was the *first time* I'd ever gotten a daylight look at anyone I'd met photographing at night! Later I followed him down the mountain to the little town of Baker, on the Utah state line, where we had a hearty breakfast. After breakfast he gassed up the big Suzuki, waved good-bye and pointed the bike westward, ready for a full-day's ride on Highway 50 (the loneliest highway in America) towards Reno and points beyond. I drove back to my campsite and prepared for a second night of photography—

—Which didn't happen because that night it *did* rain!

The day after my rained-out night was typically clear and sunny, but I'd managed to get my photos the first night and so began my day's drive to Las Vegas. If you've ever driven in Nevada you know there's a lot of empty space and knocking back the miles I got to thinking about the *community of night photographers.*

They're an atypically friendly bunch! A lot friendlier than many 'typical' photographers.

Most of the 'typical' photographers I encounter have overlarge egos. They can be paranoid, secretive and untrusting. The photography business is competitive and no photographer wants to give another any advantage. And those ASMP meetings I mentioned before? That's the American Society of Media Photographers, a professional organization of which I used to be a member. I quit the organization in the early 1990s after attending too many of their meetings where I'd hear other 'professional' photographers talk about 'keeping rates up' and not doing 'work-for-hire' and then the next day they'd be out cutting each other's throats and dropping their 'day rates' just to get some low-budget job away from a 'competitor.' Friendly backstabbers.

Yes, there's a lot of ego in photography; it's human nature I suppose, but it's unfriendly and unhelpful. Unfortunately Western culture is based more on *competition* than *cooperation* — his is why we have photography 'contests' and 'juried competitions' and even 'competitive bidding' for commercial work. We've created a society that is *afraid someone else is going to get what we've got*, even if it's just a picture.

So it's a refreshing surprise when you encounter photographers that are friendly and helpful, especially in the middle of the night.

Since I've now met four groups of night photographers I'm going to call it a trend and not a one-off *anomaly*. I've yet to meet a night photographer who was a jerk, so I'm going to give credit to the group. And I don't shoot in groups. I don't do workshops where everyone shoots the same photo over each other's shoulder, and I don't work with an entourage or more than one assistant. Usually I work alone, which is quite fine by me. And I've done plenty of night-shoots where I was all alone with the stars and coyotes...

...But it is nice to have company. Especially at night in an unfamiliar place. Humans have always found 'the dark' to be a scary place, so it's comforting to know someone is around to 'watch your back,' even if it's someone you just met. I'm not sure why night photographers are so friendly; it might be because, well, it is night and we should be tucked in our beds, but instead we're out in the middle-o-nowhere pointing our cameras skyward, hoping to capture something amazing. Maybe it's seeing that 'something amazing,' like a bright shooting star and sharing the 'wow!' experience? "Perhaps it's the subconscious respect we have for others who are out doing the same thing we are?

Subconscious respect, that's why I think night photographers are nice to each other. Night photography has its own unique technical difficulties. Aside from the obvious photographic stuff some astronomical knowledge is necessary, and there's finding a good location with an interesting foreground, and getting there, and dealing with weather, and sleep deprivation... no, night photos aren't mere snapshots, and you can't do it with your damn iPhone either!

It's like, *hey look, here comes another night photographer. So you've foregone a good nights' sleep and you've hauled yourself and your equipment out here to do something difficult. Good for you! So have I, so join me and together we'll shoot the photos we both came here to make. You and I aren't that different from one another. Look up. It's a big universe and there's room enough for all of us. Would you like me to hold that light for you?* And I'll wait while you 'light paint' the Serpent, it's only a thirty-second exposure, I'll get my shot in a minute. I'll help you get your picture and you can help me get mine, even if 'help' is just staying out of the way. It's nice to get a great photo, but it's even nicer to make a new friend — even if you won't recognize them in the morning — such is life as a member of *The Community of Night Photographers.*

How to Dress and Behave
at your own Gallery Opening

*D*on't be a dick. Don't be a slob.

That's pretty straightforward. One does not need to belabor the point. It's either your show or your artwork is part of a larger show, so be nice, be friendly, talk to people and don't be a dick. It's simple!

Recently I was sent an 'Artist Agreement' (contract) to exhibit in a Fine Arts Fair. It contained standard boilerplate language that ensures the signer of the contract (me) will cover the ass of the Big Corporation that wrote the contract. It was fairly typical except for this:

If Artist elects to attend Exhibition, Artist shall contact [redacted] at least 15 (fifteen) days before Exhibition. A representative shall be in communication with the Artist. If you elect to attend, you agree that you shall dress and conduct yourself in a manner which is within the norms of a conservative art exhibition. You agree to abide by the code of conduct to be sent to you by [redacted]. You agree that if you violate any provision of this paragraph and/or the referenced code of conduct to immediately leave the premises of the Exhibition upon request. You acknowledge that failure to honor the request to leave may result in your being involuntarily removed from the premises. You agree to hold [redacted] and the Exhibition harmless from any liability resulting from such action arising out of Artist's conduct violating this paragraph.

Seriously? How to dress and behave is written into a contract?

You've got to be kidding me. I emailed the contract-writers with this question:

I've never seen anything like this in a contract before. Do you have a lot of problems with poorly dressed and misbehaving artists? I assure you as a mature adult over the age of fifty, I do know how to comport myself & dress properly for any occasion. Could you please send me the 'code of conduct" and the 'dress code' for this event? Go ahead & have your representative contact me. I had considered attending but should I? Is there any benefit to my presence there? Does the gallery even want the artist present? Please let me know if my presence would be beneficial or even wanted.

And this was the reply I received:

This is a standard clause included based on what we witnessed at some of the openings we attended, especially the ones which had open bars. It is business, not personal.

Artists are welcome to attend. It is up to you if you would like to. If it were a solo show, I would definitely encourage you to attend. Since this is a group show, it is different — we have to be respectful to all 5 participating artists and cannot have one artist promoting his/her work at the expense of the others. I hope you can appreciate it and can relate to it.

There's a whole lot wrong with both the contractual obligation and the answer to my question about it. First of all, as a mature man of fifty-plus years of age I really do know how to comport myself at an art show. Secondly I am insulted; the last time I was lectured on what to wear and how to behave was when my Mommy was sending me off to Sunday school, and that was a very long time ago! Thirdly, there *are no* 'standards' in the art business, so don't try to sell me that 'industry standards' bullshit, this industry *has no standards*. I've been in this business for over thirty years, believe me, if there were any standards, I'd of found them. Fourth, it is personal! Sure it's 'business' but it's 'personal' too. You can't tell someone how to dress and act without it being personal. And no, I don't appreciate it. Sure, I can relate to the fact that you are afraid I might embarrass you but your contract has no clause preventing you from embarrassing me. What if you act like a dick? Can I have the 'art-bouncer' throw you out? Ah, but here's the tell:

...cannot have one artist promoting his/her work at the expense of the others...

That's the real reason! No, I won't 'step on the toes' of the salespeople. You don't want me there. I'm not attending. Thanks for helping with the decision.

I had wanted to attend the Art Fair but now I'm afraid I might inadvertently piss someone off. I was looking for an excuse to go to [the location of the art fair] but 'behavior rider' of the contract kind of pissed on my parade. Not that I'd planned on misbehaving, I just don't need a lecture in the contract about how to behave. The gallery really does not want me there. This isn't all that unusual. They seem to be enthusiastic about my work, but not so enthusiastic about me. And again, this is not unusual. *They are afraid that I might somehow screw up their ability to make money off my artworks that I paid them to exhibit.*

I ought to just go on my own. Pose as a buyer. I should show up at their booth and get all excited about Dale O'Dell's art. I should act like I'm going to buy. I should ask them, 'is the artist present?' and then get all bummed out and walk away when they say 'no.' That could be fun!

Or maybe I'll call up an old friend who lives in the same town as the art fair and ask him to attend — just to check out my gallery and make sure they're *behaving themselves.*

I suppose if I were a Big Sports Star with a twenty million dollar a year contract, then a 'morals clause' would be appropriate. But this ain't no multimillion dollar sports contract; in fact *I* paid *them* a fee just to look at my artworks, and I'll pay a percentage back to them if anything sells. They really have no right to tell me how to act. They should trust that I won't embarrass them or, more importantly, *myself.*

Oh well, like I wrote, I have been in this business for over thirty years, so I've seen a lot of stupid contracts; I won't even get into the one that began, '…agrees to be your exclusive representative *throughout the universe…*'

How about I write into the contract that gallery personnel has to behave 'properly' just the same as me? What's good for one is good for the other, right? No? Really? Why is that? Oh right, you wrote the contract.

How 'bout you people just sell my artwork? Meanwhile I'll be in my studio behaving myself, as always.

CHAPTER

TOO RICH TO RELATE

It was a gallery where I really wanted to exhibit. Famous photographers had exhibitions there. It had a prestigious reputation and it was the biggest, nicest gallery in small town known for its wealthy residents and tourists. I made an exhibition proposal and to my surprise, I got a meeting, representation, and a show. I usually don't get this 'lucky.'

For the exhibition I personally drove and delivered all the artworks to insure on-time and damage-free delivery. It was a large gallery and I supplied a lot of artwork including framed artwork at 30x40 inches. I hung most of the show myself. I did a lot of work that many artists don't, but I wanted to insure my works got there intact and were hung the best way possible. I did my part and contributed a lot of free labor above and beyond merely creating the art.

As it turned out I didn't get the whole gallery for a Solo Exhibition but had to share the space with a second artist for a Two-Person exhibition.

On opening night my works blew the other guy's away. The crowd filled the half of the gallery where my works hung and when it got too crowded they'd venture over and check out the other guy's art for a moment and then come back to mine. Everyone in attendance was complimentary and enthusiastic about my pictures. The local newspaper's art critic wrote a glowing review of my works; a few weeks after the opening I returned to the gallery and presented a well-attended Gallery Lecture. Everything went about as well as I could hope except for one thing.

Not a single print was sold.

For the entire duration of the exhibition the gallery managed to sell a couple of small cheap prints and a few books. With my framing and printing expenses along with travel and lodging, the exhibition put me deep in the hole. I am an artist and not a Rich Man. When I make an expenditure in one area, a sacrifice is required in another.

So, I'd had Big Exhibition in a Big, Prestigious Gallery with Big Crowd at the opening, positive reviews in the paper and I'd accomplished absolutely nothing aside from some ego-stroking.

After the exhibition I returned and retrieved a lot of my art-works. The gallery asked me to leave the large-scale prints and a few standard-sized pieces, so I did believing there was still poten-tial for sales. As expected the artworks I retrieved myself made it back to my studio in an undamaged condition. The artworks that remained at the gallery were subsequently loaned to a local college and businesses for exhibition.

And again nothing sold.

So-called 'experts' have told me I need to exhibit in more 'prestigious' galleries and this was one of those kinds of galleries. Everything went well and something should have sold, what hap-pened?

I had to think back and carefully analyze what had happened because things were not as they seemed. Early in the process I'd met with the gallery director a number of times and he kept men-tioning a mysterious, absent owner. An absent owner is a clue. It's important that a business owner be involved in their business and if they're not, something could be amiss. When I finally met the woman she was nice and friendly enough, but didn't seem to catch the art-history references I made during our conversations. There's another clue, a gallerist who doesn't know art might be problematic.

I think if Art is your business, you ought to know something about Art.

On another occasion I recall the gallery director mentioning his paycheck exceeded the amount of money earned by the gallery during previous months. Yikes! That's bad; company expenditures are exceeding company income! How do they make payroll? As it turns out the woman who owns the gallery is married to a Rich Dude. And not just any rich guy, but a stinkin' rich one, probably a *billionaire*. She's the spouse of a one-percenter. So, basically, I had to figure that this gallery is a plaything for its Rich Lady owner and a tax write-off for her Thurston Howell-type husband. If payroll can be met without making any sales, then there's not much motivation to sell — it's not like their livelihood depends on art sales (like mine does).

The above are clues, but don't necessarily add up to anything especially bad. Bad Things aren't usually found out until after the deal is done, and that's the way it worked again.

Later I got a call from the gallery informing me that the Rich Couple was visiting Arizona and they'd bring my large-scale works to me. Great! I told them, just please pack them carefully so the frames aren't damaged in transit. When they arrived in my driveway I went out to help carry my artwork in and noticed they were all piled on top of each other in the back of the SUV. There was no care taken in packing whatsoever and every frame returned to me was damaged in some way. I complained and they just rationalized it away as 'not that bad, it can be repaired' and left. No replacement offer was made, they didn't care.

I had to replace all the frames at my own expense before I could exhibit those pieces again. And here I must restate that when I buy expensive things like frames I must sacrifice in another area — like food or fuel or things like that. I don't think Rich People can relate.

Finally I got an email about returning the one remaining framed piece the gallery still had. I asked the gallery director to use Federal Express for the return of that print for two reasons, one, Federal Express is the most economical carrier and, two, UPS in my community has a 100% record of destroying artwork. When I got the print back it had been shipped via UPS and, sure enough, the frame and plexiglass were destroyed. When I contacted the gallery director he was apologetic but disbelieving and asked me to 'prove' damages by photographing the damage and sending him the pictures for a liability claim.

I didn't send the pictures. I've been down the road with UPS regarding damage claims in the past and UPS never pays claims. They always blame it on whoever packed the box. In this case the gallery used an outside service (thereby relieving themselves of any responsibility) and they did a lousy job packing. I also mentioned that I felt the 100% damage-rate combined with a complete lack of sales left me with a rather negative experience. I wasn't mean or insulting, but I did feel it was necessary to let the guy know.

I got a typical rationalizing email back telling me (as usual) that they'd *never* had this problem before and it only happened to *me*. Oh, how many times I've heard that! Then he felt it necessary to lecture me on all the expenses the gallery had incurred for me. They had to pay for printing of invitations and mailing and all that, and I needed to understand that.

And I do understand. I understand that if your business is the exhibition of art, it must be promoted. And my two person exhibition was promoted, but it wasn't just for me, it was for the other guy on the invitation too. A gallery director shouldn't snivel about routine expenses like promoting the show. That's their 'business expense' just as the time, effort and materials I use to create my art is my own business expense that I don't complain about.

I also understand that a check written for invitation-printing by a Very Rich one-percenter doesn't require the sacrifice of a check written by a poor guy. It's not the same.

So in the end a failed exhibition with a few expenses incurred by a gallery that's not really in the business to sell art is no big deal to them. For me, it's a substantially bigger deal. I lost money and ended up having to spend even more money to replace things destroyed by the gallery.

What I learned from this is there are some people who are so rich they don't have to run a profitable business or give a damn about those of us who give them, for free, the product they sell. This gallery isn't really a 'gallery' but rather a plaything for the rich spouse and a tax write-off for her husband. For me, I now *require* the galleries I work with to be as into selling art as I am in making it. I pay closer attention now and if they screw up little things I figure they'll screw up Big Things and I won't work with them. I don't mind working with Rich Folk (it's really a require-ment in this business) but if they're not serious, or uniformed about art, or just absent and detached, then I have to think twice about working with them. I'm not fucking around here and if the gallery isn't serious they're probably going to end up as an expense for me and another 'negative experience.'

Really, getting my unsold artwork back in the same condition I delivered is not an unreasonable expectation.

THE CHASM REMAINS

It seemed like a good idea when I registered for 'Altering Perspectives,' the SPE (Society for Photographic Education) regional conference. Although I'm not currently teaching photography, I have in the past, would like to again, and I give private photography lessons, so I hoped to learn about the current state of photographic education at the conference. Also, since I live in a small town, it seemed like a good opportunity for some photographic intellectual stimulation. Being with other like-minded photographers might be a good opportunity to learn, meet some new people and do a little networking. Or so I thought.

In the interest of Full Disclosure I must say that I've taught at Prescott College, the host of this SPE conference, in the past as an adjunct and have applied for full-time positions in their photography department for which I was not hired. I have seven years teaching experience at the University and Community College level and I have a degree in photography and thirty-years' experience as a freelance photographer (both commercially and fine-art). Since I'm a working photographer I couldn't attend every presentation and panel discussion but I did attend enough to get a good feel for the conference and I even sat in one photography class led by one of the SPE presenters.

From a technological standpoint the digital revolution of photography is understood and accepted, although I did detect some uncertainty and fear of change. Some of the presenters seemed resentful that they "had to learn each version of Adobe Photoshop" instead of re-teaching unchanged darkroom practices. From the artistic standpoint I didn't detect much of an alteration of perspectives at all. One disturbingly unchanged aspect I noticed is the insular nature of the educator-photographers. They seem to be members of a closed society and either unwilling or unable to acknowledge any aspect of photography outside their familiar comfort zone. As Bill Jay wrote in his book *Occam's razor* (Nazraeli Press, 1992), the "Chasm between Artist and Commercial Photographer is Wholly Destructive;" sadly, that chasm remains as wide as ever.

I had hoped these educators would address some of the pressing issues in the photographic industry today; things like pay-to play schemes, predatory business practices of some who buy and publish photography, the 30-year stagnation of the editorial day rate, the cheapening of photography as a result of royalty-free and microstock distribution of imagery, etc. These are but a few of the things that the next generation of photographers must deal with. They must be informed of these things and devise strategies to cope in an increasingly changed world of both the fine- and commercial-arts. Frankly, the current generation hasn't done such a banging job. But none of these issues were addressed. In fact, with the exception of one brief mention of "licensing of images" *none* of the business aspects of photography was addressed at all. To quote Bill Jay again, the educators at the SPE conference seemed more interested in "training assistant professors" than training photographers. Since the emphasis of this conference was the fine-art side only, I can only speculate that these photography teachers cannot teach what they do not know.

Granted, Prescott College is a Liberal Arts school and does not teach 'practical photography.' Conversely, institutions like Brooks Institute (out-of-business since 2016) emphasize marketable skills over 'art.' Students do choose colleges they attend based on their perceived future needs and wants, but unless the student is exposed to all aspects of photography, they're only receiving a partial education. Since SPE is a national organization of photographic educators it seems to me that it is a disservice to photography students to emphasize only fine art photography and exclude other aspects of photography. How about some balance? Perhaps, unknown to me, there are SPE conferences that do emphasize practical photography? However, since the theme of this conference was 'Altering Perspectives,' I had an expectation of 'perspectives,' as plural, and not such a narrow, singular viewpoint. The speakers at the conference presented themselves as 'artists who teach.' I find that to be a backwards statement. In my view they are 'teachers who make art.' That's a very important distinction as 'artists who teach' leads the student to believe their instructor is some Great Artist, financially successful *from the sales of their art*, who's sharing their insights with up-and-coming photographers when, in fact, their instructors rely upon teaching and not their art to pay their bills. I personally know a number of photographic educators who have never made a photograph for money. They've never done an editorial or advertising assignment, licensed a stock picture or even shot a simple portrait. Yet their students believe they're 'learning real-world skills' despite the fact that their instructor has no experience whatsoever in the 'real world.' I'm sure I've stepped on some Big Egos with the previous statements so let me justify that statement with the definition of 'professional' from the American Heritage Dictionary; a 'professional' is, "Engaged in a specific activity as a source of livelihood."

This lack of 'commercial' or 'practical' knowledge was underscored when I asked the SPE presenter who led the class I sat in if he'd ever done magazine assignments to support his art (his work easily fit the 'editorial' category). He answered, "No, no magazine would allow him to shoot the way he does." My experience tells me his answer was but mere assumption. Since editorial magazine photography is predominately low-budget, photographers are allowed and encouraged to be creative. I certainly was when I was shooting editorially. Clearly his experience is in grant application and not bidding on assignments.

And speaking of Grants, the primary funding for many 'art photographers' (aside from university paychecks), it occurs to me that it's a heck of a lot easier competing with dozens of photographers for an editorial commission than it is to compete with thousands of photographers for limited grant money. Unfortunately, if your teacher can only tell you about grant funding and not how to *work* to fund your art through the practical application of photographic knowledge, then you're a victim of your teacher's limited knowledge or bias. I find it more palatable to work to fund my personal art than to beg for money, but maybe that's just me?

'Meaning' was a hot topic. One presenter lamented that some of his students knew more about Adobe Photoshop than he did, but that was okay, he could teach 'meaning.' Really? How fucking arrogant! Do photos have intrinsic meaning or do we apply meaning? Does it matter? Is 'meaning' even teachable? How does this teaching of 'meaning' help students repay their college loans? If our photographs are supposed to have 'meaning' doesn't that disallow the viewer's own interpretation of the art? Advertising imagery is 'art' that every viewer is supposed to 'get' the same 'meaning' from, but isn't fine art a little more open to interpretation? And all this 'meaningful' imagery is just so serious. I saw very serious pictures, shot by a serious photographer, of Mexican immigrants crossing the southern U.S. border that were presented in a book and gallery exhibitions. I don't go to galleries to be educated about things like immigration issues that, in my view, is editorial photography best presented in print magazines or on the web and not in an art gallery. To me (and I'm not alone with this view) when I look at 'art' I'm viewing the subject through someone else's eyes; I'm seeing something different, an interpretation of a subject that I cannot stand before and see with my own eyes. It's the subject and *the artist's interpretation or presentation of that subject* that makes the art interesting to me. All of the exhibitions held concurrent with the SPE conference were of very serious art and none of them really showed me subjects photographed in any way that was new to me. I couldn't identify much of the art exhibited as some-one's; I was unable to view the work and say, 'that's so-and-sos' picture, stylistically most of the imagery was not distinctive of its creator; all that mattered was subject and artist-statement. This was true of five of the six exhibitions held during the conference, there was one exhibition that was different, but no one saw it. I'll get to that later.

I came away from the conference ambivalent. I witnessed very little 'Altering of Perspectives.' A fine-art-only photographic edu-cation still strikes me as insular and elitist; a realm of their own making. Again, they don't seem to be educating photographers at all, but rather, assistant professors. It seems to me their students are limited in their expression because if they get outside the 'box of preconceived expectations' they will not be rewarded. Too many educators' points of view are narrow and become the student's point of view because they're not exposed to anything outside the instructor's comfort-zone. That's the way it seems to me and my perception is a result of studying photography at the university level, obtaining a degree, and then working for thirty-plus years as an actual photographer. No doubt my perspective would be differ-ent if I was an 'educator-photographer' but I'm not a member of that club. *All* of photography is my 'comfort zone' and I don't make preconceived mental categories for this or that sort of photography, I want to see it all, and not be biased by labels. I want to be chal-lenged and get outside my comfort-zone. I believe that photograph-ic education should include *all* aspects of photography without bias. Certainly this kind of serious, 'meaningful,' art photography is needed, useful and welcome. It adds to the depth and diversity of the art form known as photography, but can't we be less narrow and embrace *all* aspects of photography. It's not all about gallery shows and 'meaning.'

All in all, I'm still glad I attended the conference. I didn't learn what I'd hoped to because the conference was too narrowly focused. I did learn that I'll never be welcome in this particular 'club' of 'fine-art photographers,' they're too exclusionary for me. I will conclude by getting back to the exhibitions held concurrent with the SPE conference. There were six exhibitions held during the conference. Three were at Prescott College, one was at the local community college, one was at a local Bar/Restaurant frequented by Prescott College students and one was held at a downtown gallery. *None* of the art photographers and educators (that I'm aware of) attended the exhibition at the downtown gallery. Why? I can guess that they were busy at the conference, and I could also guess they weren't interested in that particular exhibition because the artist was *not one of them*. I don't know. I do know that exhibition was very heavily promoted, it was listed in the participants' information packet, posters were displayed at the conference and invitations were on the table at the conference center with all the other exhibitions. The downtown gallery is open until 9pm, seven days a week and a mere half mile from Prescott College, it's closer than the Bar/Restaurant exhibition and the community college exhibition. They knew about it, and could have gotten there easily. Yet none of the SPE attendees saw fit to have a look, I suspect the imagery (if it was seen at all) may have been way too outside their comfort zone. They just weren't the least bit interested in anything that was different from their own. I was at that exhibition and I ran into a Prescott College student I'd seen earlier in the day at the SPE conference. She too noticed that none of the SPE participants were present. I asked her what she thought of their absence. She replied, "Oh they'd declare this artwork 'commercial.'" "What products could you sell with these images?" I asked her. She came back with, "None. It's not commercial at all; it's just *not their kind of art*." Interesting insight from an *art student*.

The exhibition ignored by the SPE conference-goers was mine and we specifically timed the opening reception to happen when the SPE people were in town. We assumed photographers would be interested in all kinds of photography, but we were wrong.

This isn't sour grapes. Teachers and students don't buy art and my interest is in selling, but I'd be dishonest to say I wasn't hurt just a little. I mean I was open-minded enough to attend their conference and visit the galleries where their work is shown; one would think they'd be interested in all aspects of photographic art — but they're not. Are they elitists, uninterested in things they don't readily relate to? Possibly, but I do know they didn't avail themselves to readily available art and, as photographic-art educators, that's self-limiting. I was heartened that one photographic educator (who didn't attend the SPE conference) did attend my show, I'll conclude with that story, which took a 'meaningful' turn. The next paragraph is *not fiction*.

Towards the end of the reception for my exhibition an old friend came in, perused the artworks, and joined a conversation with me, my wife and another photographer. Since our friend is a Psychic (this is the same Psychic I wrote about in my book, *Photographic Memories*) I told her, "I need to come see you for a reading, I'd like to learn about a friend of mine who passed away a few months ago." (My recently deceased friend was a Professor of Photography and one of my old classmates. In college we got along well, but as I'm now a 'professional' and he was a 'professor' that inevitable chasm had developed between us in the context of 'art.') The Psychic immediately, with no hesitation whatsoever, said, "You mean Michael?" My wife glanced at me with a look that said, uh oh, here goes the Psychic naming names until she gets a hit. But I replied, "Yeah, that's him. My wife asked, "Who the heck is

Michael?" I explained that, although my photography professor friend went by his middle name, and that's the name we knew him by, his given name was in fact, Michael." (There was no way the Psychic could have had this information in advance.) My wife got goose bumps. The other photographer's eyes got as big as saucers. Eerily, the Psychic had nailed it! She went on to say, "He's with you now." Okay, admittedly this is out-there stuff, but it's not that out-there to me, so I said, "I hope he likes my pictures." "Oh he does," she went on, "He says you've 'perfected perfection.'" (Just the sort of phraseology the guy did use.) Wow, I thought, the nicest compliment of the evening, and from a photography professor at that!

Isn't it ironic that *none* of the photographic educators attended my exhibition except the *dead* one? It's too bad he had to move 'to the other side' before he could accept photography outside his narrow sphere. How long will it take the rest of the educators?

WHEN THE STUDENT SURPASSES THE TEACHER

Nothing had prepared me for that moment. A flood of conflicting emotions washed over me. I was simultaneously awed, jealous, proud, happy, a little sad, speechless, surprised and amazed. Mainly I was happy, a little bit for me and a whole lot for her. Let me back up and set the scene that had me so flummoxed. The moment of my emotional chaos occurred in 2016, but its roots go back thirty-four years.

I met this girl, Jennifer, in 1982. It was my senior year of college and my last semester; it was Jennifer's first freshman semester. I was on the cusp of obtaining my photography degree and she was just beginning work on hers. As it goes with the usual college hierarchy, seniors and freshmen didn't mix much, but I noticed her around the photo-labs and studios. She'd be around during those impromptu photo-critiques that spontaneously occurred in the photo department; whenever I'd be showing whatever I was working on I'd see her among the other students. While she was noticing my photographs, I was noticing *her* because she was pretty, really pretty, the fashion-model kind of pretty. Since every senior-level photo student never has enough fashion-type photos in their portfolios, I talked her into modeling for me. We spent an afternoon in the studio and I shot one of those very typical, early 80s post-punk/new-wave kind of photos that were so popular at the time. We got to know each other, had a fun time, and I got a very nice (for the time period) fashion photo. I made a big 16x20 inch print of her, put it in my portfolio, and graduated.

In 1983, a mere seven months after I graduated college and after being unceremoniously sacked from not one but two corporate jobs, I came to the realization that I wasn't corporate material. A friend of mine, who was not corporate material either, had been sacked shortly before me had taken a job teaching airbrush at *The Art Institute of Houston* suggested I apply for an open position in the photography department and made an introduction for me.

So I applied for that teaching job and found myself doing the portfolio dog-and-pony show for the *Art Institute's* head of photography. Since I'd been out of college for less than a year I had not yet had the opportunity to replace all the photos in my college portfolio with 'new work from jobs' so my portfolio was still about three-quarters college work, including that picture of Jennifer.

Flipping through my portfolio he stopped on the page with the picture of Jennifer. "She's a student here." He said.

Not wanting to contradict the man attached to the ass I was kissing to get that job I simply stated: "I photographed her last spring at Sam Houston State University."

"She's taking photography classes here." He restated.

"Must have transferred."

Was my only reply.

I got the job, a few weeks later classes began and, sure enough, Jennifer was in two of my classes.

I remember working really hard to impart as much knowledge as possible to my students. Because it had been less than a year since I'd been a student myself, I wanted to be *better* than my professors, and they were very good. My job as teacher was to teach my students the teachable things; techniques and procedures so the talented student would then have the necessary skills to express themselves. I never tried to teach 'talent' or 'meaning' or 'expression' or any of the art-school things that screw-up students. I never tried to direct their story-telling, I merely provided the grammar they would use to tell their own photographic stories.

Regretfully, I don't really remember very much of my students' work, but it has been thirty-plus years so maybe my faulty memory is excused. What I do remember is that Jennifer was one of the few students who had a vision or personal style. I clearly remember walking through the black and white darkrooms in the mornings before class began. I'd look over all the prints on the drying racks and I knew which photos were hers.

I also recall many Mondays, listening to my students' stories about 'partying all weekend,' and then being asked what I did on my time off.

"I worked in the darkroom all weekend." Was my frequent reply. Most students would just roll their eyes, probably thinking, *nerd*. But, unbeknownst to me at the time, I was getting through to a few of them, not necessarily in classroom lectures, but *by example*. It turned out, for some like Jennifer, it was what I *did* and not what I *said* that was the most influential. It was this example that impacted Jennifer the most, but I wouldn't know about that for another thirty-two years.

I really enjoyed teaching and was good at it but I got fired from that job after a year and a half. I made the fatal mistake of being better than my boss, the department head, which is something detrimental to job security in academia. So I moved on and Jennifer's class graduated in 1984.

By 1986 I had started my own studio and had lost touch with Jennifer.

Over two decades passed before I saw her again. I've forgotten the exact year but it was around 2010-ish. By then I was living in Arizona and she was living in Los Angeles (I don't recall how I knew this, I probably Googled her). I had to go to L.A. on business and looked her up. We sort of picked up where we'd left off. She was struggling somewhat (as I was too) and we talked and 'compared notes' and shared some of the high and low-lights of our bumpy career paths. During our Chinese food lunch I recall thinking to myself, *I'm not the mentor anymore and you're not the student anymore, we're both equals and we're equally screwed in this weird business of art and photography.*

I saw her again a year or so later in Los Angeles and she'd made significant strides. She'd produced a *lot of very good work* and she had a licensing agent and things were looking much more positive. We stayed in touch but it wouldn't be until 2016 that I'd see her again. I'm glad we stayed in touch because that meant I knew she'd moved from Los Angeles to Palm Springs. That also meant that I would see her again after I wrapped a photo-shoot nearby at The Salton Sea and Borrego Springs.

We were enjoying dinner and drinks in the dark and moody bar at *Mr. Lyons* in Palm Springs when the conversation turned to art. Jennifer spoke very enthusiastically about the new artworks she was making and I was anxious to see her new portfolio. Out came her phone, a few taps and swipes later she's got Instagram open (oh, Instagram again!) and here's her new stuff. I scrolled through her Instagram feed until I suffered a 'cardiac event' and felt my heart ripped in two opposite directions simultaneously.

My heart returned to a normal rhythm and pumped just enough freshly oxygenated blood to my brain for me to form the thought: *Oh my god, this is freaking brilliant!* I was truly blown-away. Her new works were fully-formed and fleshed-out, it was clear that she wasn't experimenting but had found her way with clarity and confidence. The imagery was a clear departure from the obviously excellent works I'd seen in L.A. a few years prior. Her new works were bright, colorful, smart, witty, thoughtful, unique, original and, for lack of a better term, *freaking brilliant*. And they weren't photographs, this was pure digital art.

Basking in the cel-phone-glow of her imagery I felt my heart shift directions and relocate itself one-hundred-eighty degrees and suddenly I felt instantly sad and, somehow, sorry for myself. It was a fleeting feeling that didn't last but a moment, but what happened to me? What was this wave of sadness that just washed over me?

It was the sudden realization that *the student had surpassed her teacher!* Looking at her portfolio I saw no hint, no vestige, no thread whatsoever that traced a line from *these images* back to anything I'd taught her. What I was seeing was so new, so uniquely hers that I couldn't help but feel a twinge of sadness because *nothing I'd ever said or taught was left in these images, she was now far beyond any influence from me.* My illogical sadness quickly passed and my heart swelled and I felt pride. I had succeeded as a teacher!

Because the student should surpass the teacher!

And so we shared a wonderful meal and conversation that went long into the night. We discussed the *important things* like life and art and she clued me into some things I never knew. Way back in 1983 when I'd first interviewed for that teaching job I'd left my portfolio with the department head so he could 'show it to the higher-ups.' I don't know if 'the higher-ups' ever saw my portfolio but Jennifer did. Apparently the department head showed my portfolio to Jennifer who told him to, "Hire Dale, now!" For all these years I thought it had been some guy in a suit up the hall who'd given the green light to hire me, but it had actually been a 22 yearold blonde chick in the Photo One class that got me the job! Thank you, Jennifer!

As we reminisced about the 1980s she mentioned the One Thing that was her biggest influence. It had been my throw-away line, my flippant response of, "I worked in the darkroom," to the question, *what did you do last weekend?* She'd heard that, and she'd been one of the party-girls that weekend, but when she heard my response it prompted a thought in her: *I should get to work.* And she did!

After thirty-four years it was *she* who taught me an important lesson. For her it never was about the classroom lessons about f-stops, or shutter-speeds, or printing, or any of those things. Sure, she'd learned those lessons but the real lesson she'd learned from me had come from example and it was a work *ethic*.

She saw me 'doing the work' and then she 'did the work' too. That was it. That's all.

I've been 'doing the work' for my whole life, and so has Jennifer. Now, more than three decades after we were student and teacher, we stand together as semi-successful artists who *did the work*. In academic circles teachers talk about 'training the competition,' but that's a cliché. The fleeting feeling of sadness I felt when reviewing her new works was a result of Western Societies' competitive culture; for just a moment I saw her as 'competition,' and that's wrong. For a nanosecond I thought, *she's better than me!* And that thought was wrong too. Her works aren't any better than mine and mine aren't better than hers, she's simply the best at what she does and I'm the best at what I do. She'll always be better than me at making *her* pictures. *Her* pictures are something I cherish and respect, her artwork shows me a world I cannot perceive, they're a window into her world, a place I only visited through her eyes and art. The *only* reason I (and others) can see the world the way she does is because *she did the work*. I cannot claim any influence of her imagery whatsoever, that's all her! The only credit I can claim is providing *motivation by example*. At the time I didn't even realize that, "working in the darkroom all weekend" was a lesson, but I applaud Jennifer for *getting it*.

I think I'd like to acquire one of Jennifer's artworks for my personal collection but she's really good, and I don't know if I can afford one. Maybe she'll be open to a trade? I think I should offer two of mine for one of hers, she's that good.

One final note, from a different perspective.

There was a time when I was the boy who exceeded his professor.

For me it came quickly and differently but since I've now experienced this from *both perspectives* it's worthy of sharing.

Parental finances forced me to drop out of college in the summer of 1979 and it took me until 1981 to earn enough money to complete my degree. During my time away from school I had a number of photography-related jobs, the most recent at the time was in an audio-visual production studio where I worked on largescale slide shows (these were the pre-PowerPoint days). In the A/V job I also became an expert in E-6 processing and I created optical special effects, which was a very specialized area of photography.

I returned to college in the winter of 1981 and during the reenrollment process I met with my Academic Advisor, Dr. Emmette Jackson, who was also the head of the photography program. He went over my freshman/sophomore transcripts (which were all A's in photo-classes) and he spent a lot of time examining my newfrom-work portfolio of optical special effects.

"You've made considerable advances during your time in the workforce, Dale, I'm having a hard time fitting you into classes where you'd actually learn something you haven't already done, so I'm going to design some independent-studies specifically for you." Dr. Jackson informed me with a serious tone.

"Can I do that?" I wondered aloud. "Is that legit?"

"Sure." He explained. "You and I will design specialized independent-studies, I'll approve the study, you'll work directly with me and I'll be the one determining your grade at the completion of the independent study."

"So I don't have to take the E-6 class?" I asked, incredulously.

"Oh hell no!" He laughed. "You'd been souping E-6 film at a pro-lab while you were out of school, so you're competent and up-to- speed. I'm going to go ahead and give you three hours credit and an A for that class."

And then he dropped 'the bomb.'

"As a matter of fact, we're offering audio-visual sideshow

production this semester, since you've been doing just that you can teach the class, you know more about it than I do."

What?! Did I hear that right? I know more than he does?

"Sir," I asked cautiously, "Can I do that?"

"Of course you can! Your resume tells me you've been producing optical effects, processing E-6 slide film, and programming six, nine, twelve and fifteen projector shows all synchronized with Clearlight computer-controllers. All we have here is an ancient Wollensak two-projector dissolve unit, you'll be fine. I've never done any slideshows that big, *you're the expert.*"

"I'm the expert?"

"Hell yeah, your resume and portfolio say so. I'll give you the syllabus, tweak it as you see fit, I'll take attendance and the class is yours."

And there, in an instant, direct from the mouth of the professor who intimidated the hell out of me as a freshman and sophomore, was a declaration that *I knew more than he did.* I was surprised and *honored.* Curiously, Dr. Jackson seemed completely unfazed by his words and my reaction to them.

Professor Jackson's response to *me surpassing him* was remarkably ego-free. He wasn't bothered a bit because his perspective was from the position of professional teacher and success to him was being surpassed by his student. My momentary mixed feelings about Jennifer surpassing me was from the perspective of teacher and *working artist.* My artists' semi-erect ego was briefly punctured by Jennifer's amazing artworks only to be re-inflated moments later by realizing that, as a teacher, I had succeeded. Dr. Jackson had none of my mixed emotions because he was no longer working as a photographer but instead, purely as a photography teacher. Although his Bachelor's and Master's degrees were in photography his PhD was in education, so his judgment of me was from the perspective of a professional *educator* and not a photographer. To him it wasn't a big deal, to me it was *everything.*

Emmette (we got to a first-name basis quickly and remain good friends to this day, thirty-four years after my graduation) actually taught me more by *example* than in the classroom, which is the same as it was with me and Jennifer. I think there may be a correlation of teaching styles at play…

When the teacher does their job right, the student should surpass them. Most students don't because many students don't finish what they start, *they don't do the work*. For those who do, it's because they've taken all the lessons, both the formal lessons of the classroom and the informal 'life lessons,' and applied them to their own work, kept up that work, and eventually ended up in a place that surpassed their mentors.

Professor Jackson provided me with a map. He was fully aware that by the time I left that map he'd given me everything I needed to blaze my own trail but not get lost. I did the same for Jennifer, the only difference being when she left the map she found me at the periphery. As she and I stood there, just off the edge of the metaphorical map, she smiled and said she'd used-up the map I gave her but that was OK, she'd traded it for a GPS, and we should go the rest of the way together. None of us had really surpassed anyone, we got just what we needed to become who we are.

From Jennifer's 2016 Artist Statement:

Jennifer majored in photography at Sam Houston State University. There, she met her first mentor, Dale O'Dell. One afternoon, she walked into the on-campus photo-lab and noticed a group of people all gathered around O'Dell, who had some of his new photographs placed in front of him. As Jennifer stretched over the crowd to see, she remembers commenting out loud; "That's *what kind of work I want to do*." She subsequently transferred to The Art Institute of Houston, where by another act of fate, O'Dell became her teacher. At that point, Jennifer knew she was on track, and that something special was happening to her.

Dr. Emmette Jackson passed away on July 16, 2016 at the age of 75. I will forever miss him; to this day I still try to make photographs that meet the high standard he set.

CHAPTER

PAID PORTFOLIO REVIEWS
ALL THE SATISFACTION OF SPEED-DATING

I finally paid for a photography 'portfolio review' by 'industry experts' at the MEDIUM photography festival in San Diego. MEDIUM was a new festival and it was their first year. The festival was well-organized and efficiently run but I only participated in the portfolio review.

Perhaps I'd been too cynical about this, but having low-to-no expectations meant my expectations were easily exceeded. Everyone was friendly and cordial and no one was overtly negative.

I met with two museum curators, one gallerist and one graphic designer. The graphic designer was someone who was not on my list and I don't know why they assigned me the guy. I even told him when I sat down that I "didn't have anything relevant to show, and if he wanted, we could just blow off the meeting" but he was interested in my works and we ended up having a very nice conversation. When he said, "I need to find the right client so I can use you" that was an honest compliment and I'm glad I kept the meeting. (He never found the 'right client' and I never worked for him; nice sentiment, but with the typical lack of follow-through.)

I'd been assigned the graphic designer instead the gallerist I'd wanted to see. The gallerist I didn't meet was one of the people doing reviews at the MOPLA festival (Month of Photography, Los Angeles) earlier in the year. I'd sent a digital press kit to this gallerist after being rejected by MOPLA. (The MOPLA gatekeepers had declared my photography unworthy and unfit to be reviewed, and I was not allowed to participate in their paid photography reviews.) I don't know if this person was avoiding me (I think so) or if there was an actual scheduling conflict. One seldom finds out just how these decisions are made. But, as it turned out, the meeting with the graphic designer was nice enough.

One of the museum curators did fit my expectation of *not knowing just how to relate to my work and not being able to explain exactly why*. She was nice, but not especially enthusiastic about my artworks. I suspect my works were just too outside her 'comfort zone.' She had little to say and didn't have much information to offer.

The other curator was a person I'd been trying to meet for over a year. I'm glad I finally got to meet her. Again, like the other curator, she was more interested in 'traditional, straight photography' but she seemed engaged with the work. She noticed the subtle humor that infuses my work and appreciated it. She also provided some 'outside the box' information. She told me that the museums and high-end galleries don't really have an appreciation for anything remotely humorous and will reject it outright. That was new and interesting news for me and is very useful. She also provided good contact information for other alternative exhibition venues. All in all it was a good enough meeting.

The gallerist I met was also positive and, although my work wasn't right for her gallery (they all say this) she also mentioned some alternatives. She responded especially positively to my new works-in-progress, Quantum Realism, and wanted to see more in the future. This is good!

So, all in all, it was not a horrible experience. Here are some of the things I learned:

It occurs to me that there are some times in one's career that are better than others to participate in a portfolio review. I waited too long to do this. At this point in my career (35 years, so far) I know who I am and am comfortable with my own works. I'm not 'searching' and I'm not going to change what I do at this point in my life. My work reflects who I am and I cannot be someone other than me. I also think that having your work reviewed *too early* in one's career isn't especially beneficial as the 'experts' information might be confusing or unhelpful to a young artist. It seems to me that the best time for a review is early/mid-career. Too soon and you risk being overwhelmed, too late and the information you receive has diminishing returns. Work for five years or so, get yourself somewhat established and then go for a portfolio review.

I asked all four reviewers if my work 'is photography.' The graphic designer said he didn't care; which I feel is the 'correct' answer. The other three declared my work as 'definitely photography.' I still disagree but it looks like 'the system' wants to put me in the 'photography-box' anyway. I suspect there are a couple of reasons for this. One is this was a *photography* review so all the reviewers are naturally inclined to view things in photographic terms. When I mentioned influences from outside the photography medium they were all out of their element. This speaks to the insular and self-referencing nature of photography that I've written about before. The other reason I'm lumped-in with photography is because 'digital' is so closely tied to photography and it's such a new medium that doesn't have its own history and therefore is more easily considered to be 'photography.' I mentioned to one curator that I felt that 'photography' is a term that is descriptive and the viewer has a certain expectation. My works violate one's expectation of what a photograph is supposed to look like and my use of the term 'photo-digital' is more honest. She seemed to 'get' where I was coming from, but still said my works were 'photographs.' I'd like to discuss this in a more in-depth context with other 'experts' because it's them and not me that will determine future definitions of what's a photograph and what's 'digital art.' I still think 'digital' will eventually be declared a separate medium and I still don't consider myself a 'photographer' anymore.

I told the gallerist: "I want to work with galleries that are as enthusiastic about selling art as I am creating it." She got that. I suspect the gallerists that do these portfolio reviews are more serious than the ones who don't. That means *these* are the folks you want to exhibit your works (despite miniscule chances).

Having a lot of shows is good. Having shown in prestigious galleries are even better. Apparently I'm at a point where it's more important *where* I show than if I show. The cliché it's who you *know* remains true. I guess now I've got to figure out who's important and convince them to exhibit my works.

One portfolio review session is probably enough, unless you want to meet someone specific.

OK, now I've done it and got it out of my system. I don't need to do another one. These things are supposed to be good for 'networking,' but that never works for me, I'm too introverted. I can now say I've paid to have my photography reviewed by 'industry experts.' I can also say the review had no career impact whatsoever.

The only "Wow" I got came from another photographer.

CHAPTER

The Van Gogh Effect

Even those who didn't study art history know Vincent Van Gogh had a rough life. He had some mental health issues and never sold a painting during his lifetime. It's easy to understand that would be rather depressing.

Now, after his death, he's recognized as one of the greatest artists ever. His paintings are in the Greatest Museums. His works are worth millions. He's been vindicated by Art History.

Artists know the Van Gogh story and I think it's what keeps a lot of us going. We work and work and we produce art. We deal with all kinds of unpleasant things like:

Rejection.

Poverty.

Being marginalized and misunderstood.

Not being taken seriously.

Yet, we work and work and we produce art. And we hope.

We hold out hope that perhaps, one day, someday, even if it comes after our death, our artworks will be acknowledged. Maybe a posthumous exhibition or inclusion in a Museum Collection. Or a book. Or our names may be mentioned among the greats.

This hope is called

The Van Gogh Effect

And it's what keeps a lot of us from quitting.

Knowing that Vincent never got his due while alive, but did after death, can keep an artist going. Deferred gratification — even beyond the grave. We hope and hope that our genius will be recognized, that our works really do have value. And most of all, we hope the person tasked with clearing out our studios after our funerals will understand the significance of our art and not toss it all in a dumpster.

CHAPTER

LIMITED EDITIONS, LET'S DO THE MATH!

After the 2012 Houston, Texas Fine Arts Fair I received this criticism from the gallery:

Your work generated a lot of interest. One feedback we wanted to share with you was related to the size of the edition. Several collectors indicated that they would like to own unique/more exclusive pieces.

So I emailed the gallery with this question:

Can you tell me what an 'exclusive' edition size is?

And I got this reply:

As far as the size of the edition is concerned, some collectors thought that 250 was too large and that the piece they are getting was not unique.

I expected a reply with a number, so I asked again (which I should not have had to) and got this answer:

I have seen artists doing it in one of two ways: either limiting the edition to 10 prints or mounting prints on panels — whether aluminium (sic) or wood and positioning them as originals.

Well, that's not helpful at all! The most useless, and false information, is ...mounting prints on panels — whether *aluminium (sic) or wood and positioning them as originals.* Printing on panels or aluminum (correctly spelled) is not an 'original,' it's another print made on a *different medium.* Presenting a print on a different medium and calling it 'original' is a *lie and is unethical.*

My *Certificate of Authenticity* states: *Other limited editions are available in other sizes and media.* That means 'other sizes and media' are not originals but are prints on another media. I include this information so the buyer will know exactly just how exclusive an image they're getting. In my view this is called 'doing business honestly.'

So, mounting *prints on panels — whether aluminum or wood and positioning them as originals...* is dishonest and I won't do that. I'm a little surprised that a gallery would suggest that; after all they're supposed to be 'experts' (which clearly, they are not).

The real issue here is 'exclusivity,' or the perception of exclusivity; this is not a new issue and I've been hearing this same old thing for decades. Quite frankly it is nonsense and I'm tired of it.

This 'exclusivity' business goes back to painting, which is a one-of-a-kind genre. Painters make one painting and sell it (if they're well-known and represented by a good gallery) for a large sum of money. Sometimes the painter will scan or photograph their painting and sell *reproductions* for a vastly smaller sum than the original. This is a very old business model and it works for artists who produce one-of-a-kind, single works. Unfortunately the 'painting model' has been forced upon photographers, and now digital artists, and it's not a good fit. In photography the idea that *the negative can be printed again and again* limits exclusivity and it also limits price. Anything that's not a one-of-a-kind cannot be sold for one-of-a-kind prices and photographs are much cheaper to buy than most paintings. The 'photography model' also holds true for digital art; just replace the term *negative* with *digital file* and we're singing the same song.

So if one painting can sell for $10,000 a lucky photographer might get $1,000 for a single photograph. This is why many art collectors begin collecting by buying less expensive photographybefore they spend tens of thousands on paintings. This is also the reason photographers must sell multiple copies in order to making a living commensurate with their painter counterparts.

Photographers, and now digital artists, have created limited editions to provide some 'artificial rarity' or 'exclusivity.' The market doesn't seem to recognize that each print from a negative or each print from a digital file is, in fact, an original.

My edition size for the particular body of work I showed at The Houston Fine Art Fair is two-hundred-and-fifty prints, 250. I arrived at this number after analyzing artworks that were editioned between 10 and 1000. I made my decision on the knowledge of the realistic prices I could ask, my need to earn a living and on being able to offer some form of 'exclusivity' based on the size of the edition. I also have another motivation that most artists I know don't share; I *want* people to own my works, so I make more than one copy available.

Let's do the 'limited edition' math and find out what 'exclusive' really means:

250 = size of edition.
7,000,000,000 (7 Billion) population of Earth

Now let's figure out what percentage of 7 billion 250 is:

250 x 100 =25,000
25,000 divided by 7,000,000,000 = .00000357

This shows that 250 is .00000357 of one percent of 7 billion. That's pretty darned exclusive!

The standard argument against this formula is that 7 billion people *do not* collect art. This is true. In fact over 2 billion people on planet Earth live in abject poverty, so no, they don't collect art. Let's choose a smaller number of 'global art collectors' and take a guess of 500,000, a half million people planet-wide who do collect art.

Let's do the math again, with different numbers:

250 = size of edition.
500,000 = estimated number of 'global art collectors'
250 x 100 = 25,000
25,000 divided by 500,000 = .05

This shows that 250 is .05 (five one-hundredths) of one percent of 500,000. That's still very exclusive!

I think the arithmetic shows that even a 'large' edition of 250 is very, very exclusive. And that still puts 250 of my originals in the homes of collectors.

The mathematics shown above proves that an edition of 250 is in fact very exclusive. Now let's continue the math and figure out the income potential for the artist:

My price for this particular edition is $600.00 per print (unframed, print-only). If I were to sell out the whole edition of 250 I'd earn $150,000.00 — but that number isn't entirely correct The gallery keeps a 50% commission so my real earnings for selling out the edition is $75,000.00. And let's figure $5000.00 in expenses to produce and ship the artworks leaving a net $70k for selling out an *entire* edition.

Is this not as much money as you'd thought? Art may be subjective but math is objective and doesn't lie. This is where the numbers fall.

Forget that crap about 'prints on panels and aluminum' and let's now do the math for a 'gallery acceptable exclusive' edition:

10 = size of edition.

$600.00 each = price of artwork.

$6000.00 = total income from selling out an edition of ten.

-$3000.00 = less 50% gallery commission.

-$300.00 = production cost

$2700.00 = net profit to artist for selling out an edition of ten.

So an 'exclusive' sold-out edition of ten nets the artist about $2700.00 and that is not 'earning a living.' You can't afford to continue making art at these rates and edition sizes — despite what your gallery thinks.

Once you've sold out your 'exclusive' edition of ten you're done. You'll never earn another dime from that image. And guess what? The gallery is done with you too! They've earned as much as they can from your 'exclusive' edition and if you don't have something equally popular that they're willing to exhibit you're all done and the gallery will just find someone else's 'exclusive' art to sell.

The gallery cares about 'exclusivity' but it's at your expense and they don't care about your ability to earn a living.

A gallery might argue that for an edition size of ten, to raise prices. Every artist would like to sell their art at the highest possible price but that isn't feasible for everyone. 'Unknown' artists can't command as high prices as 'known' artists. Galleries that are perceived as 'high end' can justify higher prices than other galleries. And photography and digital art does not command as high a price as painting and other 'one of a kind' works do. One must be realistic and understand their position in the 'art food chain' when setting prices.

I think this notion of 'exclusivity' is snobbish and elitist. And I also believe, based on arithmetic, an edition of 250 is 'exclusive.' Again, two-hundred-and-fifty pieces measured against a collector-base of five-hundred-thousand people means the buyers of my edition are among only five one-hundredths of one percent of the total number of art collectors.

Really, isn't 0.05% exclusive enough?

FIFTY BUCKS!

"I wouldn't set my alarm clock for fifty bucks!" is a line borrowed from the photographer I worked for back when I was an assistant. In my book *Photographic Memories* he was mentioned in a chapter under the pseudonym "Ed." "Ed" was sort of an asshole; this opinion was shared by many, not just me. He wasn't one of those malicious kinds of assholes but he could be brutally non-politically correct at times. I recall once Ed was on the telephone with a client who was in hardcore nickel-and-dime mode. I listened as Ed's half of the conversation went from reasoning with the client, explaining the costs of photography, to heated and angry. Finally Ed yelled into the phone, "Fuck you, you cheapskate, I wouldn't even set my alarm clock for fifty bucks!" And he slammed down the phone. He'd just lost another client and he didn't care.

Ed didn't care about losing that client because he knew the value of his work. He also had enough experience that he knew that cheap clients are most always problematic. Cheap clients don't value photographers' work; they nickel-and-dime on the front end and then add more work they didn't budget for during the shoot. They won't pay for the additional things they demand during the shoot, seldom pay advances and they usually pay invoices late, if at all. Nobody needs a cheapshit client, they suck. This was an instance where Ed's *asshole-ness* served him well. Overhearing that conversation was one of the few educational things I took away from my year assisting Ed. As it turned out, I'd borrow that line more than a few times myself.

Photographers (and virtually everyone in the art business) are constantly being marginalized and pressured to work cheap, or for free. In business we get very little respect and the business-boys think they can run roughshod over us. Unfortunately they usually succeed. Because photographers aren't organized as a group we're easily fractured because there's *always* someone who will do the job or license the picture cheaper. Often times our fees are set by our clients. They tell us, "This is what we pay, take it or leave it." They get away with it because if you leave it, someone else *will* take the deal and the client still gets their picture at the fee they set. There are so many amateur and cheapshit *photographers* that if you pass on some shitty deal, the client can find another photographer *within minutes*. Only those photographers at the very top of the 'fame and recognition' pyramid have any power against this, the majority of us are utterly powerless.

I've left small piles of money on the table when I've refused to devalue my work. I don't care if they don't value my work, I do, and it is priced accordingly because I know how much it costs to produce good art. I don't take myself too seriously and overvalue my work, but I don't let ego get in front of business and take shitty deals. I cannot stay in business and do assignments at a loss or license stock photos for less than it cost to produce them. Lesson number one in business school is *profit*. You cannot profit, and therefore stay in business by working at a loss. This is simple math.

I first heard Ed utter the alarm clock line in 1985. I've just used it again for the umpteenth time in 2012. It's never going to change and it'll probably get worse.

An email from an Art Director arrived in my inbox. She'd seen one of my pictures on an Art website and wanted to know if the image was available for commercial license. I replied in the affirmative and asked all the standard stock photo questions in order to determine the use-fee. She replied with the specifications and I worked up a quote, then reduced the number by *fifty* percent, and emailed her a quote for $250.00. She replied with, "We usually pay $50.00, is there any wiggle-room?" I'd submitted a fair fee I felt was on the cheap side but she felt I was still 80% too expensive. I replied with a counter-offer of $100.00 and mentioned it was a rather unique image (not something she can get anywhere, from anyone). Apparently they wanted me to do all the wiggling and wouldn't budge from their offer of $50.00. We couldn't come to agreement and they didn't license the picture. Typical!

I wasn't too bothered about the non-sale because I'm all-too used to this sort of thing; it's almost standard-operating-procedure. For fun, I put a post on my Facebook page that read: *No, I will not license the picture you want for $50.00. If you're paying amateur prices, contact an amateur photographer. To quote an old friend, "I won't even set my alarm clock for fifty bucks."*

One of the first Facebook comments (from a photographer) was this: *$50.00????? Really????? I won't even ask.....last shot I licensed I got 2k for it......* A little later the same person added this: *none of the real shooters do a shot for 50.00.....*

Later, a different photographer commented: *I'd rather make 50 bucks than no bucks.*

The final comment in the thread came from me, in response to the above photographer: *That you would take $50 for a $500 photo is EXACTLY what's wrong with the photography business today. Sorry, but that doesn't help our industry.*

And therein lies the problem, neatly illustrated by a thread of Facebook comments. There's *always someone* who'll do it cheaper! There's *always someone* who will devalue their work. There's always someone who will eat shit and acquiesce to the insane demands of some faceless corporation.

In my view fifty bucks is no bucks. Aside from the devaluation of my work, fifty bucks won't fund my retirement account nor will fifty bucks save me from bankruptcy, so why bother? An extra fifty bucks (bringing my fee to an 'acceptable' $100) is nothing to the Big Corporation that wanted to use my picture. Yet they wouldn't budge. They wouldn't budge because they don't have to! They've been spoiled by thousands of photographers who'll do exactly what that last Facebook commenter does. They've been spoiled by all the Microstock imagery available for less *than a cup of coffee.*

It doesn't help that every wanker with a cell-phone camera thinks they're a photographer either!

What the photography industry needs, and will never get, is a licensing clearinghouse like BMI/ASCAP in the music industry. We need to organize and establish a *floor*, a standard minimum amount for licensing a picture for commercial reproduction. This will never happen for a whole host of reasons. Those opposed will say establishment of a standard minimum (but not maximum) is somehow 'price-fixing' or 'socialism' or erodes our 'freedom.' Photographers are also notoriously independent-minded and would reject the idea despite its benefit.

The bottom line here is things aren't going to change. Photographers *won't* organize. All we can do as individuals (like I have done) is to take a pass on shit deals. If more and more of us would refuse to license imagery or shoot new works on the cheap our clients would come to realize our work has value, and if they want to use it they'll have to pay a *fair fee.* This is not unreasonable. But it's never going to happen. It's too bad for us but great for the picture-user. Photographer's rugged individualism provides the freedom to cut each other's throats in business.

I guess I'll just sleep in; I no longer have a need for an alarm clock.

CHAPTER

DEATH AND HAPPINESS

Sitting at the computer staring into the Photoshop workspace, the phone rang. It was the mother of an old friend from college with the news that he'd died last month. Colon cancer. Diagnosis and then dead two months later. We'd met in the late 1970s in college, were fellow photography students and friends. We drifted apart, both geographically and in worldviews over the years, but we stayed in touch. What a shock, dead at the age of 51 (the same age as me!).

After graduating college I went to work. He stayed in school. He really liked school. He liked the cloistered environment of college and he really liked college girls. I'm pretty sure 'chasing pussy' kept him in school; he was motivated that way. While I was establishing my studio he was studying architecture. After nine years of college he graduated and took a job as a draftsman in Chicago.

Once when I was in Chicago on assignment I got together with my old friend. He wasn't a happy man. He didn't like architecture despite the pay. He missed the college girls. And at the age of 30-something, he was still doing all the things college boys do, the things I'd long since 'outgrown.'

So he went back to school and got himself an MFA in photography. Although he had absolutely zero photography experience (never shot a brochure, ad, or simple portrait) he had that two-year Master's degree/teacher's Union Card and got himself a job teaching photography. It seems his dreams had come true, he was back in the sheltered academic environment, and the college-girl pussy was readily available. With those goals met one may think he was a happy guy, but he wasn't.

A couple of years ago he came through Arizona and stayed with us for one night. During the evening, when I'd left the room, he hit on my wife. I guess that pussy-chasing thing knows no bounds — or honor! I avoided discussing art with him. He's a professor and I'm a professional, and the two don't often agree. I had little interest in his work as it's done for fellow academics; and he had no interest in mine — academics don't respect professionals. He was still a profoundly unhappy person. He'd always held out for something better. He'd refused tenure because he wanted to keep the door open for a better position. He went through 'disposable' women because there might be someone better coming along. He never owned a home because there might be something nicer. He was never settled, never got comfortable with who he was.

I checked him out on ratemyprofessor.com. Extremes! Loved or hated. Aside from the few "wonderful teacher" comments the rest were horrifying; "killed my dreams," "favors women," "if you don't make pictures like his, you'll fail," were the common comments. He graded hard. I've found that art professors who are unsure of their own talent and ability tend to suppress students and he was one of those. He never tested himself in the marketplace because he might fail, and really couldn't teach what he did not know.

He took himself and his work seriously — too seriously to have fun. Now he's dead at the age of 51. He died alone in a rented house with a body of esoteric personal work that will end up…….. Where? In a dumpster? (I hope not.)

Death (especially a young, sudden, death) makes one pause to consider their own mortality. What's life all about? Does life have intrinsic meaning or do we apply meaning to our lives? Was it worth it for him to always 'keep that door open?' Was it worth it, never establishing a long-term loving relationship because something better may be over the horizon?

What's the point of living for tomorrow when tomorrow may never come? I think he had it good and that better thing had come along, but he failed to recognize it. In his lifelong quest for something better, he never appreciated what he had.

I wonder if he found happiness in death? Doubtful. He's probably looking to upgrade to a nicer part of Hell or Heaven, and chasing women....... I'm saddened that he's dead, and sadder that although 'he died doing what he loved' he never found happiness.

ALWAYS remember the philosophy of comedian Red Skelton: *"Why take life seriously? Nobody gets out of it alive anyway."*

CHAPTER

I Thought I Was Better

After digging through over one-hundred years of family history, with forty-one of those years in the same house, I finally found a box of my own personal history. This happens to almost everybody; our parents die, we've got to go through their stuff, and sometimes we find some of our own stuff in the process.

I came down from the dusty attic with a box and said to my 85 year-old aunt, "After three weeks of going through the family history, I've finally found some of my own. Indulge me for a moment while I show you some pictures."

"I guess this is important to you?" she replied, disinterested.

Silly me, I should be used to this by now, after all, I do have a history with this family. Never mind, Auntie, I'll look at it later, alone.

And I did. I brought that box home with me. I couldn't bring everything, there just wasn't enough space in the car, but I brought enough to get a good reintroduction of my early photography. The box contained black and white prints mostly; prints made by me, in my old darkroom in the garage. There were a few negatives, a few thirty-five millimeter transparencies, and some early photography awards. My personal history and the roots of my own artistic development, all in a box no one cared about but me. Back home, on the comfort of my own studio floor, without uninterested family members present, I examined the contents of that box (labeled '1974') with the eyes of a mature artist with 37 years' distance from his origins and came to a somewhat less-than-comfortable conclusion:

I thought I was better than I was.

My memories didn't quite square with the evidence spread out on the floor around me. Apparently I was not a genius. I'd been a decent-enough young photographer but I certainly wasn't the brilliant artist I thought I'd been. Sure, sure, we all tend to inflate our resumes, obituaries and memories and maybe I'd indulged in some personal ego-stroking when thinking about my own artistic beginnings, but the view with today's eyes is I was more *adequate* than brilliant, back then.

I'd like to think I've gotten better over the years, which may taint the perception of my early artist-self. I do recall conversations with other photographers back in 1974 and we all were going to be brilliant when we 'grew up.' Well, we grew up, but I'm the only one who stuck with it and attempted to attain the 'brilliance' we all thought we'd acquire. Those other photographers from 1974 are now accountants, business-people, parents, employees, cubicle-monkeys and non-artists. So maybe my 'brilliance' wasn't in the art, but was merely sticking with the art? It is also possible I am a fool, but at least I can claim to be a thoughtful and introspective fool, with his own personal art-history. I can trace my foolishness back to its origins. And I can see the roots of my own artistic development in those early works. No, I didn't drop from the womb as the instant, Salvador Dali-esque type genius I thought I was — I had to work at it. And I'm still at it, but now I can analyze where I was and compare it to where I am. As they say in politics, I'm 'making progress, moving forward.'

But how did I get here?

First, and most obviously, it was *not* the result of genius. In the majority of my early works I saw no evidence of genius or brilliance, but there were a few images that showed 'the spark,' and I'll get to those later. The first and foremost thing I noticed when

going through those early pictures was that I was a good technician. I remember easily learning the 'science' part of photography
and it shows. Most of the prints had not faded in these past thirty-
plus years even in the uncontrolled environment of my parents'
house attic. Fixing and washing was apparently done properly. And
most of the prints (mainly 8x10 inch and 5x7 inch B&W RC paper)
are of normal contrast and exposure. Technically my old prints are
good, but science is easy to learn (if you try) and to me, a lot of
what went on in the darkroom was more like following a recipe
than 'making art.' The 'making art' part for me was done in the
camera, compositionally, and not in the darkroom (with a few
notable exceptions). When I look at the artistic attributes of my
early work, it's rather pedestrian. It's obvious I learned the 'rule of
thirds' and other compositional standards. I learned how to 'pan'
the camera correctly and my sports photos, while unremarkable,
were in-focus and composed well-enough. As a young, entrepre-
neurial sports photographer at my brother's little league baseball
games, I recall selling quite a few prints of 'kids-in-action' to their
parents. Although there's nothing to indicate I had a future with
Sports Illustrated, I did well enough. I also learned early on to
make do with what I had. What I had, as a young sports photographer, was an Argus A-4 camera with a 44mm lens with a leaf-shut-
ter that had to manually cocked for each exposure and a wonky
film advance knob. Certainly not the 600mm, motordrive kind of
pictures we're used to seeing in sports magazines today, but merely adequate (not too many pictures of center-fielders though).
Making do is something I learned early, and still have to do today.

My landscape photographs were as banal and unremarkable as
the Texas landscape where I lived at the time. As primarily a black
and white photographer my early works showed no eye for light.
The recognition and exploitation of 'good light' was something I
learned later — much later. A sensitivity to 'good light' wasn't
something I learned in college either; I learned it from a year-long

assistant/apprenticeship with another photographer who did have an innate ability to find and use great natural light. 'Light' for me was an acquired skill and I don't see any evidence in my early works that I had any 'natural' perception when it came to light.

I found very few portraits, snapshots or 'people pictures.' I owe this to my life-long introversion and (somewhat) dislike of other people. It was pretty cool to find 1970s era concert photos of rock bands like *Yes*, *Supertramp* and *Jethro Tull*. Those were merely 'adequate' pictures as well, notable only by the fact that cameras haven't been allowed in most rock concerts for a long time now.

Compositionally I was 'safe.' Apparently I'd read, learned and followed the compositional 'rules' and I saw no 'non-standard' or 'innovative' or 'risky' composition in my early works at all. I consider myself a 'formalist' to this day but I do try to 'shoot outside the compositional box' from time to time, although still it's not natural for me. When I look at these works now, I feel that at the time, if there were 'rules' to be followed (art-rules or photographic-technical) I followed them and exploited what was considered 'safe' but I really didn't take any chances until much, much later. I can now see that I was trying to fit a 'standard' and wasn't confident enough to 'break the rules.'

All in all I was a rather adequate photographer with above-average technical abilities for my youth. This discovery was rather disappointing as I'd held my early photography in such high esteem — until I saw it again. Not that 'adequate' is all that bad; I just thought I was better. Cognitive-dissonance dictates that I must reject a 'feeling' that conflicts with a 'fact.' I'd 'felt' I was better, but the new 'facts' of those old prints laying on my studio floor tells me I must reject my warm, fuzzy feelings about my early artistry and pay attention to the 'fact' that I just wasn't quite as good as I thought I was.

But among the boxes of unimpressively adequate photographs I did find some that showed 'the spark.'

The pictures I found where I can reasonably construe there was a 'spark of brilliance' were the ones that I'd either 'directed' or used some darkroom-trickery. The studio photos, the posed actors in the high school play, and the set-up shots were my best. When I'd 'imposed myself' on the situation had resulted in the best photography. I did better when I 'took control' or 'directed' than when I just showed up and took the shot. I didn't know it at the time, but apparently I was a much better 'advertising' shooter than 'editorial.' I found composite prints I'd made at the age of fifteen that were nearly as good as Jerry Uelsmann's. I'd built miniature sets in forced-perspective that I'd photographed for my high school newspaper that won awards. My Kodalith high-contrast film experiments were successful. Basically, what I found was my 'straight' photography was average while my 'special effect' or 'set-up' imagery was superior and showed 'the spark.'

Interestingly, now that most of my work is digital, I don't think like a photographer much anymore. Back then, not thinking like a photographer (despite advanced use of darkroom techniques) provided me the means of making the best imagery. When I was 'one of the photographers' my work was merely adequate, but when I set-up the shot, or directed the people in the picture, or printed two negatives on one piece of paper or built a set to be photographed, only then did my work contain the spark of what it's become today.

I also kept at it, which helps as success is the result of not quitting.

Since I thought I was so much better than I really was indicates I had a healthy ego — perhaps too healthy. My Dad, whose recent death was the cause of this re-discovery of my own art-history, used to criticize me for 'thinking too highly of myself.' I tried (and failed) to explain to him, back in the day and more recently, that since he didn't think that much of me, I had to do it myself. I mean if you don't think highly of yourself or your work (to a point, keep the ego in control) who will? Have confidence! Perhaps it was my delusional sense of artistic self-worth that made me keep at it?

And I'm glad I kept at it. I have gotten better. I have something to contribute. I thought I was a genius but I wasn't; I thought I was more talented, and I was wrong. But here I am anyway. And maybe in the end, hard work is no different from genius? No, I wasn't as good as I thought I was and I'm OK with that. I do think I'll keep those old pictures to myself — I don't want to spoil anyone else's delusion. And regarding that Ego thing, if I really did think *too highly* of myself and my work, do you think I'd of admitted it, written it down and shared it?

CHAPTER

WITNESS TO HISTORY, THE DIGITAL REVOLUTION
OF PHOTOGRAPHY
I WITNESSED THE BIRTH OF DIGITAL AND I ATTENDED FILM'S FUNERAL.
HERE'S HOW IT WAS FOR ME. I WAS THERE.

My first encounter with computers was in high school in the 1970s and the experience was remarkably annoying. I really had no idea what punch cards were for and the only words that ever came off the ancient dot matrix printer were *'illegal command.'* A few years later in college during the early 1980s the only contact I had with computers was to make fun of the geeks in the computer lab as they struggled to learn programming languages like C++, Cobal, BASIC and FORTRAN. Had I known then that by the 21st century those guys would basically own my ass, I'd of been nicer! I should have learned coding.

When I graduated college in 1982 I was fortunate enough to have a corporate job lined-up. It was an in-house corporate/industrial photographer job but it was also so boring that at about six weeks into it, I started looking for other, more creatively satisfying work. The unfortunate thing about that job was that it only lasted three months, a glorified summer job. I got 'laid off,' but when I lost that job I had another one lined-up because I'd already been looking.

While looking for that second, post-college, post-corporate job, I'd been peeking over the horizon to the not-too-distant-future and I really felt that computers would intertwine themselves with photography pretty soon. I could see the digitalization of photography coming. So, despite the low pay I took that job after getting sacked from my corporate 'summer job' and when to work for a company as a photographer and *computer artist*. This was 1982, eight years before Adobe Photoshop 1.0. I worked that job for less than two years and the industry changed significantly during that very short time.

The company provided computer-generated and 35mm optical slides for corporate slide show presentations. Most of their clients were banks and we created a lot of computer-generated slides of pie charts and graphs and boring things like that for financial meetings. Occasionally a client would need photographs included in the slide shows and we used a FOROX optical printer to create those slides. There never were a lot of FOROX operators in the world but I'd been trained in the late 1970s and had experience with the FOROX and that's what got me the job. Once I'd been hired and proved myself as an experienced FOROX operator I was really anxious to get trained to use that big computer down the hall.

That computer was a Genigraphics 100B and it filled an entire room. I don't know the exact cost of the thing, but I heard numbers in the quarter-million dollar range. Now, by today's desktop standards, that machine is a POS, but it 1982 it was amazing stateof-the-art tech. If memory serves, the hardware was from General Electric and the graphics software came from NASA. The graphics were 2D and we could use only 256 colors. The whole darned thing ran on an IBM-DOS mainframe. The computer had a small color monitor, a digitizing tablet (not unlike the Wacom Tablets we use now, but the pen was wired to the tablet) and there were a series of buttons on the left side of the digitizing tablet. Those buttons were the closest thing we had to a *graphical user interface* at the time and by pushing certain buttons the computer would do certain repetitive tasks (today, in Photoshop, those things — scripts — are called 'actions'). I recall the last button in the row was to *refresh the screen*. I have no idea about the RAM or video cards of the day but a fast computer artist could do a lot of work while not seeing anything on-screen. Then by clicking that fourth button the screen would refresh (which took a few moments for processing) and the artist could see his latest work. All of our client's works were stored on 8-inch single-density floppy disks that held a whopping 256k of data.

Next to the darkroom was another dark room that contained a *film recorder* — something we don't hear about much anymore. A film recorder is a really cool device with a camera lens and a hires video monitor that converts the digital data to scan lines that are exposed onto film. Most of our work was output to 35mm Ektachrome slides (we had our own in-house E-6 lab) that were projected during those banking meetings.

A graphics computer, a film recorder, a FOROX optical print-er and an in-house photo-lab; this was all way-cool state-of-the-art stuff for 1982! As a 23 year-old fresh out of college, top of my class, with a photography degree, I had at my fingertips the most advanced creative tools in the world. I had a head full of ideas and was set to charge headlong to The Future of Art, but the company I worked for had much more pedestrian ideas.

Already, in 1983, I could see the vaporware beginning to solid-ify; it wouldn't be long before what we were doing would 'go desk-top.' The IBM PC was already two years old. I felt that within a few more years the companies' core business, chart and graph graph-ics, would be gone. Predicting that simple graphics would move to the desktop computer I felt that the evolution of our business would be creative illustration for print. When I expressed my futurist views to management they shut me down, nobody was interested in what the kid thought. They so much didn't want to hear what I had to say that they put me on the night shift, alone, so I wouldn't bother anyone. It was the dumbest thing they could do to an employee like me.

Nightshift work for the computer graphics company entailed proofreading and fixing any mistakes made during the day and revising last-minute slides. All this was sent to the film recorder followed by processing the exposed film. Developed film was edited and mounted in slide mounts, collated and packaged for delivery. I absolutely hated the night shift (don't work by night, don't sleep by day) but I could do my job in four hours or less leaving me at least four hours a night to *do my own creative work and experiment! And I did!*

While alone with the technology I did quite a number of things that ultimately furthered my own career as a computer artist and special effects technician:

I created a portfolio of creative computer-illustrations. Although the company had no interest in this, the market was interested.

I developed 'hybrid' photo-digital artworks using the Genigraphics computer to create CGI elements that I combined with photographs using the FOROX camera.

I spliced a 36-exposure roll of Kodachrome 64 into the middle of a 100-foot roll of Ektachrome and tested the film recorder's ability to image computer graphics on the more archival Kodachrome film. (Too contrasty.)

I used multiple-exposures in the film recorder to render images with more information than could be recorded in a single exposure.

I created CGI images using two exposures, one for the main image and a second exposure for 'glowing highlights.' I programmed the film recorder to 'pause' between exposures and would go into the (totally dark) film recorder room and place a sheet of diffusion material over the film recorder's CRT and make the second exposure. The resultant double exposure would have 'glows' that otherwise couldn't be achieved digitally.

I photographed various textures that could be sandwiched with text or other slides and duplicated using the FOROX camera creating a 'grunge' or 'distressed' look which predated any layering in Photoshop by more than two decades.

I pushed the technological/creative envelope as hard as I could and did a *lot* of creative things that the company had no interest in. As a result of my 'personal productivity' while working the night shift I was able to take my new wiz-bang, razzle-dazzle, computer-generated portfolio and:

Pick up creative freelance work that I would do on the companies' equipment at night. (This is the work the company wasn't interested in nor did they believe the work was out there.) I used the money to supplement the low pay from my 'regular' job.

I printed some of the works and exhibited them in galleries.

Used my new CGI work to obtain a contract with a Stock Photo Agency. (At a time when 200+ images were required 'for review' for an agency to consider you, I was offered a contract after showing only *four* computer-generated illustrations, *nobody* had digital art at the time but me.)

This is my own personal history of the analog to digital revolution to date. A lot of others were doing similar things at the same time but most of them were on the technical side. I didn't really care about *how* the computer did what it did, all I cared about was using new tech to make new art. My perspective was that of artist only.

After a little over than a year I had to leave that job despite all the hi-tech, wiz-bang, way-cool gadgetry. The pay was so low I was barely getting by, management was incompetent and I could see that their business model, which would remain unchanged, would fail sooner than later. (The company went out of business in 1986.) Before giving notice I ran all my digital files though the film recorder and got everything on film, and I copied all my digital data. At the time I didn't know just what kind of computers I'd get my hands on in the future, but I knew I would, so I was prepared. For the remainder of the 1980s I rented time on others' workstations, outsourced some work to photo labs that had Genigraphics equipment or the very similar Dicomed computers. I continued to create hybrid photo-digital works using an optical printer of my own design. Often my optical works were mistaken for digital works (something I allowed my clients to believe) and I stayed competitive in the marketplace until Adobe Photoshop came around in 1990.

In 1991, one year after the commercial introduction of Photoshop, I attended a week-long workshop in Santa Fe, New Mexico and learned, then Mac-only, Adobe Photoshop 1.0. Although we were manipulating photographs I still had an advantage over my fellow students because of my background in the computer-generation of artwork, and I was already familiar with film recorders. In 1991 we were outputting our work on film; the Epson printer wouldn't come along for a few more years. Aside from learning the basics of Photoshop, I learned about scanning slides and negatives, which was extremely important as the digital cameras of the day really weren't ready for primetime. When I left the workshop I was reasonably competent with Photoshop but so poor I could not afford to fully 'go digital' until 1994 when Adobe Photoshop 3.0, the first PC version, came out.

The only computer I could afford in the early 1990s was a well used IBM 286 with a monochrome monitor which I used primarily as a word-processor and to generate labels for 35mm slides. In retrospect, as much as I wanted to be an 'early adopter' my inability to afford the hardware saved me from wasting a lot of money in an era when we were learning our way, RAM was godaw-ful expensive, and upgrading was nearly constant. Some photo labs were acquiring Macintosh-Photoshop workstations and I continued to rent time on the equipment as needed.

I'll be honest. We didn't know what the fuck we were doing with digital imaging in the early days — but we really, really want-ed to do it.

During the pre-digital camera era we scanned our film to get the image into the digital environment but in the early 1990s there were very few viable desktop scanners so we went to service bureaus for drum scans. Kodak was a great help with this when they intro-duced the Photo CD in 1992. But early on we hardly knew what kind of file to save; do you want a GIF, or maybe a TIFF? The JPEG was not yet available. And on what media do you store that newly scanned image? Even then digital image files were too large for flop-py disks of any size. New removable media hit the market like the fragile SyQuest SQ-400, 42 megabyte Data Cartridge which we used early on. There were some tape-drives available. I recall using a thing called a Bernoulli Box to bring scans to the studio from the scanning service bureau. (The Bernoulli Box technology would eventually morph into the Zip Disk.) After the Zip, Iomega brought out the larg-er capacity Jaz Drive, which failed in the marketplace. Eventually the cost of CD burners came down to the point where they were affordable to the average consumer so we used them extensively. This was all long before DVDs, USB hard drives, USB thumb drives, Secure Digital, or Compact Flash cards, or 'the cloud.' These were days when even 'fast' computers were slow and RAM cost upwards of fifty dollars per megabyte. For a long time I kept work-ing optically because accomplishing the same thing digitally was just too damn expensive!

The movie industry was way ahead of still photography when it came to computer-generation and manipulation. There's a lot more money in movie-making so it's logical that the film industry would embrace 'digital' early and in a big way. In 1982 the movie "Tron" was released. "Tron," though dated-looking today was utterly groundbreaking at the time. What most movie-goers didn't realize was "Tron" was mostly digital-looking rotoscoped optical effects and not computer-generated at all except for some of the backgrounds, which were done by Genigraphics. I was doing almost exactly the same thing when I was combining Genegraphics computer-generated elements with photos using the FOROX camera to create photo-digital hybrid images. Two years later, in 1984, "The Last Starfighter" was released. All of the spaceship and space battles were computer-generated. Again, today, the space scenes in "The Last Starfighter" look like aged, 8-bit video game graphics; a lot has changed in the last 30+ years. In another two years Disney would release "Flight of the Navigator" in 1986. This movie also featured a computer-generated spaceship but the cool thing is it was chrome and reflective. We were all amazed at the texture-mapped reflections moving along the silver-chrome spaceship. In 2001 we were equally amazed at the moving, computergenerated fur on the creatures of "Monsters, Inc."

Throughout the 80s and 90s we saw computer-manipulation and computer-generation of imagery move from the laboratory, to the university, into industry and ultimately to the mainstream consumer. Some other players of the early days were: Scitex, Silicon Graphics, Quantel Paintbox, Gerber Systems Technology, Intergraph, Lexidata, Bell Labs, Boeing, NASA, JPL, Digital Graphics Systems, Spectragraphics, Computervision Corporation, Raster Technologies, Chromatics Inc., Dicomed, Electronic Information Services, Aurora Systems, and Cranston-Csuri. Some of America's finest research labs and universities were working on computer-imaging, both in the art and physics departments including: MIT, Rice University, Sandia National Labs, New York Institute of Technology, Oxford University, Purdue University, State University of Groningen in the Netherlands, and the University of Houston.

By the end of the 20th century, thanks to digital technology, a new art form was born — Digital Art. You'll only read that here because I'm the only one who's put a date on it –I was there, so I know a little something. Art historians are late to the digital party.

By 1990 we had clunky Adobe Photoshop 1.0 and the writing on the wall became permanent. Photography was 'going digital.' By 1994 we had Photoshop 3.0 for the PC and the new version included *layers*. By 1995 I retired my optical printer and began doing special-effect and composite work digitally. But we weren't quite there yet...

It would take almost a decade for commercial clientele to catch up. Nobody could handle a digital file for reproduction, they still wanted film. I found the workflow a little strange, but that's the way business was done at the time and I had no choice except to adapt. We were at a film in — film out stage with digital image-processing in the middle. I was sending 35mm film out for scanning (usually the inexpensive but practical Kodak Photo CD format), doing retouching and creative 'darkroom'work digitally with Photoshop, and then outputting back to film. In a few more years I'd bring scanning in-house with a Nikon 4000ED scanner, but I never acquired my own film recorder (very few of us did). That meant going back to an expensive photo lab/service bureau for outputting to film. After trying virtually everything there was at the time I settled on outputting to 8x10 inch film using Light Valve Technology. The 'LVT'was basically a great big film recorder and I could output to very impressive 8x10 inch Ektachrome color transparency film. I think the cost of those 8x10 inch transparencies was over $200.00 each back then so I began creating files where I would gang 4 to 6 medium-format size images on one piece of 8x10 film to bring individual image costs down. We'd then deliver transparencies to the client or stock photo agency which, for reproduction, were *scanned* and printed via offset printer. It was an expensive pain in the ass which, thankfully, went away when our clients caught up and 'went digital' themselves and then we could just send a digital file.

But then there was printing, which was still catching-up. We could make LVT negatives or transparencies and take them into the darkroom and make B&W, Cibachrome or Type-R prints but it added an additional generation, an extra step, and expense. What was needed was a way to go direct from the computer to a digital printer and skip the chemical darkroom step. In 1991 *Nash Editions* opened shop. Started by musician and amateur photographer Graham Nash, *Nash Editions* used rare, expensive and state-of-theart- for-the-moment IRIS printers which were early Giclee' printers. (Giclee' is a French word for 'sprayed ink,' which is the same thing as Inkjet.) Quality work by *Nash Editions* proved the inkjet processviable for digital printing, even large-scale and, even more importantly, they changed the *perception* (especially of the museum and gallery folks) that a digital print could be a viable end product and not a mere 'proof.' Nearly a decade later, in 2000, Epson brought the first Archival Pigment printer to the market, the Epson Stylus 2000P, and now an artist could make their own, exhibition-quality fine-art print right in their own studios. The next generation of Epson (and Canon) pigment printers upped the quality of B&W printing to rival a silver-gelatin print from the darkroom.

By the first decade of the 21st century a modern photographer or 'digital artist' could afford to bring every step of the digital imaging process in-house and have total control without using any outside technical services. My own system consisted of the computer with built-in CD and Zip drives, a large CRT color monitor, a Wacom digitizing tablet, a 35mm film scanner and a pigment inkjet printer. That computer had an impressive 128 megabytes of

RAM, today box-stock computers come with *gigabytes* of RAM! That computer was superseded many times by 2017.

By the year 2000 'digital' had a stranglehold on photography. Already darkrooms were disappearing and computers running Adobe Photoshop began filling the void. Darkroom skills were giving way to 'learning an application (Photoshop).' Film wasn't dead yet but it was facing mortal competition from newfangled digital cameras. I recall seeing some early prototype digital cameras and they were awful, and expensive, and low-resolution. I was at a meeting at my stock photo agency in New York and met a photographer who was all impressed with himself because he had one of those new digital cameras. I ask him to show me the thing and the poor guy couldn't even figure out how to turn it on, much less take a picture! Yeah, I'd be using film for a while yet. One hitch in the workflow was time. Because of digital technology, business was speeding-up, deadlines were tighter and things had to be done faster. Time constraints were problematic with the normal delays of sending film out for processing and then sending the resultant slides out to be scanned. Life would be so much easier if the pictures out of the camera were already digital. Digital cameras needed to get better, and they did!

After watching that goofball in New York struggle just to turn on his digital camera I decided I would not be an early adopter of the digital camera. I intended to wait until they got better, faster and cheaper. Besides, I already had every film camera and lens I needed, I was in no mood to start buying new cameras all over again. Eventually I had to...

My first digital camera was a 3.3 megapixel Canon G-1. I bought it in 2000 for the too-high price of about a grand! It wasn't a SLR but the image on the tiny preview screen was from the sensor, so it was like an SLR as I was seeing the image through the taking lens. 3.3 megapixels isn't super high resolution, a straight print from the camera might hold up to 8x10 inches or a little bigger, but at the time I think about six megapixels was state-of-theart, so it wasn't far off. My intent was to use the camera in the studio to photograph products against a chroma-key background and paste the product into another, higher resolution background photo. This worked fine for a while. Digital cameras were evolving faster than an aggressive tumor but I resisted upgrading every time something new hit the market. I recall camera resolutions rising from 3 to 4 megapixels and then to 6 (I upgraded to a 6MP DSLR). Next was 8 megapixels and I got one of those, then 10, 12, 15, 16, 18, 20, 22. Today my maximum-resolution, full-frame DSLR is a 22.5 MP beast and it's been superseded by cameras with 50 megapixels and more. I even bought a 4 MP point and shoot camera with a Foveon sensor just to see how those images looked (good sensor, slow processor). In the beginning of the digital camera sensors were small, so you lost your widest wide-angle lens and that was a problem — especially for a guy like me who favors the 20mm! We got our wide angle lenses back with new design super-wide-angle lenses and full-frame sensors that kept a 20mm lens at 20mm. Fortunately digital cameras are not as fragile as I'd feared early on, but they are decidedly un-sexy. Digital cameras are little more than processors with lenses and my original Canon G1 was as much of a brick as my fifty year-old Argus C-3. From a historical perspective the 'digital revolution of photography' took about fifty years, from the late 1950s to the early 00s.

From the perspective of the consumer the 'digital revolution' took only about a decade, from 1990 to 2000. Rapid evolution; or at least it seemed that way to the consumer. I consider myself, and my contemporaries in the field, to be bridge artists in that we began our careers at the end of the film/analog era, came of age during the transition and will end our careers fully digital. It's been quite an exciting time to be a photographer... and a little scary... and confusing!

I'd like to think I was fairly prescient during the transitional times, much of my prediction-anticipation turned out to be correct, but there were things I got wrong and other things I never saw coming. Most of us thought film would be around a lot longer than it was. No, film isn't 'dead' but film or 'analog photography' has become a retro-niche-specialty. I watched as my darkroom became little more than a storage-space for inkjet supplies as so much of the papers and chemistry of the photo-lab was discontinued and no longer available. There were black and white prints I'd made all the way into the 1990s that I could no longer produce the same way; the papers, developers and toners were no longer manufactured. By the time I bought an Epson R2400 printer (one of my favorites) black and white inkjet prints were now indistinguishable from darkroom-made prints and I knew that was it for my darkroom days. Today (2017) there remain a number 'analog' photographers dedicated to film and the darkroom. I commend them for their dedication to 'tradition' but don't let them convince you they're any better than a 'digital' photographer, because they're not. They're not special and the marketplace doesn't give a damn about how they make their photographs. I do hope they buy enough film to keep it alive.

I didn't and many of my photographer friends did not anticipate the digital 'camera.' We figured we'd be using the same cameras as always except we'd using *digital camera backs*. We'd envisioned a digital back for the camera that contained the sensor, processor, battery and memory. You could install the digital module to the back of your camera and shoot digital photos, or remove it, reinstall the 'normal' camera back and go shoot film. This never happened. New digital cameras backs don't open to load film, instead all that space is used for the sensor, processor(s), memory and other stuff involving ones and zeros. If this had been a workable idea perhaps film would still be viable? It's really too bad because by the late 1980s film research and development had really reached a zenith — the last films that were manufactured were the best we'd ever had and were getting better. The digital camera killed all new R&D for film.

Without the need for film-transport mechanisms and the advancement of the super high resolution electronic viewfinder (I do believe the optical viewfinder will eventually go away, superseded by the mirrorless EVF) it is now time to rethink the ergonomics of camera design. Since digital cameras are little more than handheld computers with lenses, they can evolve into a new form and no longer have to 'look like a camera.' Eventually someone's going to come out with a new-design camera body that will be very different from the cameras (and cel-phones) we're using today.

We didn't anticipate that cell-phones would soon include still and video cameras giving rise to 'mobile photography' and 'iPhonography.'

I didn't foresee the internet. When I first got 'online' I saw rather quickly that the portfolio website would replace the physical portfolio. It was very cool in the early days of the internet to be on the phone with an art director or gallerist in a distant city and *both* of us could be viewing and discussing the *same* images at the same time via a website on the web. There was an immediate savings in shipping costs to send out a portfolio and getting it back. After that it became convenient to digitally deliver image files via email or FTP, saving more shipping fees.

The stock photo industry was profoundly changed forever for the worse by digital cameras, cell-phone photography and the rapid dissemination of imagery via the web. Throughout the 1980s and accelerating through the 1990s the stock photo industry was rapidly being sold off to corporate opportunists who never gave a damn about photographers or photography. By the early 00s they no longer had to publish and mail expensive print catalogs of images to clients — their clients could now visit the companies' website and download a stock photo. This also eliminated the picture researcher job as it was now being done, for free, by the pictureuser. And with digital cameras and cel-phones making photography easier more pictures were being made than ever before (an estimated 1.2 *trillion* photos were shot in 2017!). New stock photo 'suppliers' took on the amateurs because with digital images they no longer needed the space to archive prints and transparencies. File cabinets holding thousands of slides were replaced by server farms containing *millions* of images — all in the same space! Although the stock photo business was being done more efficiently and cheaper the new corporate masters reduced photographer's commissions making it impossible for a professional to earn a decent living through the license of stock photos any more. To make matters worse, they flooded the market with so many pictures that it drove the price down to the point were now you can license a photo for less than the cost of a cup of coffee.

'Digital' really killed the photo-lab business. With less film to process because of digital cameras, and fewer prints to make because so much is merely displayed on video screens the only labs that survived are the ones that adapted to digital, cater to professionals, and expanded their businesses to include things like signage graphics and other 'print industry' things that transitioned to digital.

I've done the art historians' job once already by clearly stating that 'digital art' is a new art-form in and of itself. For now, the socalled experts continue to lump 'digital art' in with photography (primarily, I think, because the ubiquitous software is called *photo* shop) but not all digital art is 'photography.' Even when working with photographic source-material there is a digital line that when crossed defines the resultant artwork as no longer a photograph but something else — digital art. I don't know if art historians are clueless, gutless or just don't care, but I'll do their jobs for them one more time with this declaration: The post-surrealist era began in 1990. Adobe Photoshop, introduced in 1990, allowed for cutting, pasting and compositing of realistic imagery unlike anything before. This opened new doors of surrealistic-style expression that had been closed to all but the craftiest and clever of photographers. The new digital technologies allowed for new interpretations of abstract-expressionism, impressionism and especially surrealism. Besides this, Salvador Dali died one year prior, in 1989. His death ended the classical surrealist period and the next year Adobe Photoshop ushered in the post-surrealist era. Fifty years from now we'll see if the art history books agree with me.

'The transition' is now complete, photography is officially digital but there are enough practitioners of old-school film photography to keep 'analog' photography alive as niche-specialty, but what does the future hold? Prediction is tricky business. Here's what I think is coming in terms of *input, image-processing, output* and *market*.

Input: Will continue to be digital, film will become a specialty niche. As old film is scanned and digitized scanners will remain but will be less common and perhaps no longer manufactured for desktop use. The megapixel wars are not over! To guess, 100 megapixel, full-frame 35mm sensors may become cheap and 'standard.' There will be many smaller sized sensors designed for small cameras and cel-phones. I don't think the Bayer Pattern sensor will last and I'm not sure the three-layer, film-like, Foveon sensor is the answer. I think we're going to see new sensors, probably curved, and they won't require firmware color interpolation. Dynamic Range, or 'latitude' as we used to say in the film days, will continue to increase to levels rivaling or exceeding the human eye. No more "exposing for the shadows and printing for the highlights." Sensors will most likely be sensitive to wavelengths beyond visible light. I can envision a switch or button on the camera allowing the photographer to toggle between making pictures by visible light, infrared or ultraviolet light. Perhaps other wavelengths or even night-vision too. The curved-sensor design will allow for really cheap lens manufacture and fixing things like chromatic aberration, coma and barrel distortion will be done with inexpensive software (ultimately lens-correction will be built in to firmware) thus allowing good image quality from really cheap lenses — virtual lens technology. We may even have tiny 'cooling systems' built in to cameras to suppress the noise generated by sensor heat build-up. I think the mirror-box and pentaprism of the SLR will go away, replaced by ultrafast, ultra-hi-res electronic viewfinders. Future cameras will be mirrorless. For now there is impetus to make cameras smaller but I think in the future there will be a push to make some cameras larger just to make them easier to hold. They won't be heavier though, lightweight composites will be used more and more. The camera itself is due for a major redesign. Of course the surveillance industry will benefit from smaller, low-energy consuming cameras with higher resolution. We're going to see more cameras everywhere, more dash-cams, more backup-cams and more wearable cameras. I predict that the police will continue to murder people and when they do their body-cams will usually and mysteriously 'fail' at just the 'right' moment. Technology always advances at a faster rate than human nature.

Image-Processing: All roads will continue to lead to Photoshop, for a while. Adobe Photoshop is a deep and complex program with a steep learning curve. Already we have simpler and lower-cost image-processing alternatives in the form of Lightroom, GIMP, Photoshop Elements and others. I do believe that Photoshop already is, and will continue to be, the 'industry standard,' but there will be alternatives. Computers themselves will continue to get better, faster and cheaper. Some day we may have superfast quantum computers for the desktop, imagine how fast a filter effect could be applied to a huge file with a quantum computer! Voice recognition will eventually get to Star Trek levels of functionality, but I don't know if that would benefit digital artists. Instant wi-fi transmission of imagery will allow for a photographer in the wilderness to be micromanaged by someone in a cubicle thousands of miles away. I don't think software will ever replace a photographer's compositional skills. Light-Field Technology may become commonplace (assuming it even works, which is questionable today) allowing for refocusing of images after they've been taken. In filmmaking and video high-definition will get higher and higher. Photography will be less 'optical' and more 'computational.'

Output: Most images won't be output/displayed beyond a phone, tablet or computer screen. It seems backwards to me but as megapixel counts rise, display size gets smaller. The same people who used to insist I use a 4x5 camera for a postage-stamp size reproduction now insist on 50 megabyte files for... postage-stamp size *display*. 'Display' will supplant 'reproduction' for many uses. Prints will only be important to collectors of fine art images. Still photography and videography will essentially merge, one device doing both. Stock photography will cease to generate revenues with those images becoming essentially free, or had for pennies. Professional photography will shrink supplanted by 'citizen journalists,' eBay-adequate product photography shot with cel-phones will take much of the work away from studio product photographers. As photography becomes easier and easier more and more people will be doing it thereby eliminating the need for a trained, professional photographer. Inkjet printers from Epson and Canon are already amazing and will continue to improve. Since inkjet printers already match or exceed the quality that came from the darkroom printer, future improvements will most likely be in terms of greater speed and user-friendliness.

Market: Predicting business trends is problematic at best, so I'll keep this brief. I think there will be fewer and fewer actual 'professional' photographers working in the future. Because of increased competition from 'people with cel-phone cameras' photographers will not be able to specialize due to lack of work and will have to become 'generalists'who shoot everything. Wedding photography will hang on for a while — at least until brides and grooms get tired of cheesy wedding portraits and realize that they can just get all the guests to shoot and share photos from their phones. Small product photography studios will need more 'large' product shoots (like cars and private planes) to get by. Small products will be shot by adequate amateurs with cel-phones, good enough for eBay quality. Fashion and architectural photography will become even more of a specialty, but with fewer full-time practitioners. We're going to see a lot of aerial photos until the drone fad fades. Stock photography will become, in essence, free photos. More and more 'general photography,' will be done by 'people with cameras/phones' who aren't trained in photography. Professional photographers will be the ones who can 'get the difficult shot' that non-trained 'people with cameras' cannot. Sports photography will remain. As far as the paparazzi goes... who cares? We're already seeing a purge in newspaper photographers in favor of free pictures from 'citizen journalists.' We will continue to have 'war photojournalism' because only professionals will be willing to be shot at to get photos. (There will be plenty of war to cover, unfortunately.) In terms of 'fine art' we may see more 'analog' and 'film' photography simply because the process is too difficult for the average digital photographer, which makes the product (the darkroom print) more unique and valuable. The contemporary museums and galleries will probably continue be dismissive of 'digital art' for a long time preferring to stick to what they think they already know. Photographic fine-arts will remain a closed-society of elitism. The university photography degree will probably cease to be offered, an 'iPhonography' class will probably be offered in the art or media departments instead.

Conclusion: Where we were — where we are — where we're going: No doubt there are many unforeseen changes hiding just over the horizon. Because of digital the mindset and philosophy of photographers, especially fine-art photographers, has changed in many ways. As of 2018 all this is still relatively new and I predict it will take at least one generation for things to find a new equilibrium. Photographers who know lighting, either set-up in the studio or recognized on location, will always have a skill that coders cannot write software to do. Composition is another innate + teachable skill that cannot be replaced by software. Photographers no longer have to be as clever as they once were because software will allow for nearly unlimited creative options. For me, I miss (a little) the days when I needed to do a special-effect shot and had to figure out how to do it. I had to build actual things like miniature sets to photograph, or know where I could double-expose to buildup an image. I had to have some mechanical engineering skills that are no longer required thanks to software. I had a bag of 'chemical engineering' skills I used in the darkroom —'secret' toner dilutions, developer combos and dilutions, etc., etc. That knowledge is no longer required, it's been supplanted by software too.

The 'digital transition' profoundly changed the technical aspects of photography and it changed the aesthetic too. The thing I wonder about the most is what the future art historians will have to say about this epoch? Like Beaumont Newhall's incomplete and not quite accurate history of photography I fear that future historians will get it wrong, or worse, they'll only scratch the surface and ignore many, many innovative artists of today who just aren't recognized. There is a ton of digital art to be seen on the internet; will future art historians have to patience to dig through it to find the true innovators? Doubtful. What will they say about the intense transition period of 1990-2000? Historians love categorization, how will they define non-photographic digital art? Will digital artists be considered impressionists, abstract-expressionists, surrealists? Or will historians create a ghetto for 'digital' impressionists, abstract-expressionists and surrealists and thus separating them from others who create the same except in a more traditional medium. Will they look back at our work and declare it 'experimental?'

I've already heard the same anti-digital arguments today that were anti-photography arguments fifty years ago, will historians get over it? Today digital art is expressed in a myriad of ways, will future historians recognize the contribution from us, *the very first photo-digital artists in history?* Or, will our works be dismissed because they're misunderstood, out of context, in the future?

For history, I'm doing what I can to write down thoughts on all this as it happens. And I'm making archival pigment prints of my work that will last just as long as a properly-processed B&W print from the darkroom. Will whomever finds my work after I'm dead recognize what they've found? Will they care?

CHAPTER

RETURN TO ANTELOPE CANYON
JUST ANOTHER 'BUCKET-LIST' PLACE TO SHOOT A SELFIE?

Diverse natural beauty makes Arizona a photographer's paradise. As a long-time Arizona resident I often act as tour-guide for traveling photographers. In February of 2018 I found myself guiding a group of photographers to some of the more obscure photographic locations in the state. They also wanted to photograph the well-known sites too, including Antelope Canyon. It had been years since I'd been to Antelope Canyon — so long ago I'd photographed it on film, so I joined the guys for the Antelope Canyon photography tour. I'm glad I did, and I wish I hadn't. Compared to my previous visits to Antelope Canyon this time it was uniquely unpleasant. Popularity isn't always a good thing.

If you're not familiar with the name *Antelope Canyon* you'll recognize the photos. The images of the undulating sandstone walls and light-beams of the slot canyons near Lake Powell have become iconic. Pre-2000, few people had ever heard of the place which was also known as 'the slot canyon' or 'the corkscrew.' Post-2000, it seemed as if everyone in the world knew about Antelope Canyon and just had to go there. In a very short amount of time photographs of Antelope Canyon transitioned from rare and beautiful to cel-phone-commonplace. Beauty gone banal.

My own 'discovery' of Antelope Canyon were photographs in a book by photographer Bruce Barnbaum. His 1986 book featured a chapter of photos from an unnamed 'slit canyon.' Although

Barnbaum did not discover the canyon now known as 'Antelope Canyon', and did not disclose its location, he did inadvertently popularize the place. My thoughts after looking at Barnbaum's photos were, I want to go there — I want to shoot that. But where is it? It took some research, pre-internet, but I eventually figured out where it was located and set out to photograph Antelope Canyon in 1988. I had a topographic map, a compass, and a pick-up truck…

…The truck was 2WD and it wasn't long before I was stuck, axle-deep in sand as I attempted to drive to the 'slit canyon.' After abandoning the truck I managed to find one of the lesser-known canyons in the area and got some good photos. I never found 'upper' or 'lower'Antelope Canyon because the rest of my day was spent hiking out, finding a wrecker and going back and getting my truck unstuck. Although I got the shot, by the end of the day I was dehydrated, exhausted and pissed-off. "Damn," I said to the wreck-er driver, "Why don't the Navajos just manage the place and charge everyone twenty bucks a head to drive them there in a 4WD!?"

Twelve years later they were doing exactly that. At the tail-end of the film era (with the best films ever invented) I returned to Antelope Canyon in 2000. That time I did not need the topograph-ic map, compass (or 4WD) as I simply drove to the location out-side of Page, paid $5.00 to enter tribal land and paid another $20.00 to one tour-operator for a ride to Antelope Canyon. I rode to the canyon in a 4WD truck with about six other people and had plenty of time for photography. With only seven of us in the canyon it wasn't crowded at all. When the driver told us it was time to leave I handed him another twenty dollar bill and asked if I could ride back with the next group. That was no problem and it gave me over twenty minutes with the empty canyon all to myself! Only when I was alone in the slot canyon did I truly feel I was experiencing it properly. When I returned to my darkroom and processed the film I was very happy. I got the shot and didn't need to go back to

Antelope Canyon again — until the traveling photographers put the idea back in my head in 2018.

I checked into Antelope Canyon tours for them and learned that in the ensuing 18 years virtually everything had changed due to the canyon's greatly increased popularity. The three photographers had photographed Antelope Canyon the previous summer and it was very crowded. The tour operator told them then, "Come back in the winter and you'll have the canyon to yourself." So they came back in February. Antelope Canyon has been massively commercialized and there are at least a dozen tour-guide operators. They do not coordinate with each other which means multiple simultaneous tours crowd the canyon. Nobody "had the canyon to themselves." And prices have gone up; the tour I took eighteen years ago for $20.00 is now $45.00. That's not too bad but that's for the 'tourist tour' and no tripods are allowed. The 'photography tour' (tripods *required*) costs $146.25. For our money we got extra time in the canyon but there was nothing we could do about all the other people crowding the canyon on all the other tours.

Leaving the tour company's downtown Page facility, Nate, our Navajo guide, drove us to the canyon (only the four of us, we were the only ones on this photo-tour). Nate told us about "shooting fast" and how he'll do his best to "hold up the crowd" as long as possible for us to get our photos. We were a little concerned about his mention of "crowds" and his advice to "shoot fast" until we arrived and saw over a half-dozen tour-operator vehicles already there and crowds lined up outside the canyon. It was looking like a giant clusterfuck!

Wildlife and sports photography are "shoot fast" situations, but landscape photography is a slower, more contemplative process. I was so rushed I didn't have enough time to concentrate on the canyon or the photography! We were "shooting fast" only to clear the way for all the other people. It was canyon-wall to canyon-wall full of people! Packed! Antelope Canyon isn't big. Some passages are so narrow you can stand in the center of the canyon and touch both walls with your hands. Imagine fifty fat guys in a hallway, all trying to squeeze past each other. I tried to make myself as two-dimensional as possible, flat Dale squished up against the canyon wall as the All-Star American Beergut Band marched past, followed by fifty more, skinnier foreign tourists, followed by more obese Americans, followed by more and more and more people. The guides do a commendable job holding people back long enough for a photographer to get a long exposure but it's not a good photographic experience. And everyone takes the same photo. The guides stop and point and say, "Here's this shot, point your camera here." It's become a photographic festival of slot-canyon-clichés! I had no time to stop, think, turn around, look or consider a different shot, it was "shoot here and move on, shoot there and move on." I was miserable! Thirty years ago I may have gotten stuck in the sand but it was a much more pleasant photographic experience than in 2018, trying to shoot a photo among a horde in a hallway! I liked this place better in 1988, before it was 'discovered.'

And 'discovery' is the problem. It's just too crowded to photograph — or to be experienced properly. Sadly, Antelope Canyon is no longer 'special,' its specialness erased by the footprints of a million tourists. The tours make it accessible, but now, commonplace. The canyon is overused and overcrowded and *will* suffer the inevitable human-caused wear-and-tear and decay. Access should be limited. But any sort of 'conservation' of Antelope Canyon is impossible for now because so much money is being made by the tour operators. Imagine ten tour operators bringing ten tourists to the canyon each hour, seven days a week at prices per person between $45.00 and $146.25. That's a cash-canyon!

I will not return, ever. If I want to photograph another slot canyon I'll hire a Navajo guide and go find one of the 900+ slotl canyons scattered around the Lake Powell area. But you may be wondering, *should I go to Antelope Canyon?* That, of course, is an individual choice and I would not dissuade anyone based on my own experience. I would say that if you're claustrophobic or introverted a tour as they're run now is probably not for you. If you don't mind crowds or a lot of people invading your personal space and you've just got to see it, then go. If you're a photographer I can guarantee you will *not* get $146.25 worth of original photos out of the place. You will get your own version of what is now a cliché. To avoid frustration enjoy others' photos because you won't shoot anything different yourself, it's nearly impossible.

Antelope Canyon is a rare and beautiful work of natural art, but it's too easy to visit and that brings the crowds. It used to be a special, hidden, hard-to-find place that if you did find it, rewarded you with spectacular photographs. Now it's just another backdrop for a selfie. A deep canyon but a shallow experience.

CHAPTER

DON'T STARE AT THE SUN
THE GREAT AMERICAN SOLAR ECLIPSE OF
AUGUST 21, 2017

Humans have accurately predicted solar eclipses since ancient Mesopotamian times. Given that the occurrence of a total solar eclipse is about once per continent per human lifetime it is highly likely that during your lifetime an eclipse will happen over the landmass on which you live. *You should see the eclipse.* An eclipse is a unique astronomical event that you should witness one at least once, even if you must travel a great distance. You'll never see (or feel) anything comparable. It cannot be overemphasized, each and every human being should see at least one total solar eclipse.

I traveled a great distance, 1100 miles, to witness and photograph the Great American Eclipse of 2017 and it was worth every highway mile, overpriced hotels, bad fast-food, a minor sunburn and even spending one night sleeping in the car. I saw the eclipse from the automotive homage to England's Stonehenge, Carhenge, which is located in Alliance, Nebraska.

The summer of 2016, when I first learned of the 2017 solar eclipse, I had a photo-shoot already in the planning stages for 2017. I'd be photographing 'land art' installations featuring automobiles including *Carhenge.* The August 21 total solar eclipse would span the entirety of the North America and I wondered, *will the shadow fall over Nebraska?* A quick Google search and, yes! The moon's shadow would traverse the sky directly above Alliance,

Nebraska. I scheduled the photo-shoot in Nebraska for August 21 and would get two subjects — Carhenge and the eclipse. How cool is that?

Not as cool as I thought. I taught myself about Solar Filters, protecting my eyes and my camera's sensor, exposure data, and all that. I read a lot of books and visited a lot of astronomy websites and many 'experts' were saying the same thing about optimum viewing locations — go to Alliance, Nebraska. The highest proba- bility of clear skies is in the middle of the continent, away from the coasts. Since it was looking like I would have a lot of company on the Nebraska plains I tried to book a local hotel room a full ten months before the event. Not cool. All lodgings in Alliance and nearby Scottsbluff, Nebraska were totally booked! And they were booked at the 'special eclipse viewing' rates of $400-$900 per night instead of the usual $60.00! Luckily I found a room at a less than extortionate price, thirty miles away in Bridgeport, Nebraska. Then I read in the Scottsbluff newspaper that the Alliance Chamber of Commerce would be expecting 10,000 'eclipse visitors.' (The population of Alliance is 8500.) This is going to be a 'Solar Woodstock' event!

During the 'eclipse research' phase I was reminded of all the mythology surrounding eclipses. Primitive men did not understand eclipses and ascribed supernatural explanations for what they were witnessing. Hopefully, and despite national anti-science senti- ments, no one still believes that eclipses are caused by the sun being eaten by a frog, wolf or dragon; or the sun being stolen by dogs or bitten by a bear. Despite our collective scientific knowl- edge of orbital dynamics there still is a lot of pseudoscience that comes from the New Age and Astrology communities. Notions like a disruption of the Earth's magnetic field and people's own bodily systems may have some validity while other ideas such as evil omens, beginnings and endings, life-changing events and enhanced emotions have no scientific causation or correlation.

Three weeks before the eclipse I 'rehearsed' photographing the sun using a timer set to two and a half minutes — the duration of totality; just how many photos can I shoot in one-hundred and fifty seconds? There's nothing quite like the pressure of photographing a thing that will fry your eyes if you look at it, only comes around infrequently, lasts less than three minutes, and you really can't practice or test for it. This ain't no wedding portrait! Testing, practicing and rehearsing paid off. I got the shot while I saw others struggle with equipment, not getting the shot or really observing the eclipse. Luck favors the prepared.

Driving north on highway 25 through Colorado I saw signs on the highway warning of 'heavy eclipse traffic' but saw none of it. On the road between Sterling, Colorado and Alliance, Nebraska I prepared myself for traffic like I'd seen on TV from Oregon, but encountered none. I rolled into the Carhenge parking lot at 10:30AM the day before the eclipse without incident or delay. There was no overnight parking or camping allowed at Carhenge but one tenth of a mile up the highway a farmer made his bean field available to campers for forty-five dollars a day. I happily paid the fee (happy that it wasn't a hundred bucks — which I would have paid) and claimed a spot on high ground.

Relieved that I'd staked out my special spot on Earth today to photograph the sun tomorrow I had a full day to kill before the big astronomical alignment. With ten thousand-plus boneheads with cell-phones coming in from all over, we were happily surprised to have free wi-fi in the bean field! Verizon even trucked in portable cel-phone towers so we could all update social media, real-time. There were souvenir sellers, t-shirt sales, food vendors, and ice and water was for sale. Plenty of Porta-Cans too. Ten miles down the road, in Alliance itself, there was an Indian Pow-Wow, softball games, rock bands playing and all the churches put out food for the weary eclipse-travelers. All in all, the city of Alliance, had a wellorganized plan and there were no incidents of theft or violence of any kind. I felt confident that after the eclipse nobody would burn things or overturn cars the way they do when some sports team wins a championship. Everyone was nice, friendly and well-behaved. One old guy passed out from the heat and the EMTs took him away and that was *it*.

I had a tasty BBQ sandwich from one of the vendors for lunch and watched a steady stream of eclipse-viewers fill the bean field the rest of the day. By late afternoon Sunday the field was nearly full of RVs, tents, teardrops, and various kinds of shades and shelters. I watched City Dads struggle with brand-new tents. A parade of white legs walked by. There must have been ten million dollars' worth of Canon, Nikon and Celestron glass pointed skyward. On Sunday the Alliance airport had a fly-in breakfast and was overwhelmed by 250 private planes — a certain famous actor/pilot was allegedly there but I didn't see Han Solo or the Millennium Falcon anywhere. In the afternoon I wandered around the bean field and down the hill to Carhenge and talked to people: Camping next to me was Alex and Austin, a couple of guys from Bismark, North Dakota, fully prepped with beer and eclipse glasses. Janice and her two daughters were nearby, setting up multiple telescopes and cameras. There was Halter-Top Hanna, the unwashed New Age-Hippie chick laying out crystals to be 'charged' under the special 'eclipse light.' Shaman-Sam looked ready for a photon-bath, whoa dude put on a shirt! I met Sonny (real name!) an 'eclipse-chaser' who proudly told me, "This is my tenth eclipse!" I didn't meet any flat-Earthers or climate change-deniers. Everyone was happy to be here, like me.

They came in large numbers from all over. Most people I spoke to traveled between 250 and 500 miles to see totality. After the eclipse I spoke to the proprietor of the Meadowlark Hotel in Bridgeport where I stayed two nights; the Sunday before the eclipse she had reservations for people from China, Japan, Australia, France, England and Austria. Crowd size estimates had about 5000 people in the immediate area of Carhenge, 10,000 when the surrounding areas were included. For the entire Alliance area the estimate was 20,000 eclipse-viewers!

On Monday August 21, 2017 millions of people temporarily migrated to the path of totality that stretched from Portland, Oregon to Charleston, South Carolina. They all did this to see the moon's seventy-mile-wide shadow, traveling at 1800 miles per hour pass over them for about two minutes!

On eclipse day we woke up to a fright, it was completely fogged-in! *Well, if I don't get the shot it's not my fault.* Janice, my camper-neighbor came over, tablet in hand and said, "I've got a NOAA weather app here that says the temps dropped last night, we hit the dew point and this is just ground fog that ought to burn-off in an hour." She was right! And thanks again to the farmer for the free wi-fi!

Actually, the scare with the fog just made seeing the eclipse even more precious.

While the fog dissipated the Bismark boys made a coffee run and we began our day fully caffeinated. Another guy wandered through the campground selling cinnamon rolls. Eclipse excitement grew as thousands of tripods, cameras, telescopes and binoculars were set-up. My set-up included a main camera, a full-frame Canon DSLR with a 400mm lens (which is an 8x magnification); a Lumix micro four-thirds camera as back-up for the main camera; and Canon G9 which was a back-up for the back-up. I also ran a Kodak HD video camera and took a few photos with my Android phone. I was well rehearsed and ready for the show to start.

When the show did start it was hard to tell. Someone in the crowd yelled out, "First contact," and we peered sunward through our eclipse-glasses to see a tiny notch taken out of the sun by the moon. I shot photos about every fifteen minutes to document the progression of moon occluding the sun. Without looking at the sun through eclipse-glasses, you really didn't know there was an eclipse happening until the moment of totality, yes, Sol is that bright. During the first phase of the eclipse everyone was shooting photos or looking through telescopes. Janice was struggling with camera alignment and I assisted her from time to time. No one was competitive and everyone helped each other to get the best photos and have the best experience. A few minutes before totality a panicked man came by asking for tape, duct tape, anything! He had a homemade, 3D-printed holder for his solar filter that had broken at just the wrong moment. I handed him a roll of duct tape, the second most important thing in my camera bag, and told him, "Take it, make your repair and get the shot, bring the roll back later." He thanked me profusely and was off.

Only at the moment right before totality did the light change enough to be noticed, and it only darkened like a cloud had passed over the sun. Solar filters came off the cameras and everybody got ready...

Totality!

And then it was dark. Sunset all around. Birds quiet and crickets chirping. It had gone from midday to twilight in an instant and it was weird... And it was indescribably spectacular. Through my telephoto lens I could see the diamond ring, the sun's photosphere, the solar flares and prominences and *everything!* I got the shot! And I got the shot again! Totality was magic, an incredible sight. I will not use a tired, clichéd sex metaphor here, but it was over way too quick! Two and a half minutes later, third contact and totality was over, the landscape brightened and the moon began to uncover the sun. The crowd cheered. Wow! Just wow!

The air temperature had dropped about ten degrees during totality but we only noticed afterwards, when it began to warm up again. I continued photographing the waxing eclipse but many were already taking down tents and packing up to leave like it was the eighth inning of the ballgame and they're going to beat the traffic (they didn't). The guy with the broken solar filter holder returned my duct tape and gave me a big hug, "Oh man, you saved the shot, thank you, thank you, thank you!" I was happy to help out and I'm happy he got the shot. Never travel without duct tape.

I can completely understand how a total solar eclipse would scare the living crap out of Neanderthal Man. He knew (unlike a certain Cheeto-toned 'world leader') not to look at the sun so he wouldn't see it coming. He'd be going about his day, hunting and gathering or whatever, and then suddenly day would turn to night. Without understanding the science behind what had happened he'd better sacrifice a virgin quick, you know, to appease the gods.

By about 1 pm it was just a regular day again— except I was standing in a hot bean field with 10,000 new friends, the sun high in the sky. I packed up, bade farewell to my eclipse friends and bugged-out. Ten miles later I found that traffic I'd missed the day before and spent the next three hours driving thirty miles to Bridgeport. Oh well, I'm glad I didn't catch this traffic on the way in.

After check-in and a much needed shower all of the memory cards from the eclipse cameras went into secure case and into my shirt pocket, never to be away from my person until I returned to my studio. The images on those cards were more precious than gold! Then it was off to the bar and dinner. The restaurant was nearly full and everyone was still buzzing about the eclipse earlier in the day. Even the waitresses stopped serving long enough to go out in the parking lot and see the eclipse.

I spent the next day in Bridgeport as well. I drove back to Carhenge, picked up a few extra photos minus the crowd and shot a few more photos of the (relatively clean) aftermath. I had a second photo-shoot in Utah and it took me a few extra days to get home. Driving alone across Colorado and Utah gave me a lot of time to think and 'process' what I'd witnessed:

An eclipse can be called a 'fixed astronomical event.' The solar eclipse that just happened was going to happen exactly as it did no matter what. If there were no humans or any other conscious entities on Earth to witness the eclipse, it would have occurred exactly the same way unseen. And this is where I think it gets interesting, not to be a nihilist, but nothing has any intrinsic meaning of its own and all 'meaning' ascribed to the eclipse-event is *applied* by human observers. So, in terms of 'meaning,' we get out of it what we bring to it. The New-Ager-types got their crystals charged or chakras cleansed or whatever, the scientific-types gathered data and perhaps greater understanding of the universe's clockwork. Others were merely curious, satiated by a new experience. For some it was an excuse for a party, for kids, a day off from school. Everyone got something positive out of it and with those good feelings multiplied by ten or twenty thousand souls, well that's palpable positivity — a shared experience, good for everyone.

For me it was a range of feelings. Immediately after totality I felt profoundly exhausted. Was my fatigue caused by a sudden change in gravity or energy? Did the eclipse itself cause my sudden tiredness? Possibly. But more likely the culmination of planning, preparation, travel, discomfort, and the anxiety of only having two and a half minutes to get a photo *and actually getting the photo* suddenly being fulfilled might be a more realistic cause for fatigue. As a photographer I successfully met a unique technical challenge and as an artist I'd generated new imagery for future works. I'd witnessed a beautiful temporary 'light event' more incredible than a Pink Floyd concert! I met a whole lot of interesting folk in the bean field and shared a communal experience. But moreover, as a human, I felt my place in the universe. Seeing the eclipse in its full totality glory underscored my humanity. I am here! I am alive! I have perceived this rare and fleeting thing and have made it permanent in my memory. It is significant because I have seen it and it is real because others saw it too. I see, therefore I am! The eclipse would have occurred just as it did even if no one saw it, but without witnesses there is no Wow Factor.

Wow! Wow times millions of witnesses!

To conclude, here's the opening paragraph again. I really mean it Given that the occurrence of a total solar eclipse is about once per continent per human lifetime it is highly likely that during your lifetime an eclipse will happen over the landmass on which you live. You should see the eclipse. An eclipse is a unique astronomical event and you should witness one at least once, even if you must travel a great distance. You'll never see (or feel) anything comparable. *It cannot be overemphasized, each and every human being should see at least one total solar eclipse.*

Afterword

Exactly one week after the positivity of the eclipse negativity again reigned supreme as hurricane Harvey flooded Texas. It seemed as if, for only one day, everyone forgot about their troubles, ignored the daily horrors of the Presidential shitshow, and collectively enjoyed a rare, and joyous, astronomical event. Sadly some people didn't believe the warnings *not to look at the sun* and injured their eyes. Google reported a significant increase in the number of searches using the words 'my-eyes-hurt.' Ophthalmologists reported newly blind patients with eclipse-shaped crescents burned into their retinas. And on TV we saw President not-a-role-model staring at the sun, eyes unprotected, until someone told him not to. It's sad, but it's hard to feel bad for people who willfully injure themselves because they think the warnings are 'fake news' just to sell more eclipse glasses.

Even though I've been working professionally for 35 years I still learned one important photographic lesson — sandbags! Right after totality, when the temps began to rise again the winds increased. The winds were so strong they blew over my main camera and tripod. Oops, there goes six grand of camera and lens crashing to the Earth! Fortunately the soft grass and the lens' filter-holder took the impact and nothing was damaged except the solar filter (I did take the last couple of shots with my back-up camera). This will not happen again as I now own four, twenty pound sandbags that I will use to stabilize the tripod in the future.

This was the first 'digital photography' eclipse in America and *millions* of photos were shot of the event. For those that got the shot, they all look pretty much the same. A few photographers set up and shot that one 'hero' photo. For me, adding the partial and totality shots to my library will make for some very cool composite images.

The next total solar eclipse that will be seen in the USA will occur on April 8, 2024 and the path of totality will go through central Texas. Totality should last a little over three minutes. As much as I despise the state of Texas I may have to go there and shoot another eclipse now that I have some experience.

If you're looking for technical information on photographing solar eclipses buy a detailed book. I will mention that it's important to practice or rehearse your photography. Get a solar filter and go out and practice. Record your exposures so you'll have a starting- point for the real thing. You can't rehearse for totality so my best advice for that is, remove the solar filter and bracket, bracket, bracket! Learn to shoot fast, you'll only have a few minutes. And steady your tripod with sandbags!

THAT'S NOT A REAL BIGFOOT!
ORIGINALLY PUBLISHED IN THE JUNE 2018 ISSUE OF
FIVE SENSES MAGAZINE

If you read Alan Dean Foster's article, *Your Science Conspiracies may be Charged at a Higher Rate*, in last month's *Five Senses*, you got a taste of the ridiculous things Conspiracy Theorists believe, like how the Rothschild family "controls the weather." Taking the path of least mental effort it's easier to believe a rich family controls the weather than it is to learn some weather science. Mr. Foster's article presented a long list of conspiracy theories credited to the Rothschild's including "Bigfoot."

Ah ha! Bigfoot! Now that's a conspiracy theory I'm know something about! I absolutely assure you there are people all over the world who believe there's a real Bigfoot creature out there. These people are *true believers* and they will NOT be dissuaded, facts-be-damned!

There was the guy who brought me a picture of Bigfoot for photo-analysis. He was so biased and absolutely positive he'd found a 'real' photo of Bigfoot that when I didn't confirm his bias he got angry and called *me* a liar. He could not accept he was wrong, so I had to be. He stormed off before I could tell him how I knew the photo was fake: It was *my* photo! He had a stolen copy of one my Bigfoot photos!

This isn't the first time I've run into *Captain Confirmation-Bias*. So many *true believers* are cocksure their photos of Bigfoot,

UFOs, Space Aliens, Lake Monsters, and other weird things are real. I can point out the strings holding up the UFO model and they just say I'm stupid. I can show them my own background photos, models, props and even the Certificate of Copyright from the Library of Congress and they still refuse to believe. They're hopeless.

Please note! Dale is a phenomena illustrator and NOT a hoaxer. If you should ever find one of Dale's UFO or phenomena pictures presented as 'factual' anywhere, PLEASE contact Dale so the record can be set straight.

The above disclaimer is on the 'information' page of my website and refers to the fifty image gallery of Bigfoot and other phenomena. Over the years I have created hundreds of phenomenological illustrations for publication. My pictures illustrate others' stories of strange phenomena and never once have I photographed a 'real' space alien, ghost or Bigfoot — never! Unable to photograph the 'real thing' (assuming it exists at all) I use photographs and computer-generated elements to create photorealistic illustrations. None of my imagery should fool any reasonably competent photo-analyst.

Today the job of the photo-analyst has become ever more important because of hoaxers with computers who disseminate fake pictures and muddy the waters of legitimate research. But not all hoaxers are Photoshop wiz-kids so, thanks to the internet, they steal and re-appropriate others' works and present them as 'legitimate.' Now (as predicted) they're stealing from me.

When I put the *phenomena* gallery on my website I added the disclaimer with the knowledge that eventually I may have to set the record straight. Early on I was contacted about copyright issues, but often I'm contacted by curious people who'd seen my images on TV (Ancient Aliens) or elsewhere and wanted to know if they were 'real' and were disappointed when I told them I'd created it instead of actually photographing it.

Then came an email from a documentary filmmaker in England. She was in pre-production on a film about the British version of Bigfoot, the 'Dogman,' and had been given a packet of photographs of 'Dogman' (allegedly) shot by a local witness. Most of the photos were typical of Bigfoot pictures in that they were of poor quality and unsharp; but one stood out because it was of higher quality and showed a clear, distinct Bigfoot — or Dogman, in this British case. The photo was so different from the others it aroused her suspicion and she began investigating its provenance. Her investigation led her to a British print magazine that had the exact same photo in it, with a credit line for Alamy, a British stockphoto agency. She then searched Alamy, found the photo, and learned who created it — me! She emailed with a thumbnail of the image and asked me to verify if it indeed was mine and for other information about it. I verified it and let her know I did a lot of phenomenological and cryptozoological imagery and that image, along with *all my* 'paranormal' imagery are illustrations and *not real*. I provided a link to the disclaimer on my website, thanked her for informing me of the misleading use of my image, and that was it.

Until the call from the American filmmaker. His story was similar to the British filmmaker's, and he was calling about the same photo! He was considering a 'Bigfoot' film documentary but was so overwhelmed with hoaxes, fraud and fakery that the project just wasn't worthwhile for him. He too had acquired my (Alamy, stock) photo, traced it to me, and called. He'd been briefly involved in the (now shelved) British Dogman documentary film and provided more information. He even provided the name (and aliases!) of the original Dogman hoax-perpetrator in England! This new information set me on an internet quest to find the hoaxer, which I did easily thanks to her YouTube channel, the 'Simlish Dog Lady.' The 'Simlish Dog Lady' is quite a hoaxer, and aggressively full of crap! I commented on her YouTube Channel and called her out. This led to me connecting with other British Dogman/Bigfoot-cryptozoology groups and leaving comments and making statements about the differences between 'real' photos, hoaxes and illustrations. I even reconnected with the original British filmmaker and sent her a longer and more detailed email. She published my email and my (now controversial) Bigfoot photo online to debunk the Simlish Dog Lady's claims.

Apparently the Simlish Dog Lady is quite a thorn in the side of the British Bigfoot/Dogman research community. (And yes it is a 'community.')

This is all pretty funny… up to a point. It's one thing for the hoaxer to 'appropriate' my imagery to feed their ego, get some attention in the form of clicks and 'likes,' or maybe even get a TV or movie deal but dear Dog Lady went too far. Unfortunately she involved the police with a hoax claim that "Dogman took my dog," and sent the local Bobbies on a fruitless search which wasted time and resources. When she tried to present my stolen photo as evidence, the Bobbies were smart enough to recognize a picture that was 'too good to be true.' The British Police eventually called me and I verified the photos' inauthenticity and we had a good laugh at the Dog Lady's expense.

I really do appreciate the humor of the situation. Considering all the current controversies in the media I'd much rather be debating the veracity of a photo of a thing we can't even agree is real than the other stuff in the news today that is real like misogyny, racism, corruption, etc. etc. Yeah, Bigfoot is harmless silliness compared to that!

My phenomenological and cryptid imagery is not real and is not presented as real. I've always made that very clear, but once the imagery leaves my possession, it's out of my control. People believe what they want to believe, it's called *Confirmation Bias*. People like the Simlish Dog Lady already believe, they don't have to be convinced. My photo merely confirmed her already-held bias, that 'Dogman' is real — and my picture proves it for her (she did cross a legal line when she claimed it as her own). She's not a skeptic and she's not going to question the image. *Cognitive Dissonance* does not allow people to change their minds when confronted with new information that conflicts with an already-held belief. It's easier for a 'believer' to call me a liar than to consider themselves wrong. They're wedded to their preconceived notion — irrespective of the facts. It would be too uncomfortable for the believer to admit they were (willfully) fooled.

In this new, dangerous, era of so-called 'fake news' one must take the position of open-minded skeptic regarding *all information*. We must be especially critical of 'photographs' in this post-Photoshop era too. Follow the examples set by the filmmakers who contacted me; check it out, think critically, ask questions. The camera doesn't lie but liars take pictures and liars with Photoshop can make pictures. In the end it doesn't even matter if a picture is 'real' when it furthers the agenda of those who *won't think critically*, like dear Dog Lady.

The credibility of the source, provenance, logic, and conventional wisdom are some factors we must employ when considering the authenticity of an image. Consider the context of an image: if it's published in some tabloid like *The Weekly World News*, it's *probably* fake; if it's published in *Time* magazine, it's *probably* real. *Probably* being the important word here. A publication's credibility is a factor, but it's essential think critically. What's the provenance of pictures on the internet? Do you know who created the image? Are they credible? Perhaps the metadata has been stripped from the image, why? Always be skeptical.

The Simlish Dog Lady believes what she wants. Luckily, she chose to steal one of my photos to prove her 'Dogman' sightings and the provenance of that image drew a line straight back to me and I debunked her claim (of both 'reality' and her ownership of the image). The British Bigfoot/Dogman researchers appreciate me debunking my own image but as you may guess, those who believe the Dog Lady believe that I'm the liar. It's not in their interest to believe the facts.

Be thoughtful, critical, and wary of everything you see. If it's raining, don't assume the Rothschild family caused it. And if you come across a really high quality picture of Bigfoot, don't assume it's real because it's probably one of mine.

CHAPTER

THE PORTFOLIO OF LOST PHOTOS

It has been widely reported by those who study NDEs (near death experiences) that upon death of the body the recently deceased person experiences a 'life review,' a movie-like replay of the life just lived. According to Dr. Penny Sartori, author of *The Wisdom of Near-Death Experiences*, "During the life review living images of a person's life are literally played out and relived from a third person perspective. The life review can include all of the important events in their life as well as the insignificant." Psychologist Dr. Michael Newton Ph.D. has also written extensively about life reviews in his book *Life Between Lives*.

Obviously all reports of the life review come from people who have had near death experiences and were revived; permanently dead people don't come back to tell tales. But the life review is not a new concept, it has been reported for centuries but only in recent years has the experience of "...my whole life flashed before my eyes..." been taken seriously enough for academic study.

Some 'experts' still discount the life review experience as the effects of an oxygen-starved 'dying brain' but quantum physics verifies the nonlocal aspects of consciousness and lends some scientific credence to possibility of the phenomena. As one who has extensively studied parapsychology and mysticism, I certainly believe in the reality of the life review. I'm (mostly) looking forward to mine.

I'm not looking forward to being, "...confronted with the consequences of [my negative] actions and feeling the effects [my] actions had on others." But "…feeling elated after experiencing from the other person's perspective how [my] actions had helped someone," seems pretty nice. *(Satori, The Wisdom of Near-Death Experiences, 2014)*. I suppose a complete life review must include the bad and the good.

Assuming the transition from the physical plane to the non-physical plane reintroduces us to 'all there is' I do have a list of standard questions like: Who killed JFK? Who killed Marilyn Monroe? O.J. really did it, right? And, was 9/11 an inside job? But, and more importantly, I've got some personal things I'd like to see. Since it'll be my *life* review I should see this stuff.

I want very much to see every photograph I've missed or lost!

I want to see the very first photos I shot at camp when I was nine years old. I remember shooting them, but I never saw the pictures because 'the film didn't come out.' I want to see the picture I lost last month because of a hard drive crash. And I want to see all the photos I lost in between; the missing roll of film, the image from the damaged and unprintable negative, the ones ruined by the lab. I want to see all the photos I didn't shoot because I didn't have a camera with me at the moment, and the ones I didn't shoot because I talked myself out of it. I want to see all the photos I missed because of my own bad timing or bad luck.

I want to see all the lucky shots I wasn't ready for and I want to see all the ones I should have shot but didn't because I just wasn't paying attention. I want to see the images I didn't get because of my own stupidity, inattention or bad timing.

I WANT TO SEE THEM ALL! I WANT TO SEE MY OWN 'PORTFOLIO OF LOST PHOTOS.'

Of course I won't be able to share them because they'll only be visible in my own life review, but I want to SEE them. I want to feel bad for missing the good ones and I want to feel relieved for missing the ones I never needed anyway. I want to compare them to my memories of them, I want to know if I've romanticized my 'losses.' I want to see what might have been.

If I reincarnate (and I hope to avoid coming back to this big dumb planet) I *will not* be a photographer again and I *will not* attempt to re-shoot those lost shots. However if I do have to come back to Earth I plan on being rich as shit! I'll be an Arts Patron and I'll set about re-acquiring all the photographs I *did* get in this lifetime. And by *then*, all the work I've done *now* might actually be worth something!

ABOUT THE AUTHOR

DALE O'DELL is a photographer, digital artist and author. His photographic and digital artworks have been exhibited in over two hundred solo and group exhibitions and his commercial works are published internationally. Dale has written about photography, art and aesthetics for most of the leading photographic publications. He studied Photography and Philosophy in college at received a B.S. in Photography from Sam Houston State University in Huntsville, Texas in 1982. Dale has worked as a corporate photographer, optical effects technician, computer artist and educator; he opened his own studio in 1986.

When not making or writing about art Dale is a motorcyclist, occasional musician, remote viewer and paranormal researcher. He lives in Prescott, Arizona with his wife, Bernadette, and Bruno the Chihuahua.

OTHER BOOKS BY DALE O'DELL

Photographic Memories — A look at life through the Lens
(A companion volume to this book.)
Human/Nature
The Surreal Landscape: Woodlands
The Surreal Landscape: Desert
35/50 A 35-Year Retrospective
Dogs of Summer
Invisible Light — Infrared Photography
Tales of Loneliness and Abandonment
Abstractica
Quantum Realism
Ephemera
Four Portfolios
Alone in the Dark

www.ingramcontent.com/pod-product-compliance
Lightning Source LLC
Chambersburg PA
CBHW071252220526
45468CB00001B/95